The Ballets Russes and Beyond

Belle-époque Paris witnessed the emergence of a vibrant and diverse dance scene, one that crystallized around the Ballets Russes, the Russian dance company formed by impresario Sergey Diaghilev. The company has long served as a convenient turning point in the history of dance, celebrated for its revolutionary choreography and innovative productions. This book presents a fresh slant on this much-told history. Focusing on the relation between music and dance, Davinia Caddy approaches the Ballets Russes with a wide-angled lens that embraces not just the choreographic, but also the cultural, political, theatrical and aesthetic contexts in which the company made its name. In addition, Caddy examines and interprets contemporary French dance practices, throwing new light on some of the most important debates and discourses of the day.

Davinia Caddy is Senior Lecturer at the School of Music, University of Auckland. Her articles and reviews have appeared in publications including *Journal of the Royal Musical Association*, *19th-Century Music*, *Cambridge Opera Journal*, *Music & Letters* and *Opera Quarterly*.

New perspectives in music history and criticism

General editors: Jeffrey Kallberg, Anthony Newcomb and Ruth Solie

This series explores the conceptual frameworks that shape or have shaped the ways in which we understand music and its history, and aims to elaborate structures of explanation, interpretation, commentary and criticism which make music intelligible and which provide a basis for argument about judgements of value. The intellectual scope of the series is broad. Some investigations will treat, for example, historiographical topics, others will apply cross-disciplinary methods to the criticism of music, and there will also be studies which consider music in its relation to society, culture and politics. Overall, the series hopes to create a greater presence for music in the ongoing discourse among the human sciences.

Published titles

Leslie C. Dunn and Nancy A. Jones (eds.), *Embodied Voices: Representing Female Vocality in Western Culture*

Downing A. Thomas, *Music and the Origins of Language: Theories from the French Enlightenment*

Thomas S. Grey, *Wagner's Musical Prose*

Daniel K. L. Chua, *Absolute Music and the Construction of Meaning*

Adam Krims, *Rap Music and the Poetics of Identity*

Annette Richards, *The Free Fantasia and the Musical Picturesque*

Richard Will, *The Characteristic Symphony in the Age of Haydn and Beethoven*

Christopher Morris, *Reading Opera Between the Lines: Orchestral Interludes and Cultural Meaning from Wagner to Berg*

Emma Dillon, *Medieval Music-Making and the 'Roman de Fauvel'*

David Yearsley, *Bach and the Meanings of Counterpoint*

David Metzer, *Quotation and Cultural Meaning in the Twentieth Century*

Alexander Rehding, *Hugo Riemann and the Birth of Modern Musical Thought*

Dana Gooley, *The Virtuoso Liszt*

Bonnie Gordon, *Monteverdi's Unruly Women: The Power of Song in Early Modern Italy*

Gary Tomlinson, *The Singing of the New World: Indigenous Voice in the Era of European Contact*

Matthew Gelbart, *The Invention of Folk Music and Art Music: Emerging Categories from Ossian to Wagner*

Olivia A. Bloechl, *Native American Song at the Frontiers of Early Modern Music*

Giuseppe Gerbino, *Music and the Myth of Arcadia in Renaissance Italy*

Roger Freitas, *Portrait of a Castrato: Politics, Patronage, and Music in the Life of Atto Melani*

Gundula Kreuzer, *Verdi and the Germans: From Unification to the Third Reich*

Holly Watkins, *Metaphors of Depth in German Musical Thought: From E. T. A. Hoffmann to Arnold Schoenberg*

Davinia Caddy, *The Ballets Russes and Beyond: Music and Dance in Belle-Époque Paris*

The Ballets Russes and Beyond

Music and Dance in Belle-Époque Paris

Davinia Caddy

CAMBRIDGE UNIVERSITY PRESS
Cambridge, New York, Melbourne, Madrid, Cape Town,
Singapore, São Paulo, Delhi, Mexico City

Cambridge University Press
The Edinburgh Building, Cambridge CB2 8RU, UK

Published in the United States of America by Cambridge University Press, New York

www.cambridge.org
Information on this title: www.cambridge.org/9781107014404

First published 2012

Printed in the United Kingdom at the University Press, Cambridge

A catalogue record for this publication is available from the British Library

Library of Congress Cataloguing in Publication data
Caddy, Davinia, 1980–
The Ballets Russes and beyond: music and dance in belle-époque Paris / Davinia Caddy.
    p.   cm. – (New perspectives in music history and criticism ; 22)
Includes bibliographical references and index.
ISBN 978-1-107-01440-4
1. Ballets Russes – History.   2. Ballet – France – Paris – History – 20th century.
3. Dance – France – Paris – History – 20th century.   4. Music – France – Paris – History –
20th century.   5. Paris (France) – Social life and customs – 20th century.   I. Title.
GV1786.B355C34   2012
792.80944361–dc23

2011035583

ISBN 978-1-107-01440-4 Hardback

For my mum and dad

Contents

Examples

Figures

Front cover
Bakst, faun from *L'Après-midi d'un faune* (1912). Print, dimensions unknown. By permission of the Bibliothèque nationale de France.

Back cover
Bakst, bacchante from *Narcisse* (1911). Print, 25 × 19 cm. Courtesy of the Picture Collection, The New York Public Library, Astor, Lenox and Tilden Foundations.

Note on presentation

All primary, French-language sources are quoted in the original French and followed by an English translation (my own, unless otherwise stated). There are two exceptions, when only the French is given: footnotes; and single words or short phrases in the main text, the meaning of which seems clear enough. Quotations from primary sources in other languages, as well as all secondary material, appear in English translation only.

Titles of productions by the Ballets Russes appear in their original French. The spelling of Russian names follows *The New Grove Dictionary of Music and Musicians*; for individuals not listed, I have followed standard practice.

Acknowledgements

There are several people and institutions to thank. For financial assistance towards the costs of archival research: the Scouloudi Historical Foundation; the British Academy; the Music & Letters Trust; the Faculty of Music, University of Oxford; The Queen's College, University of Oxford; the School of Arts and Humanities, Oxford Brookes University; the School of Music, University of Auckland; and the National Institute of Creative Arts and Industries, University of Auckland. For archival assistance: the staff at the Bibliothèque nationale de France (BnF) (especially the Bibliothèque-musée de l'Opéra and the Département des Arts du spectacle), at the Houghton Library, Harvard, and at the New York Public Library (NYPL) for the Performing Arts (Jerome Robbins Dance Division). For acquiring primary and secondary source-material relevant to this project: Phillippa McKeown-Green and her staff at the Music and Dance Library, University of Auckland. For help locating and ordering images: Elvira Allocati (SCALA Picture Library), Philippe Bretagnon (BnF), Andrea Felder and Thomas Lisanti (NYPL), Mary Haegert (Houghton), Susan Hoffius (Waring Historical Library), and Dominique Plancher-Souveton (Musée de l'Assistance Publique, Hôpitaux de Paris). For musical examples: Ross Hendy and Jared Commerer at Promethean Editions. For looking over my French translations: Emmanuelle Chapin. For advice, assistance, and for taking on this project: Vicki Cooper and Becky Taylor at Cambridge University Press.

For a forum for discussion: the Francophone Music Criticism Network (especially Katharine Ellis and Mark Everist). For enthusiasm and encouragement: Suzanne Aspden, Francesca Brittan, Michael Christoforidis, Mary E. Davis, Karen Henson, Sarah Hibberd, Elizabeth Kertesz, Helen Julia Minors, Delphine Mordey, Susan Rutherford, Emanuele Senici, Mary Ann Smart and Richard Langham Smith. For reading my work, and for inspiring me and countless others: Roger Parker. Also for reading and offering perceptive comments: Roger's graduate group at King's College, London, particularly Gavin Williams.

For the warmest of welcomes to Godzone, where this book came to completion: my colleagues and friends at the School of Music, University of Auckland (especially Allan Badley, Robert Constable, Tamara Rickett, Dean Sutcliffe and Peter Watts) and at the New Zealand School of Music, Wellington (Keith Chapin, Brian Diettrich, Elizabeth Hudson and Inge van Rij). For friendly faces and open arms: Derek Bradley, Patrick Bradley, Robyn Panckhurst, 'Gloria', Joy, Eira, Vicky, Linda and everyone at North Shore Yoga. For allowing me to take over several rooms in their house: Pauline Bradley and Gracie (*le chien crétin*). For allowing me to take over several rooms in our house, and for much, much more: Chris Bradley.

For love, laughter and opportunities: my family and friends back home in England. For encouraging my musical studies: Ruth Binks, Pat Jeffers, Andrew Jones and Joy Stockton. For training in dance: Miss Cox. For sheer goodness of heart: Jo Daley. For inspiration: my Alsager Grandma. For reminding me what's important: my brother Dominic and my nephew Joseph. And for just about everything: my mum and dad. This book is for you.

Mission Bay, Auckland, June 2011

1 ❧ Introduction: *Le Génie de la danse*

This book has shared close quarters with a painting by Henri Matisse: *La Danse I* (Figure 1.1), a compositional study for a thirteen-foot mural commissioned by a Russian textile tycoon. The original is housed in the Museum of Modern Art, New York; a glossy poster print, slightly creased and torn at the edges, hangs in my office. Yet the closeness I describe is not only physical, a measure of distance between my MacBook and my Matisse. There is also a metaphorical – though no less palpable – intimacy. Throughout all stages of research and writing, the painting has captured my imagination, its five dancing nudes continuously and variously evocative. Admittedly, the pear-shaped dancer viewed from behind – the one about to fall flat – made the initial impression. Reaching out for the offered hand but not quite making contact, the dancer appeared to embody a scholarly pursuit with which I was all too familiar: an attempt to establish connections, to reconcile different arts and different disciplines, to get to grips with something – a line of argument, even a historical reality – that tended to remain out of reach. But then there were the other dancers, their boundless energy and exuberance, their elemental physical motion. It was not difficult to appreciate *La Danse* as a pictorial pick-me-up; it seemed to radiate all that long hours at the computer could eclipse. Indeed, many more qualified than I in matters of visual art have trumpeted similar descriptions, helping *La Danse* earn a place amongst the most popular paintings of the twentieth century – even, amongst 'Works of Art to See Before You Die'.[1]

As readers may well be aware, there is also a historical aspect to the closeness between the painting and this project. A leading figure within French artistic circles, Matisse created *La Danse I* in 1909, during the so-called belle époque, the historical period dating from roughly 1900 to 1914 – and the period under discussion in this book.[2] In an interview towards the

---

[1] I refer in particular to the list compiled by British journalist Jonathan Jones (*The Guardian*, 30 October 2006) and that generated by readers in response to Jones's article (posted on the newspaper's website, 5 December 2006). In both cases, it is the final (and larger) version of the painting – *La Danse II* – that is listed.
[2] Scholars have variously defined the boundary-dates of the belle époque, some preferring to backtrack to the 1880s. Here I adopt a shorter time frame, with a central focus on the decade or so before the outbreak of the First World War.

Figure 1.1 Matisse, *La Danse I* (1909).

end of his life, the painter claimed to have been influenced by some dancing he had witnessed at the Moulin de la Galette, an open-air dance-hall-cum-cabaret in Montmartre (depicted by Renoir in a painting of 1876, now an upmarket cafe). More specifically, Matisse recalled the Galette's famous farandole, a lively, follow-the-leader and specifically French dance in which men and women held hands, running and skipping along a meandering path.[3] Is this the dance captured in paint, super-size and mountain-top? It seems likely: the clasped hands and whirling spontaneity link mural with memory, as well as with the painter's recollections of the atmosphere in the dance-hall ('gaie') and the essence of dance itself ('vivante').[4] These recollections should give us pause. Dance, for Matisse, was a conceptual theme of significant cultural puissance, one that the painter returned to more than

---

[3] Georges Charbonnier, 'Entretien avec Henri Matisse', *Le Monologue du peintre*, vol. II (Paris: Éditions Julliard, 1960), pp. 7–16; for an English translation, see Jack Flam (ed.), *Matisse on Art* (1978; rev. edn Berkeley and Los Angeles: University of California Press, 1995), pp. 189–94.

[4] Flam suggests that Matisse may also have been influenced by a Catalan folk dance performed by fishermen and witnessed by the painter in the summer of 1905. According to Flam, this Catalan dance, 'grave and stately', contrasted with the spirited French farandole, and thus confuses the issue and identity of the painting's inspiration. See Flam, *Matisse: The Dance* (Washington, DC: National Gallery of Art, 1993), pp. 23–4.

once during his career.[5] Associated with vitality, vigour and rejuvenation, dance offered Matisse an artistic subject that could be both pictorial and abstract, specific and universal. *La Danse I* embodies this expressive potential. The painting may depict the far-flung and frivolous bodies of the Galette, but it may also function metaphorically – as a visual incarnation of *le génie de la danse* (the spirit of dance) in the belle époque.[6]

Period pleasure

It has become a cliché to describe the period as dance's 'golden age', a time of unprecedented stylistic diversity, cultural prestige, commercial success and general popularity. As is well known, from the late nineteenth century dance featured on an increasing number and variety of Parisian stages, from the Académie Nationale de Musique et de Danse (otherwise known as the Opéra), the Opéra-Comique, the Théâtre du Châtelet, Théâtre des Champs-Élysées and Théâtre des Arts, to the capital's many music-halls, cabarets, circuses, salons, *cafés-concerts* and museum galleries. Besides staged dance productions, there were dance schools and private classes, dance societies, competitions and tea-parties, and dance-inspired documentary and fiction films. These various phenomena helped dancers attain a new 'celebrity' status (made possible owing to the development of print technologies and the mass dissemination of the illustrated press), as well as an international fame and fan base.[7] This fan base itself was widespread in both geographical and cultural terms. The brightest lights of the contemporary dance scene inspired literary reflection, scientific study and copycat performers, as well as ranges of clothing, accessories and plant-pots.

Perhaps it was inevitable that dance was to thrive in an era in which the pursuit of pleasure supposedly eclipsed social, economic and political concerns. Inherited stories and images depict Parisians pedalling through the Bois de Boulogne or strolling through the Tuileries, evenings spent at the

---

[5] *Ibid.*

[6] The phrase owes something to a sculpture by Jean-Baptiste Carpeaux that has adorned the façade of the Paris Opéra since 1869. Entitled *La Danse*, and featuring a winged *génie* with accompanying figures, the large *haut-relief* bears a striking resemblance to Matisse's painting of the same name.

[7] For a historically informed discussion of the rise of celebrity culture, one that backtracks to the nineteenth century (rather than focusing, as is customary, on the post-war period), see Lenard R. Berlanstein, 'Historicizing and Gendering Celebrity Culture: Famous Women in Nineteenth-Century France', *Journal of Women's History*, 16/4 (2004), pp. 65–91; also see his *Daughters of Eve: A Cultural History of French Theater Women from the Old Regime to the Fin de Siècle* (Cambridge, MA: Harvard University Press, 2001).

Chat Noir, the Folies-Bergère or Maxim's. As legend has it, life during the belle époque was precisely that – a buoyant, hopeful and carefree quotidian reality centred on a burgeoning entertainment industry.[8] This industry, itself central to a new urban economy, was no longer the privilege of an upper class with time on its hands. A Republican-endorsed *nivellement des jouissances* (democratization of entertainment) made a number of activities accessible to a wider public; subsidized rail fares attracted people from the provinces to the city.[9] As a result, audiences increased in number and diversity, as did theatres and other performance venues; and the matinee performance became a regular feature, sparking an afternoon theatre-going trend amongst families, especially women and children. Archival sources suggest that by the dawn of the twentieth century, more than half a million Parisians went to a theatre once a week. This figure, equating to roughly 40 per cent of the recorded population, may even underestimate, for it accounts only for box-office sales at Paris's main theatres, and not for visitors to the variety venues of *café-concert*, cabaret and circus.[10]

Specifics notwithstanding, the commercial and cultural fortune invested in the entertainment scene was no doubt motivated in part by the French capital – 'the capital of pleasure', as it was known across the world.[11] Newly face-lifted by the urban renovations of Baron Georges-Eugène Haussmann, Paris was toasted by contemporaries as a modern metropolis, a quintessentially commercial (rather than industrial) city. What is more, the capital was known for its theatrical aura; its new topography endorsed the spirit and

[8] According to Roger Shattuck, *The Banquet Years: The Origins of the Avant-Garde in France, 1885 to World War I* (1958; rev. edn London: Vintage, 1968), life was of 'surface aspect', a mix of 'pompous display, frivolity, hypocrisy, cultivated taste and relaxed morals' (p. 3). Also see Jean-Pierre Camard, Paul Ricard and Lynne Thornton, *L'Art et la vie en France à la Belle Époque* (Paris: Paul Ricard, 1971); Raymond Rudorff, *The Belle Époque: Paris in the Nineties* (London: Hamish Hamilton, 1972); and Nigel Gosling, *Paris, 1900–1914: The Miraculous Years* (London: Weidenfeld and Nicolson, 1978).

[9] See Georges d'Avenel, *Le Nivellement des jouissances* (Paris: Flammarion, 1913). Charles Rearick describes this 'levelling' in his *Pleasures of the Belle Époque: Entertainment and Festivity in Turn-of-the-Century France* (New Haven, CT, and London: Yale University Press, 1985).

[10] See Eugen Weber, *France: Fin de Siècle* (Cambridge, MA: Harvard University Press, 1986), p. 159; and Adna Ferrin Weber, *The Growth of Cities in the Nineteenth Century: A Study in Cities* (Ithaca, NY: Cornell University Press, 1968), p. 73. For a summary account of the Parisian theatre scene, its growth and diversity, see Catherine Hindson, *Female Performance Practice on the Fin-de-Siècle Popular Stages of London and Paris* (Manchester University Press, 2007), pp. 9–33. For a more nuanced perspective, one that conceptualizes the significance of art and entertainment in terms of national and political agendas, see Jann Pasler, *Composing the Citizen: Music as Public Utility in Third-Republic France* (Berkeley and Los Angeles: University of California Press, 2009).

[11] Hindson, *Female Performance Practice*, p. 9. As Hindson notes, an 1895 issue of *Harper's New Monthly Magazine* declared that 'Americans go to London for social triumph or to float railroad shares, to Rome for art's sake, and to Berlin to study music and economize'; yet they go to Paris only 'to enjoy themselves' (p. 13).

spectacle of staged entertainment. Haussmann had replaced Paris's winding medieval alleyways with wide, straight and tree-lined boulevards, ones that offered linear perspectives on famous monuments and buildings.[12] And not only on these. The boulevards afforded Parisians their own urban theatre; in the spectacle of the street, observers could look across the urban landscape and be looked at themselves.[13] These same observers were instructed how 'to act Parisian': pocket guides detailed what to wear (pearls during the day, diamonds at night), what to do (go to Bayreuth, or plan to go next year), what to like (grouse shooting in Scotland), what not to like (politics), and what to discuss in public (one's eventful social calendar).[14]

Paris dancing

If Paris was a metaphor for the stage – and if Parisians were actor-observers in the grand narrative of the belle époque – then dance was a symbol of the contemporary way of life.[15] In the words of André Mangeot, editor of the journal *Le Monde musical*:

On danse partout. On danse même tellement qu'on ne pense plus qu'à cela . . . tout n'est il pas danse dans notre existence? Danse du sang dans les artères. Danse des

---

[12] David Harvey offers a useful history of 'Haussmannization' in his *Paris: Capital of Modernity* (London: Routledge, 2003); Harvey draws attention to the ways in which social relations were shaped by the material and economic conditions of daily life, themselves shaped by Paris's spatial reorganization. For more, see Priscilla Parkhurst Ferguson, *Paris as Revolution: Writing the 19th-Century City* (Berkeley and Los Angeles: University of California Press, 1994), particularly pp. 115–51; and Vanessa R. Schwartz, *Spectacular Realities: Early Mass Culture in Fin-de-Siècle Paris* (Berkeley and Los Angeles: University of California Press, 1998), pp. 1–44. Incidentally, the conceptualization of the city as an active stimulus of modernity and modern art has been explored by Edward Timms and David Kelley (eds.), *Unreal City: Urban Experience in Modern European Literature and Art* (Manchester University Press, 1988) and Lynda Nead, *Victorian Babylon: People, Streets and Images in Nineteenth-Century London* (New Haven, CT, and London: Yale University Press, 2000). It is also central to T. J. Clark's magisterial thesis, *The Painting of Modern Life: Paris in the Art of Manet and his Followers* (New York: Knopf, 1984).

[13] See Schwartz, *Spectacular Realities*, pp. 1–44. Even theatre-going acquired a theatrical aspect. The foyer of the Folies-Bergère, for example, with its bar immortalized by Manet, was fixed with lights and mirrors so that spectators could see and be seen.

[14] See, for example, the unauthored guide *Paris-Parisien* (Paris: Ollendorff, 1898), pp. 398–403. Schwartz discusses the nature, construction and performativity of social roles in her *Spectacular Realities*; also see Peter Bailey, *Popular Culture and Performance in the Victorian City* (Cambridge University Press, 1998).

[15] According to the English publication *John Bull's Trip to Paris*, c.1900, '[t]he talent for acting comes more readily to a Frenchman than to an Englishman. Every Frenchman is more or less of a born actor.' See Hindson, *Female Performance Practice*, p. 14.

idées dans le cerveau bouillonnant de l'artiste, de l'inventeur et du banquier … Danse des ondes hertziennes. Danse des écus. Danse de la vie, devant la mort.[16]

(We dance everywhere. We dance so much that we only think about dancing … is not everything in our existence dance? Dance of blood in the arteries. Dance of ideas bubbling in the brain of the artist, the inventor, the banker … Dance of radio waves. Dance of coins. Dance of life, in face of death.)

Equally enthusiastic about dance and its metaphorical potential was Ricciotto Canudo, an Italian-born critic who made Paris his home in the early 1900s. In his 1907 study *Le Livre de l'évolution de l'homme*, Canudo described dance as 'le grand creuset orgiaque des individus' (the big, orgiastic melting pot of people), 'le symbole anthropologique du Feu' (the anthropological symbol of Fire) and 'un bain régénérateur' (a regenerating bath).[17] To Canudo, the essential meaning of dance was connected in metaphysical terms to 'toutes les compositions et les décompositions profondes de la vie, d'où toutes les formes de la vie jaillissent' (all the combinations and divisions of life elements, from which all forms of life spring forth).[18]

This enthusiasm for dance was no doubt stimulated by a cluster of concurrent phenomena: a burgeoning interest (across the visual arts, photography and early cinema, as well as the physical sciences and industry at large) in the concept of motion; a specifically theatrical anxiety about opera, vocal exegesis and dramatic impersonation; an intellectual loss of confidence in verbal culture (the so-called language crisis, symptomatic of early modernism); and a societal trend towards sport and recreation. (Many of these will be addressed in this book.) Yet also important was the physical presence in the French capital of foreign performers. Names will be familiar. First, before the turn of the century, came the 'modern' dancers from North America, the most notable being Loie Fuller and Isadora Duncan.[19] Although these women worked independently, performing solo (or else with students they trained), they shared aesthetic objectives: to promote dance as an autonomous art; to expand the expressive potential of gesture; and to experiment with stage effects, decor and costume. As for technique, their aim was to liberate dance from the perceived restraints of both a dramatically superfluous virtuosity and a dramatically informed

---

[16] André Mangeot, 'On Danse', *Le Monde musical*, 30 January 1914, pp. 20–1 at p. 20. Mangeot went on to ponder the essential definition of dance as a physical activity, as opposed to less specific movement. There was, he implies, no clear distinction: 'La Danse, n'est-elle pas comme le Jour, dont on ne sait à quel moment précis il succède à la Nuit? Il y a du jour dans la nuit, et il y a de la nuit dans le jour.'

[17] Ricciotto Canudo, *Le Livre de l'évolution de l'homme: psychologie musicale des civilisations* (Paris: E. Sansot et Cie, 1907), p. 148.

[18] *Ibid.*, p. 147.

[19] Fuller introduced Duncan (fifteen years her junior) to Parisian audiences, although the two soon parted company.

mime: in other words, from the choreographic mandate of 'classical' ballet. The dancers maintained a personal approach to their dancing, a desire to externalize feelings and emotions, or else to convey something of 'Beauty' or 'Nature' in the abstract. They danced barefoot, un-corseted and often in a draped or diaphanous costume.[20] Figure 1.2, a studio photograph of Duncan, shows the dancer in typically loose-fitting attire. The pose is equally typical. With arms outstretched, chest forward and neck tipped slightly back, Duncan appears as compelling and triumphant as the marble sculpture *The Winged Victory of Samothrace* – the famously headless (and armless) monument, dating from *c*.190 BC, that now stands at the top of the sweeping Daru staircase in the Louvre, Paris (Figure 1.3). This association between Duncan and the sculpted Greek goddess may be unsurprising: the dancer rhapsodized at length about classical Greece, its art, culture and ideal of the human body; she also promoted herself as the embodiment of Greek dance, at times appearing to bring to life specific poses from vases, bas-reliefs and other forms of sculpture.[21] Certainly, this seems the case in Figure 1.2. The photograph, with its soft focus yet intense chiaroscuro effect, adds to the Grecian illusion; it captures a radiance that illuminates – both literally and metaphorically – the dancer's majestic pose.

Figure 1.4, also a studio photograph, may be even more iconic. Taken by one L. Roosen, the shot depicts Vaslav Nijinsky in his role as the Golden Slave in the 1910 ballet *Schéhérazade*. Nijinsky, of course, was the star protégé of the Ballets Russes, the company that famously stormed onto the Paris circuit in 1909. Led by the Russian impresario Sergey Diaghilev, the Ballets Russes caused a sensation, their productions pored over in the daily and specialist presses, in memoirs, picture books and popular literature. Audiences and critics, enamoured by 'les incomparables danseurs russes', rushed to praise a specifically choreographic

[20] The dancers' memoirs offer useful accounts of their dancing and motivations: see Isadora Duncan, *My Life* (1928; repr. London: Gollancz, 1996); and Loïe Fuller, *Fifteen Years of a Dancer's Life* (1913; repr. New York: Dance Horizons, 1977). There is also an extensive secondary literature, including Richard Nelson Current and Marcia Ewing Current, *Loïe Fuller: Goddess of Light* (Boston, MA: Northeastern University Press, 1997); Peter Kurth, *Isadora: A Sensational Life* (Boston, MA: Little, Brown and Company, 2001); Giovanni Lista, *Loïe Fuller: danseuse de la belle époque* (Paris: Somogy, 1995); Lillian Lowenthal, *The Search for Isadora: The Legend and Legacy of Isadora Duncan* (Pennington, NJ: Dance Horizons, 1993); Sally Sommer, 'Loïe Fuller', *Drama Review*, 19/1 (1975), pp. 53–67; Sewell Stokes, *Isadora Duncan: An Intimate Portrait* (London: Brentano, 1928); and Valérie Thomas and Jérôme Perrin (eds.), *Loïe Fuller, danseuse de l'art nouveau* (Paris: Éditions de la Réunion des Musées Nationaux, 2002).

[21] For more on Duncan's Grecian inspiration, see Ann Daly, 'The Natural Body', in Ann Dils and Ann Cooper Albright (eds.), *Moving History/Dancing Cultures* (Middletown, CT: Wesleyan University Press, 2001), pp. 288–99. Incidentally, *The Winged Victory of Samothrace*, a resident of the Louvre since 1866 and one of Duncan's personal favourites, took on specifically nationalist associations in the early war years, appearing to allegorize an exalted and triumphant French spirit; see Kenneth E. Silver, *Esprit de Corps: The Art of the Parisian Avant-Garde and the First World War, 1914–1925* (London: Thames and Hudson, 1989), pp. 96–106.

Figure 1.2 Duncan (1908); photographer unknown.

'renovation'.[22] Principal choreographer Michel (Mikhail) Fokine, himself influenced by Duncan, advocated an expressive, almost psychologically motivated choreography, one that liberated the body – particularly the torso and arms – from stilted balletic conventions. Nijinsky's pose in Figure 1.4 is exemplary. The dancer's arms do not frame his body in perfect symmetry; instead, they extend outward and behind, thrusting into the foreground a bejewelled torso and naked

---

[22] See, for example, Pierre Lalo, 'La Saison russe', *Le Temps*, 28 May 1912, p. 3.

Figure 1.3 *The Winged Victory of Samothrace* (*c*.190 BC).

Figure 1.4 Nijinsky as the Golden Slave, *Schéhérazade* (1910–11); photographer, L. Roosen.

midriff. The arched neck, almost-closed eyes and ecstatic smile also betray Fokine's trademark naturalism – an insistence on the body as a gateway to the soul, to the essence of dramatic character.

A comprehensive account of Fokine's choreographic project can be found in the secondary literature, spearheaded by the archival work of Lynn Garafola. In her seminal monograph of 1989, Garafola documents the history of the Ballets Russes, describing various choreographic initiatives (the promotion of the male dancer, the 'democratization' of the corps de ballet), as well as a Wagnerian ideal of collaboration between the arts.[23] Yet, and as Garafola is sure to recognize, the defining characteristic of the company was intangible, impossible to grasp but everywhere to be seen, heard and even smelt. 'Russianness' was an exotic perfume: in the words of one critic, 'un parfum d'une insistance particulière, un charme de couleur et d'accents indéfinissables' (a perfume of a particular piquancy, a charm of colour and indefinable tones).[24] As Garafola and others have argued, Diaghilev's promotion of ballets either specifically Russian or vaguely Eastern in theme (*Cléopâtre*, *Schéhérazade*, *L'Oiseau de feu*, *Sadko*, *Petrouchka*, *Le Dieu bleu*, *Thamar*, *Le Coq d'or*) served a dual purpose. A calculated and commercial strategy, the exotic ballets helped entrench the troupe's foreign status whilst satiating a deep-seated desire amongst the French for all things Oriental.[25] *Schéhérazade*, in particular, was loaded with Oriental

[23] Lynn Garafola, *Diaghilev's Ballets Russes* (1989; repr. New York: Da Capo, 1998). These initiatives did not escape notice in the press. On the newly designed and specifically Russian corps de ballet, for example, see Mill Cissan (pseudonym), 'La Saison russe', *Comœdia illustré*, 15 June 1910 (special supplement on the Ballets Russes [no page numbers]): 'Les solistes, nous l'avons vu, et répété, sont hors de pair; mais il est plus stupéfiant de pouvoir reconnaître à chaque membre du corps de ballet une valeur de soliste. En Russie, dans le pays du *tchin*, la hiérarchie n'existe point parmi les artistes de la danse: du moins on n'y voit point de comparses, de personnages qui ne sont là que pour porter un costume, faire nombre et se grouper avec des gestes mécaniques. Non, la troupe entière vit, frémit, participe à l'action dansée ou mimée, et tel de ses artistes qui n'a point, ce soir-là, un rôle en vue, ne serait pas embarrassé pour exécuter d'emblée les pas les plus complexes.'

[24] Mte Casalonga, 'Adieux . . . (Ballets Russes)', *Comœdia illustré*, 15 July 1910, pp. 595–8 at p. 595. The Ballets Russes also inspired actual perfumes ('Parfum des Jardins d'Armide', 'Prince Igor', 'Nirvana', 'Un air embaumé'), some of which were named after Russian ballets and worn by female patrons.

[25] See Garafola, *Diaghilev's Ballets Russes*, p. 43, and Richard Taruskin, *Defining Russia Musically: Historical and Hermeneutical Essays* (Princeton University Press, 1997), p. 49. French interest in the Orient, prominent throughout the 1800s, was given new impetus at the turn of the century by the appearance of Joseph Charles Mardrus's translation of *The Thousand and One Nights*. The publication, serialized over five years in the Symbolist journal *La Revue blanche*, steered Parisians towards Oriental culture and artefacts; society women even began to emulate the Oriental 'look' in street fashion and interior decoration. For more on French Orientalism, its impact on culture and the arts, and its relation to the French colonial project, see Madeleine Dobie, *Foreign Bodies: Gender, Language and Culture in French Orientalism* (Stanford University Press, 2001); and Roger Benjamin, *Orientalist Aesthetics: Art, Colonialism and French North Africa, 1880–1930* (Berkeley and Los Angeles: University of California Press, 2003). Both books draw heavily on the critical conceptualization and political implications advanced by Edward Said in his classic text *Orientalism* (New York: Pantheon, 1978).

imagery. The decor, designed by Léon Bakst, replaced the ethereal world of nineteenth-century ballet with the colour and opulence of an imagined East.[26] The costumes, also by Bakst, were both exotic and erotic. As illustrated in Figure 1.4, the Golden Slave wore a flesh-revealing bandeau and baggy harem pants – immodest attire that served to liberate the dancer's body, to allow him a range of unrestricted movements.[27] More than this, both costume and choreography emphasized an explicitly Oriental persona: a sex-fuelled slave-lover, unbound by the laws and constraints of society, free to ravish a forbidden woman in her husband's home.[28]

But one of the Russians' 'adorables ballets', *Schéhérazade* helped trademark some now-familiar descriptors.[29] 'La merveille de danse' (the wonder of dance), 'la splendeur bondissante' (splendour bounding forth), 'la jeunesse de grâce' (youthful grace), 'plein de fougue' (full of ardour): these were but some of the terms bandied about in the press, terms that have been maintained to this day in the scholarly literature on the Russian company. Even the quickest flick through the mass of biographies and history books (many of which trumpet 'legends', 'legacies' and 'untold stories') reveals an embarrassment of 'ecstatic' reference, not only to specific productions, but to the company itself.[30] Literature on the American 'moderns' has endorsed similar epithets: 'la sensualité', 'l'esprit' (spirit), 'l'extase' (ecstasy), 'la jouissance' (pleasure). These terms coordinate nicely with the cultural dynamics of the period: they endorse the *belle* of the *époque*, along with the attendant associations of *éclat* and *énergie*. Indeed, and with this endorsement in mind, it is tempting to glance back to the Matisse painting with which this chapter began. The quintet's dynamism, spontaneity and physical zing: these

---

[26] Bakst's set, designed as a lavish seraglio, was decorated in vivid greens, blues and reds; Persian-style rugs and cushions, and gold and silver lanterns, adorned the stage, itself framed by a huge silk drape. For illustrations and accounts of Bakst's designs, see Charles Spencer, *Léon Bakst and the Ballets Russes* (1973; rev. edn London: Academy Editions, 1995); and Alexander Schouvalov (ed.), *The Art of Ballets Russes* (New Haven, CT, and London: Yale University Press, 1997). As Schouvalov notes, Bakst's *Schéhérazade* offered little in the way of authenticity; yet this was no matter to the French.

[27] Costumes and colours for *Schéhérazade* quickly influenced Parisian culture, from high couture and interior design to jewellery and even pastry-making.

[28] This type of characterization conforms to the typical Orientalist narrative, its primitive, sexual and decadent overtones. To the European audience, the Orient represented a fantasyland displaced from the body politic – and from the bourgeois behavioural conventions – of the West. Uninhibited sexuality, licentiousness and Oriental despotism served as projections of domestic fears and desires.

[29] This is not to forget the so-called neo-Romantic ballets of the company's early years, gradually eclipsed by the more popular exotic fare; see Garafola, *Diaghilev's Ballets Russes*, p. 43.

[30] Take, for example, Vladimir Fédorovski's aptly titled *L'Histoire secrète des Ballets Russes* (Paris: Éditions du Rocher, 2002). Notwithstanding its attention to important details of the Franco-Russian relationship, the book conjures a romanticized image of the Russian company, its 'frénésie' and 'passion', and 'les valeurs éternelles' incarnated in its dancing.

impressions are consistent with those of Paris's celebrated dancers, at least according to the oft-quoted reports. The painting, it appears, may be thoroughly ensconced within its context, may represent, if not a particular style or type of dance, then the essential and defining *génie* (spirit) invoked earlier.

The Midas touch

Yet what if this *génie* – conceptualized by Matisse, embodied by the Ballets Russes – rings true in only a limited sense? What if the impressions of youthfulness and exuberance are one-sided and, therefore, misleading? Raising these questions is not to deny the historical enthusiasm for dance, nor is it to cast doubt on the specific salience of the Russian company. As dance historians have not tired of telling us, especially during recent centennial celebrations, Diaghilev and his troupe achieved a rapid and remarkable ascent to fame. Generating interest across the general public and the commercial sector, the Ballets Russes earned the respect of prominent artists, critics and men-of-letters. More than this, they turned around the fortunes of ballet (then an embattled genre), and turned to gold their own choreographic creations, at least in metaphorical terms. Yet the myth of the Midas touch may be precisely that. Despite evidence of the troupe's innovative aesthetic and alluring qualities, the view that these were its only characteristics – the only terms with which it was recognized – is too narrow. Likewise, the standard conceptualization of dance of the period, inextricably bound to the Russian company, may well be limiting.

As implied above, the cumulative impact of the extant literature on Diaghilev's troupe has been to create, as much as to report, a historical identity. Academic volumes, books and articles – not to mention the numerous exhibition catalogues, photograph albums and souvenir brochures that have sprung up in recent years – have tended to lionize the troupe, to look back on its *saisons russes* with rose-tinted reverence and awe. To put this in other words, the literature betrays a common desire or discursive strategy, often leaning on overblown adjectives and tabloid-like histrionics. For example, in an article aptly titled 'The Russians Have Come, the Russians Have Come', Clive Barnes describes 'the Diaghilev onslaught which revitalized ballet', noting the magic, incantatory force of the names 'Diaghilev' and 'the Ballets Russes'.[31] Looking back on pre-1900s dance,

---

[31] Clive Barnes, 'The Russians Have Come, the Russians Have Come', *Dance Magazine*, 72/2 (1998), p. 162.

Elizabeth Kendall recalls 'the calm before the storm': 'a placid surface about to be broken by new and wild versions of the art heaving shockingly into view'.[32] With similar rhetoric, if different imagery, Deborah Jowitt reminiscences upon the 'fire' and 'controversy' of the Russian troupe, describing a 'visionary' impresario, 'windblown' and 'fragrant' ballets, and 'Mon Dieu, those dancers!'.[33] Clearly, both Kendall and Jowitt indulge in imaginative historical recreation; yet the titles of their articles are written in earnest. 'A Doorway to Revolution', 'The Ballets Russes Revolution': the 'r' word – along with the synonyms 'renaissance', 'rejuvenation' and 'rebirth' – crops up interminably.[34]

This manner of rhetorical promotion – the enumeration of the company's novel working methods, the proclamations of its pioneer status – is linked to a tendency to conceptualize the Ballets Russes as a turning point in the history of dance. This history reads as a 'rupture' narrative, one that splits into halves marked 'before' and 'after', and one that leans (dangerously, I think) on a Romanticized belief in the personal autonomy of artists – that is, their seeming removal from social and cultural realities. Diaghilev's troupe, as a historical construct, appears both independent and untouchable – in the words of museum curator Jane Pritchard, 'a giant that continues to grow'.[35]

Part of my purpose in this book is to slow down this growth spurt, to pull on the reins of the Ballets Russes bandwagon and take a moment to pause and catch breath. In the chapters that follow, I should like to think again about the company, to reconsider what we know – or, rather, what we think we know – about its contemporary status and significance. Confronting the usual history, looking afresh at the source-material, it emerges that there were other kinds of discourse, other characteristics, qualities and influences associated with the troupe, ones that may afford new perspectives on dance during the belle époque.

---

[32] Elizabeth Kendall, '1900, A Doorway to Revolution', *Dance Magazine*, 73/1 (1999), pp. 80–3 at p. 80. Kendall goes on to describe how 'Diaghilev unleashed the fantastic energy of the Ballets Russes', those 'provocative, colourful, dramatic and daring performers from borderlands at the edge of European consciousness' (pp. 83 and 80).

[33] Deborah Jowitt, 'The Ballets Russes Revolution', *Dance Magazine*, 83/2 (2009), pp. 26–9.

[34] Also see Garafola, *Diaghilev's Ballets Russes*, p. 143 (for one reference amongst many). Giannandrea Poesio notes the 'overenthusiastic tones' and 'celebratory modes' of much of the literature in his perceptive review-essay 'Perpetuating the Myth: Sergey Diaghilev and the Ballets Russes', *Modernism/Modernity*, 18/1 (2011), pp. 161–73.

[35] See Jane Pritchard (ed.), *Diaghilev and the Golden Age of the Ballets Russes, 1909–1929* (London: Victoria and Albert Museum, 2010), p. 187; this volume accompanied the exhibition (of the same name) held at the Victoria and Albert Museum, London, September 2010 to January 2011. Pritchard and the exhibition should both be applauded for bringing into view – literally and metaphorically – the variety of contexts in which the Russian troupe worked and made its name.

Revisionism

The period itself has come under scrutiny. Recent historians have contested the legend of the *belle*, juxtaposing reports of Parisian pleasure with accounts of the period's problems: anarchist attacks, anticlerical offensives, economic insecurities, stagnant population growth, inconsistent industrial development, a deceleration of the colonial enterprise, decreasing foreign trade, the rise of radical extremists, political disillusionment, agitation amongst trade unions, and reactions against bourgeois domesticity.[36] Exposing the Janus-faced nature of the era, revisionist histories have unearthed anxieties of various kinds, ones that imposed themselves on intellectual and political circles, on industry and business, on the military, the church and on society at large. This is to say nothing of anxieties within the arts. As Marius-Ary Leblond (the nom de plume of two writer-cousins) maintained in a piece for the fortnightly *La Vie*, the biggest challenge facing modern times was public incomprehension.[37] The emerging masses, it seemed, wanted to retreat from taste-making, to content themselves with the immediate and sensuous stimulations of music-hall and cinema, to grow numb under the influence of alcohol.[38] As for artists themselves, critic Louis Laloy described the confusions and contrarieties that characterized the contemporary scene:

C'était une époque troublée; coup sur coup, des révélations merveilleuses avaient frappé nos jeunes esprits, et chacun défendait son dieu. Nous n'avions en commun qu'une immense espérance et les idées se heurtaient, étincelantes comme des épées.[39]

---

[36] See, for example, Christophe Charle, *Paris fin de siècle: culture et politique* (Paris: Éditions du Seuil, 1998); Colin Jones, *Paris: Biography of a City* (London: Allen Lane, 2004), chapter 10 ('The Anxious Spectacle'), pp. 396–442; Christophe Prochasson, *Paris 1900: essai d'histoire culturelle* (Paris: Calmann-Lévy, 1999); Debora L. Silverman, *Art Nouveau in Fin-de-Siècle France: Politics, Psychology and Style* (Berkeley and Los Angeles: University of California Press, 1989); Barnett Singer, *Modern France: Mind, Politics, Society* (Seattle: University of Washington Press, 1980); Richard Sonn, *Anarchism and Cultural Politics in Fin-de-Siècle France* (Lincoln: University of Nebraska Press, 1989); Weber, *France: Fin de Siècle*; and Johannes Willms, *Paris, Capital of Europe: From the Revolution to the Belle Époque*, trans. Eveline L. Kanes (New York: Holmes and Meier, 1997). Marshall Berman's *All That is Solid Melts into Air: The Experience of Modernity* (New York: Simon and Schuster, 1982) is useful on the social and cultural effects of the modernization of city life.

[37] Marius-Ary Leblond, 1913; cited in Jacques Reboul, 'Le Public et les artistes', *Montjoie!*, 1/11–12 (November–December 1913), pp. 12–13 at p. 12.

[38] For an insightful account of the split and the slippage between 'serious' art and the 'masses', see Andreas Huyssen, *After the Great Divide: Modernism, Mass Culture, Postmodernism* (Bloomington: Indiana University Press, 1986).

[39] Louis Laloy, 'Article critique concernant *L'Histoire de la musique* de Camille Mauclair', *Comœdia* (1914); clipping, F-Pn, Ro 6019. On the perceived need for 'un art pour le peuple', see Camille Mauclair, *Trois Crises de l'art actuel* (Paris: Fasquelle, 1906), pp. 248–63; and Paul de Stoeklin, 'L'Art pour le peuple', *Le Courrier musical*, 15 January 1909, pp. 42–6. As Stoeklin notes, this need

(It was a confused period; blow by blow, marvellous revelations had struck our young minds and each defended his own god. We had in common only an immense expectancy; ideas collided, sparkling like swords.)

Laloy's words are instructive, and the emerging counter-narrative – a less-than-belle époque – especially so. For this narrative can point us to an important and provocative revision in dance historiography, one that can help wrench our usual assumptions into new and vivid perspectives. To put this another way, one might argue that the study of belle-époque dance has lost its freshness, and that our habit of historicizing the period has been doing more harm than good, doing away with the complexities and contingencies that shaped the conception, realization and reception of dance performance. This book may read as a recovery effort. It not only suggests alternatives to the broadly acknowledged innovations of the Ballets Russes; it seeks to resituate the company within a variety of contexts – theatrical, intellectual, aesthetic, even scientific – specific to the period.

Some interesting work has already been done, particularly on the American 'moderns' mentioned earlier. Ann Cooper Albright, Rhonda Garelick, Felicia McCarren and Julie Townsend have constructed 'interdisciplinary' histories of Loie Fuller, locating the dancer in her immediate social and cultural locale.[40] Garelick, in particular, and in a remarkably vibrant and wide-ranging book, has emphasized Fuller's 'deep-connectedness' to contemporary developments, from Orientalism and art nouveau to cinema and medical science.[41] Carrie J. Preston invokes a similar 'connectedness' in an insightful article on Isadora Duncan.[42] Taking her lead from the dancer's own words ('I must place a motor in my soul'), Preston exposes and explores the similarities between Duncan's dance theory, modernist performance aesthetics and Futurist ideology, drawing on a shared vocabulary of the industrial machine.[43]

---

was new, for never before had 'le vrai peuple' (meaning, he says, 'les ouvriers') existed as an entity apart from the middle and upper classes.

[40] Ann Cooper Albright, *Traces of Light: Absence and Presence in the Work of Loïe Fuller* (Middleton, CT: Wesleyan University Press, 2007); Rhonda Garelick, *Electric Salome: Loie Fuller's Performance of Modernism* (Princeton University Press, 2007); Felicia McCarren, 'The "Symptomatic Act": Mallarmé, Charcot and Loie Fuller', in her *Dance Pathologies: Performance, Poetics, Medicine* (Stanford University Press, 1998), pp. 113–71; and Julie Townsend, 'Alchemic Visions and Technological Advances: Sexual Morphology in Loie Fuller's Dance', in Jane C. Desmond (ed.), *Dancing Desires: Choreographing Sexualities on and off the Stage* (Madison: University of Wisconsin Press, 2001), pp. 73–96.

[41] Garelick, *Electric Salome*, p. 16.

[42] Carrie J. Preston, 'The Motor in the Soul: Isadora Duncan and Modernist Performance', *Modernism/Modernity*, 12/2 (2005), pp. 273–89.

[43] On the machine aesthetic, readers may also wish to consult Felicia McCarren's book, *Dancing Machines: Choreographies of the Age of Mechanical Reproduction* (Stanford University Press, 2003).

There will be little on these two dancers in the pages that follow – for reasons of space and scope. I should prefer, as mentioned earlier, to refocus on the Ballets Russes: their presence in Paris, their reception in the press, and their resonance with contemporaneous cultural phenomena. On these subjects, too, there have been welcome additions to the literature. John E. Bowlt, Professor of Slavic Languages, has upturned the usual claims of 'newness' and 'renovation' by pointing to the Ballets Russes' retrospective tendencies: in particular, to Diaghilev's fascination with the late seventeenth and eighteenth centuries.[44] Anna Winestein has situated the company within the context of an early twentieth-century cult of 'stardom' and 'celebrity', focusing on the emergence and development of the photographic image as a promotional tool.[45] In an edited volume devoted to the 1911 ballet *Petrouchka*, Andrew Wachtel tackles head-on the 'myth' of the company's uniqueness, suggesting that the Russian productions were thoroughly typical of Russian modernist theatre.[46] And, in two recent books, Mary E. Davis attempts to reweave the Russian company into the fabric of the belle époque.[47] The metaphor is appropriate, for Davis focuses on fashion: coverage devoted to the company in French fashion magazines; relations between company members and Parisian fashionistas; and similarities of style – of costume and couture, on stage and off.

These recent writings are refreshing: they tempt us to look beyond the familiar and the commonplace, to peer into surrounding social and cultural spheres. Davis's work especially interests me, because it brings to light interesting juxtapositions: a Chanel cardigan and Russian neoclassicism; composer Erik Satie and *Vogue*; 'Tango teas' and dancing 'tastemakers'. These juxtapositions, none of which is couched in polemical terms by the author, are more than evocative. They endorse a relational and dialogic approach, one that launches the study of dance onto hitherto overlooked historical terrain. This approach, which I seek to emulate in the pages that

---

[44] John E. Bowlt, 'Diaghilev and the Eighteenth Century', in Sjeng Scheijen (ed.), *Working for Diaghilev* (Groninger Museum, 2004), pp. 38–48.

[45] Anna Winestein, 'Still Dancing: Photographs and Postcards of the Ballets Russes', in Alston Purvis, Peter Rand and Anna Winestein (eds.), *The Ballets Russes and the Art of Design* (New York: Random House, 2009), pp. 95–124.

[46] Andrew Wachtel (ed.), *'Petrushka': Sources and Contexts* (Evanston, IL: Northwestern University Press, 1998).

[47] Mary E. Davis, *Classic Chic: Music, Fashion, and Modernism* (Berkeley and Los Angeles: University of California Press, 2006); and her *Ballets Russes Style: Diaghilev's Dancers and Paris Fashion* (London: Reaktion Books, 2010). Readers may also appreciate the revisionist account of the reception of the Russian company in the American press offered by Hanna Järvinen, 'Failed Impressions: Diaghilev's Ballets Russes in America, 1916', *Dance Research Journal*, 42/2 (2010), pp. 76–108; and the new biography of Diaghilev by Sjeng Scheijen, *Diaghilev: A Life* (Oxford University Press, 2010).

follow, has the potential to challenge outworn assumptions about Diaghilev and his Ballets Russes. It may even upset established hierarchies and historical wisdoms about the broader terrain of belle-époque dance, pointing perhaps towards a new and as yet unknown historical *génie*. Yet these challenges are to be embraced. Ultimately, they can help extend our imaginative reach, broadening our understanding of dance as a complex cultural practice and, in doing so, inviting us to construct interesting juxtapositions of our own.

Music and dance

A musicologist by trade, I am interested primarily in the juxtaposition of music and dance, a juxtaposition to which the Ballets Russes famously devoted serious attention. Engaging non-specialist ballet composers, doing away with formulaic and frivolous musical scores, whilst encouraging a collaborative work ethic, the troupe have long been applauded for their initiation of a new dialogue between music and dance, composers and choreographers. Fokine's recollection of his work with Stravinsky on *L'Oiseau de feu* is suggestive:

I have staged many ballets since *L'Oiseau de feu*, but never again, either with Stravinsky or any other composer, did I work so closely as on this occasion . . . I did not wait for the composer to give me his finished music. Stravinsky visited me with his first sketches and basic ideas, he played them for me, I demonstrated the scenes to him. At my request, he broke up his national themes into short phrases corresponding to the separate moments of a scene, separate gestures and poses . . . Stravinsky played, and I interpreted the role of the Tsarevich, the piano substituting for a wall. I climbed over it, jumped down from it and crawled, fear-struck, looking around – my living room. Stravinsky, watching, accompanied me with patches of the Tsarevich melodies, playing mysterious tremolos as background to depict the garden of the sinister Kashchey the Deathless.[48]

Although the reliability of this account has been challenged (not least by Stravinsky himself),[49] the impression of creative interplay is striking.

---

[48] Michel Fokine, *Memoirs of a Ballet Master*, ed. Anatole Chujoy, trans. Vitale Fokine (London: Constable, 1961), p. 161.

[49] See Igor Stravinsky and Robert Craft, *Expositions and Developments* (1959; repr. London: Faber and Faber, 1962), p. 129: 'To speak of my own collaboration with Fokine means nothing more than to say that we studied the libretto together, episode by episode, until I knew the exact measurements required of the music.' Following Stravinsky, Richard Taruskin describes the 'close collaboration' recalled by Fokine as, in reality, a 'dictatorship', one in which Fokine 'meddled' with the composer's music; see his *Stravinsky and the Russian Traditions: A Biography of the Works through 'Mavra'*, 2 vols. (Berkeley and Los Angeles: University of California Press, 1996), vol. I, p. 585.

Stravinsky is at the piano, Fokine is jumping over it: the two share ideas with mutual respect and influence.

Equally striking is the overt mimeticism of music and dance as described by the choreographer. Musical themes, we learn, not only matched up to structural divisions, individual gestures and poses; they participated directly in the dramatic scene. This close coupling of music and dance was not of the clichéd, melodramatic kind; nor was it related to the nineteenth-century tradition of onomatopoeic instrumental recitative (music that was somewhat crudely composed to sound like speech). According to Richard Taruskin, the action of the ballet – 'graphic', 'detailed', 'natural', 'realistic' – was conveyed by means of a tightly woven arrangement of musical leitmotifs and leitharmonies (many of which were based on symmetrical octave partitions).[50] To Taruskin, this musical-gestural latticework – 'the ballet's greatest merit in 1910' – was not only unprecedented;[51] it helped boost the significance of ballet on the theatrical scene. Discussing the interrelation of music and gesture, Taruskin implies its relevance to Fokine's larger project: 'to raise ballet above the level of pretty *divertissement* and show that, yes, it could be as substantial as opera'.[52]

Or even as concert-hall music. As is also well known, ballet scores during the period began to take on a life of their own: scores for *Daphnis et Chloé* (1912), *Jeux* (1913), *Le Sacre du printemps* (1913) and even *L'Oiseau de feu* were variously arranged (or left alone) for performance in the concert hall. In tandem with this practice, dancers and choreographers developed an interest in pre-existing, non-dance music: the solo American dancers (quoted earlier) were the first to borrow from the 'classical' giants (Beethoven, Wagner, Brahms); but soon Diaghilev and Fokine followed suit, appropriating music from Chopin, Schumann, Borodin, Debussy and Rimsky-Korsakov, to name a few.

Synchronizing in new (motivic and harmonic) ways with onstage movement, yet also establishing an autonomous status, music may well have helped raise the stakes and the status of ballet, and thus have had a determining impact on the reception of the Russian troupe. It may even have contributed to the so-called 'revolution' of dance, the 'revitalization' and 'exuberance' of the Russian productions. Yet the principles of collaboration, mimeticism and autonomy were not the only components of the troupe's musical aesthetic; moreover, they were not always applauded or assumed to be beneficial for the development of dance. In the chapters that follow, I suggest that our habitual view of the company's musical efforts may

---

[50] Taruskin, *Stravinsky and the Russian Traditions*, vol. I, pp. 586–637.   [51] *Ibid.*, p. 586.
[52] *Ibid.*

sometimes be turned on its head, and that close attention to music – its relation to onstage movement, its reception by the French – may help us move beyond those clichés and conventional ways of thinking that have so strongly shaped our understanding of both the troupe and the historical dance scene.

Musicology and dance

Before summarizing these chapters, it will be useful to recount the methodological and conceptual characteristics of a recent musicological enthusiasm. Long treated as peripheral to music history, dance has become one of the discipline's most fashionable concentrations, the subject of an increasing number of articles, conference papers and special editions. This literature has variously explored composers' thoughts about dance, choreographers' thoughts about music, and the relation between collaborators.[53] There has been the odd analytical study of audio-visual relations, as well as a few important and repertoire-specific projects, ones that investigate what we might call the musical embodiment of dance: Wye Allanbrook on rhythmic gesture in Mozart opera; Gurminder Kaur Bhogal on Debussy, Ravel and the arabesque; Lawrence Zbikowski on dance topics within eighteenth-century music; and Sevin Yaraman on the waltz 'as sex, steps and sound'.[54] As for case studies of dance in the theatre, Marian Smith has written a compelling history of the relation between opera and ballet 'in the age of *Giselle*', and Wayne Heisler has studied the ballet scores of Richard Strauss.[55] Notable opera enthusiasts (amongst them Maribeth Clark, Sarah Hibberd and Mary

---

[53] Roland John Wiley gave the kick to music–dance studies in his seminal *Tchaikovsky's Ballets* (Oxford University Press, 1985). Then followed (to name but a few) Charles Joseph, *Stravinsky and Balanchine: A Journey of Invention* (New Haven, CT, and London: Yale University Press, 2002); Simon Morrison, 'The Origins of *Daphnis et Chloé* (1912)', *19th-Century Music*, 28/1 (2004), pp. 50–76; Tamara Levitz, 'Syvilla Fort's Africanist Modernism and John Cage's Gestic Music: The Story of *Bacchanale*', *The South Atlantic Quarterly*, 104/1 (2005), pp. 123–49; Deborah Mawer, *The Ballets of Maurice Ravel: Creation and Interpretation* (Aldershot: Ashgate, 2006); and Stephanie Jordan, *Stravinsky Dances: Re-Visions Across a Century* (London: Dance Books, 2007).

[54] Wye Allanbrook, *Rhythmic Gesture in Mozart: 'Le Nozze di Figaro' and 'Don Giovanni'* (University of Chicago Press, 1983); Gurminder Kaur Bhogal, 'Debussy's Arabesque and Ravel's *Daphnis et Chloé* (1912)', *Twentieth-Century Music*, 3/2 (2006), pp. 171–99; Lawrence Zbikowski, 'Dance Topoi, Sonic Analogues and Musical Grammar: Communicating with Music in the Eighteenth Century', in Danuta Mirka and Kofi Agawu (eds.), *Communication in Eighteenth-Century Music* (Cambridge University Press, 2008), pp. 283–309; and Sevin Yaraman, *Revolving Embrace: The Waltz as Sex, Steps and Sound* (Hillsdale, NY: Pendragon, 2002).

[55] Marian Smith, *Ballet and Opera in the Age of 'Giselle'* (Princeton University Press, 2000); Wayne Heisler, *The Ballet Collaborations of Richard Strauss* (University of Rochester Press, 2009).

Ann Smart) have also turned to dance and to gesture, keen to explore the dynamic interaction of vocal and physical means of theatrical representation, or else the institutional politics behind music theatre.[56]

Smart, in particular, deserves attention here. Her 2004 monograph *Mimomania: Music and Gesture in Nineteenth-Century Opera* not only offers interpretive readings of the relation between music, visuals and stage movement; it outlines a compelling historical trajectory, from the overt synchronization of music and movement (in the style of the contemporary *mélodrame*), through suspicion of synchronous effects, to music less graphic and mimetic, more abstract and 'transcendental'.[57] Besides this, Smart addresses the notorious issue of operatic representation (in particular, the representation of women), exploring ways in which the visual, physical and aural dimensions of opera could variously animate the body on stage, even convey a character's power or 'physical presence'.

Its significance to opera criticism (and gender ideology) aside, Smart's monograph has much of historical and theoretical value for scholars of music and dance, not least its seamless transitions between iconographical sources, contemporary writings, composers' testimonies, stage manuals, gestural treatises and the music itself – to Smart, 'a wordless stage direction'.[58] Her close readings are carefully considered and persuasive; moreover, they bring to light some of the most pressing issues facing scholars of music and movement. I think particularly of the conclusion to the chapter on Auber's 1828 opera *La Muette de Portici* and its silent heroine Fenella. At base, Smart argues that the 'filler' music (perpetual-motion style) used to accompany the protagonist approximates a sheer bodily energy in its lack of rhetorical or

---

[56] Maribeth Clark, 'Understanding French Grand Opéra through Dance', PhD thesis, University of Pennsylvania (1998); 'The Quadrille as Embodied Musical Experience in 19th-Century Paris', *Journal of Musicology*, 19/3 (2002), pp. 503–26; 'The Body and the Voice in *La Muette de Portici*', *19th-Century Music*, 27/2 (2003), pp. 116–31; and 'The Role of *Gustave, ou le bal masqué* in Restraining the Bourgeois Body of the July Monarchy', *Musical Quarterly*, 88/2 (2005), pp. 204–31; Sarah Hibberd (ed.), *Melodramatic Voices: Understanding Music Drama* (Aldershot: Ashgate, 2011); and Mary Ann Smart, *Mimomania: Music and Gesture in Nineteenth-Century Opera* (Berkeley and Los Angeles: University of California Press, 2004). This is not to mention the influx of studies on music and gesture from cognitive and phenomenological perspectives: see Anthony Gritten and Elaine King (eds.), *Music and Gesture* (Aldershot: Ashgate, 2006) and their *New Perspectives on Music and Gesture* (Aldershot: Ashgate, 2010). As readers will be aware, the word 'gesture' here takes on a wide variety of associations, from real-time physical movement (that of a conductor or instrumentalist), through movement with special 'symbolic' meaning, to the 'translation' of such movement into notated musical form. For a summary of the 'conceptual breadth' of the term (in a review of the 2006 volume cited above), see John Rink, *British Journal of Aesthetics*, 47/2 (2007), pp. 224–6.

[57] Smart, *Mimomania*. This trajectory, as Smart points out, was nonetheless complicated by the retention of 'melodramatic' synchronizations (for comic or distancing effect) in operas such as Meyerbeer's *Les Huguenots* and Wagner's *Die Meistersinger*.

[58] Smart, *Mimomania*, p. 5.

pictorial content. This music stands 'in some way' for Fenella, but does not imitate her movements; it is 'intensely vivid and present', but non-signifying. Citing Roland Barthes ('what is truly alive cannot signify'), Smart maintains that Fenella's music strays from the conventionally mimetic (and thus from conventional analysis) because the heroine 'is no longer pausing to strike poses, represent emotions, or, in fact, to signify or narrate in any way at all'.[59]

It is tempting to put a little pressure on these words: to wonder how music can 'not signify' yet 'stand for'; how it can (nevertheless) conjure bodily 'force' or 'energy'; and why it should remain resistant to scholarly understanding. What, in fact, would or should a mimetic or 'non-signifying' music sound like? There are no histories of music closely allied with gesture or with dance, no global narratives that reach out across periods and repertoires to explain how music was conceived and composed, how it sounded in performance, and how audiences and critics responded to it. Then there is the old, hoary issue of how we are to make sense of the alliance: how music and bodily movement – two complex metaphors, neither without signifying ability, yet neither secure in its signification – can fasten together as meaning.

It may be old and hoary, but this issue has been fuelled by the ascendance of hermeneutics within the humanities: a manner of interpretive reflection seeking to identify meaning on some allegorical or metaphysical plane. Within dance studies, questions of meaning have prompted a range of hermeneutic approaches, embracing various so-called 'post-structuralist' enthusiasms (feminism, identity politics, postcolonial theory, anthropology, subjectivity). At bottom, gesture and the body are 'read' as rooted in culture: not only as 'trace' or 'symptom', passive and puppet-like in the Foucauldian sense; but as dynamic and engaging, 'performative' in their negotiation with dominant modes of representation.[60] As for musicology, slower off the mark (as usual) in its reaction to interdisciplinary trends, the field of opera studies has witnessed the most stupendous of hermeneutic

---

[59] *Ibid.*, p. 62.

[60] See, for example, Ann Cooper Albright, *Choreographing Difference: The Body and Identity in Contemporary Dance* (Middletown, CT: Wesleyan University Press, 1997); Jane C. Desmond (ed.), *Meaning in Motion: New Cultural Studies of Dance* (Durham, NC: Duke University Press, 1997); Susan Leigh Foster (ed.), *Choreographing History* (Bloomington: Indiana University Press, 1995); Mark Franko, *Dancing Modernism/Performing Politics* (Bloomington: Indiana University Press, 1995); André Lepecki (ed.), *Of the Presence of the Body: Essays on Dance and Performance Theory* (Middletown, CT: Wesleyan University Press, 2004); and his *Exhausting Dance: Performance and the Politics of Movement* (London: Routledge, 2006); Susan A. Reed, *Dance and the Nation: Performance, Ritual and Politics in Sri Lanka* (Madison: University of Wisconsin Press, 2009); and Helen Thomas, *The Body, Dance and Cultural Theory* (New York: Palgrave Macmillan, 2003). For a useful survey of the field, see Alexandra Carter and Janet O'Shea (eds.), *The Routledge Dance Studies Reader* (1998; rev. edn London: Routledge, 2010).

attempts.[61] This will come as no surprise. In opera, music is mediated by words – concrete, tangible nodules that help to join the dots connecting sound and sentiment. Leaning on libretti, scholars are eased into the extra-musical, into character psychology, strategies of seduction, dramatic moods and mimesis, as well as broader social, political and sexual issues.

To state the obvious, dance is not opera. Compared to discursive language, it has no concrete meaning. Moreover, and also unlike opera, dance tends not to exist in notated form, but only in the memories of the choreographers and performers who created it. (Staging manuals and comments in reviews may provide clues as to what movements looked like; but these clues are often vague, occasionally incongruous and certainly insufficient for historical reconstruction. Films are few and far between; and images, though helpful indicators of posture, costume and visual scene, capture only moments of an art that by definition moves.) As a result, and without the crutch of a text, scholars face immediate hurdles. How are we to describe, let alone to conceptualize, physical movement? And what of its interaction with music – famously indeterminate?

We are now, it seems, at a turning point when it comes to the issue of meaning. After a phase (the so-called 'New Musicology', now ubiquitous and no longer mentioned) in which hermeneutics ran riot, scholars are beginning to question their urge to ascribe meaning to all manners and kinds of music, whether mimetic, pictorial or (in Smart's words) 'transcendental'. As Carolyn Abbate has acknowledged in a recent essay, this tendency results in a dubious dead-end: 'no one can *give the lie* to any individual claim about a particular meaning embodied in a melody or harmonic turn, in a composer's style, in the strangest musical moment at one extreme, or the most ordinary procedure or convention at the other'.[62] Thanks to Abbate and other musicological blades, we are now thinking critically about the nature and significance of our interpretive endeavours, and pursuing with urgency and enthusiasm new subjects of study: modes of listening and spectatorship, music and

---

[61] I am thinking of a particular cluster of studies from the 1990s, ones that gravitate towards metaphysics and sexuality in equal measure: Carolyn Abbate, *Unsung Voices: Opera and Musical Narrative in the Nineteenth Century* (Princeton University Press, 1991); Corrine E. Blackmer and Patricia Juliana Smith (eds.), *En Travesti: Women, Gender Subversion, Opera* (New York: Columbia University Press, 1995); Gary Tomlinson, *Metaphysical Song: An Essay on Opera* (Princeton University Press, 1999); Linda Hutcheon and Michael Hutcheon, *Bodily Charm, Living Opera* (Lincoln: University of Nebraska Press, 2000); and Mary Ann Smart (ed.), *Siren Songs: Representations of Gender and Sexuality in Opera* (Princeton University Press, 2000).

[62] Carolyn Abbate, 'Cipher and Performance in Sternberg's *Dishonored*', in Karol Berger and Anthony Newcomb (eds.), *Music and the Aesthetics of Modernity* (Cambridge, MA: Harvard University Press, 2005), pp. 357–92 at p. 357.

performance.[63] The last is mounting a serious challenge to the interpretive method, suggesting that the musical 'work' exists not as notated text or autonomous abstraction, but rather as a real-time (essentially physical and embodied) 'presence-effect'. This renewed interest in aesthetics and experience – in our engagement with music as sound and as art – betrays musicology's characteristic belatedness: Susan Sontag railed 'Against Interpretation' (preferring 'an erotics of art') in 1966; Isobel Armstrong ushered in *The Radical Aesthetic* (and its democratic potential) in 2000; Sianne Ngal discussed *Ugly Feelings* (not ugly meanings) in 2004; and Hans Ulrich Gumbrecht celebrated *The Production of Presence: What Meaning Cannot Convey* in 2004.[64] These interdisciplinary studies illustrate a reactionary swerve: they abandon conventional hermeneutics, decrying the conceptualization of art as merely something to be interpreted, and they focus instead on aesthetic experience: to quote Lindsay Waters, 'on the complex ways in which art can hold us in its grasp'.[65]

A dual project

This book is contingent. The result of several years' thinking about music, musicology and the extra-musical scaffolding erected around each, chapters illustrate different modes of enquiry: the long-established tradition of 'close reading'; the new-fangled (yet, I think, historically evocative) non-hermeneutics; a reception history embracing music, art and issues of ontology; and a historically grounded study of the interrelations between musical genres. Readers expecting a coherent methodology will be frustrated. What I attempt is more akin to the opposite: chapters move in different directions, pursuing a variety of perspectives – each of which strives to raise more questions than it answers.

Yet this book of course is a dual project. The variety of musicological methods – my 'perspectivist' approach – supports a defined historical cause.

---

[63] See, for example, Elizabeth Le Guin, *Boccherini's Body: An Essay in Carnal Musicology* (Berkeley and Los Angeles: University of California Press, 2005); and Roger Moseley, 'Work or Play? Brahms's Performance of His Own Music', in Kevin C. Karnes and Walter Frisch (eds.), *Johannes Brahms and His World* (Princeton University Press, 2009), pp. 137–65.

[64] Susan Sontag, *Against Interpretation and Other Essays* (New York: Farrar, Straus and Giroux, 1966); Isobel Armstrong, *The Radical Aesthetic* (Oxford: Blackwell, 2000); Sianne Ngal, *Ugly Feelings* (Cambridge, MA: Harvard University Press, 2004); Hans Ulrich Gumbrecht, *The Production of Presence: What Meaning Cannot Convey* (Stanford University Press, 2004); also see his *In Praise of Athletic Beauty* (Cambridge, MA: Harvard University Press, 2006).

[65] Lindsay Waters, 'Literary Aesthetics: The Very Idea', *The Chronicle of Higher Education*, 16 December 2005, page numbers unknown.

As described in the first half of this chapter, I am interested in the history and reception of belle-époque dance, and how we might move beyond those clichés of dynamism and exuberance, beyond the acclamations of 'rebirth' and 'revolution' most often associated with the Ballets Russes. I should like to think that music could lend a helping hand: specifically, could act as a lens through which we might re-examine historical dance productions and reinterpret their significance within the diversified contexts of early twentieth-century Parisian culture.

Chapter Two is broadly centred on the ballets staged at the Paris Opéra during the pre-war years in which the Russian company was resident in the capital. Initially I seek to explore the relationship between the two companies as perceived in the French press, noting the various ways in which the Opéra was implored to take its lead from Russian choreographic and scenic developments. My principal aim, though, is to offer a 'thick description' of one ballet: a 1910 commission from the Opéra called *La Fête chez Thérèse*, set to music by French composer Reynaldo Hahn and with a libretto by Catulle Mendès. A detailed study of this ballet, especially its musical score, reveals a broad cultural resonance, one that extends from the *ballet-pantomimes* of the July Monarchy, through the extracurricular activities of composer Gustave Charpentier, to belle-époque ideals of womanhood, social parity and dancers' skirts. *Thérèse*'s institutional and historical significance, I argue, can lead us towards a possible continuity between supposedly oppositional camps (the French national ballet and the Ballets Russes) and categories (the conservative and the avant-garde).

Chapter Three presents the case study of Nijinsky's *L'Après-midi d'un faune* (1912), a ballet infamous for its masturbatory eroticism as well as its mis-matching dance. Set to Debussy's 1894 score (itself based on a Mallarmé poem), the ballet has long been considered one of the first examples of audio-visual dissonance: to quote dance scholar Stephanie Jordan, *Faune* represents a 'dual experience', a 'dissociation of sensibilities' between an 'impressionistic' music and an 'angular', 'staccato' choreography.[66] Drawing on a little-known body of primary literature, this chapter presents an alternative argument, one that, whilst allowing for the stylistic incongruity between music and visuals, suggests a new conceptualization of music as balletic accompaniment. The music–choreographic relation, I suggest, can cast a revealing light not only on contemporary balletic practice, but on the significance and meaning of modernist representational modes.

---

[66] Stephanie Jordan, 'Debussy, the Dance, and the *Faune*', in James Briscoe (ed.), *Debussy in Performance* (New Haven, CT, and London: Yale University Press, 1999), pp. 119–34.

Chapter Four details the reception of the Russian troupe in the French press: the large-distribution daily newspapers and the smaller, more specialist journals. Looking afresh at this body of criticism, I examine not only what critics wrote, but the various historical, intellectual and aesthetic forces behind their points of view. The Ballets Russes, I argue, were the subject of intense press debate, described not only in the rhapsodic, rapturous terms we have come to cherish and emulate, but in the harsh reality of belle-époque cultural politics. A locus of contemporary anxieties, the troupe became a metaphor for invasion: the literal invasion of Parisian society by seemingly dangerous and destructive foreigners, and the metaphorical invasion of 'art' itself. Detailing the press response to *Le Sacre du printemps* (1913), as well as the run of productions set to pre-existing music, this chapter teeters on the edge of some of the most notorious issues of art and its ontology, issues that continue to occupy us today.

Following the anxieties exposed in the previous chapter, Chapter Five explores the circumstances surrounding the premiere and reception of the Russians' *Le Coq d'or* (1914), an opera-ballet that featured singers on the sidelines and dancing doubles on stage. The production provoked strong reactions in the press, not least from the family and supporters of Rimsky-Korsakov, whose opera the Russians had renovated. These reactions are instructive, for they gesture to a larger critical debate, not about music specifically, but about theatrical aesthetics and staging practices; singing, dancing and standards of each; and the status and significance of opera and ballet in the early twentieth century. *Le Coq d'or*, I suggest, may be understood as an example of a widespread and essentially modernist phenomenon, one that mobilized the concept of gesture as a mode of language and experience, whilst devaluing vocal expression. The 'gesticulation of opera', specifically, lies at the centre of the chapter – and at the conclusion of this book.

Suspended dualities

Like *Le Coq d'or*, Matisse's *La Danse II* (for which *La Danse I* had served as a model) caused a sensation when first presented to the Parisian public. Hung in the opening room of the Salon d'Automne (one of Paris's annual art exhibitions), the painting overpowered and overwhelmed the spectator. According to Henri Pellier, critic for *La Petite République*:

On entre dans la première salle et le choc que l'on reçoit n'est pas précisément dans l'ordre des émotions artistiques. Les organisateurs l'ont sans doute voulu ainsi pour habituer l'œil d'un seul coup aux brutalités de forme et de couleur qu'il sera susceptible de rencontrer.[67]

(One enters the first room and the shock that one receives is not precisely in the order of artistic emotions. The organizers no doubt wanted it like that to habituate the eye at a single stroke to the brutalities of form and colour that it would be liable to meet.)

This shock was widely felt, symptomatic as much of the size of the painting (260×391 cm) as the brute simplification of line and the intense yet restricted palette. Critics variously described this reductiveness in terms of violence, madness, fury, emptiness: to Charles Morice, writing in *Le Mercure de France*, Matisse had emptied his painting of meaning and value, had approached the edge of 'le néant' (nothingness).[68] Although some critics looked to praise the painter's use of form and colour, many struggled to make sense of the painting – what it was about, what (or who) it depicted, and what it was doing taking over the exhibition wall.

Clearly, this initial reception contrasts with our response to the painting today – the impressions of *éclat* and *énergie* evoked at the outset of this chapter, echoed by a number of critics and fans. The realities of the belle époque are at odds with popular mythology; perhaps they were edited out of history, silenced by the dominant narrative of innovation and achievement. These points may be worth bearing in mind throughout the following pages, and for obvious reason. The reception of the Ballets Russes, now and then, bears a remarkable similarity to that of Matisse's canvas, pondered at length for its overblown (and threatening) presence on the wall, its annihilation of decorative art and the new mimetic order it seemed to signify.

There is a final point. According to recent historical scholarship, Matisse's paintings of the belle époque 'suspended' such dualities as modernism and tradition, representation and resistance, form and sensuality, pleasure and pain, fascination and fear, the functional and the absolute, the decorative and the primitive, the national and the foreign, the self and the 'Other'.[69] As such, it is argued, these paintings bear witness to the destabilizing effects of the historical scene, the confusions of the period and the dislocation of the individual from the mass culture and modernity of the newly commercial world.[70] It is tempting to wonder whether the Ballets Russes occupied a similarly unsettling zone, whether they, too, signified a disruptive presence within the belle époque. It is to these ideas that I shall attend in the pages that follow.

[67] Henri Pellier, 'Le Salon d'Automne', *La Petite République*, 30 September 1910, p. 4.
[68] Charles Morice, 'Art moderne: Le Salon d'Automne', *Le Mercure de France*, 1 November 1910, pp. 154–63 at p. 154.
[69] See Alastair Wright, *Matisse and the Subject of Modernism* (Princeton University Press, 2004).
[70] *Ibid.*, p. 11.

2 ❧ Ballet at the Opéra and *La Fête chez Thérèse*

History has not looked kindly on the Paris Opéra's early twentieth-century ballets. Of the thirteen works created between 1900 and 1914, when the Opéra closed temporarily (until December the following year), only one has entered even the periphery of the repertory; none has been commercially recorded. The works staged between 1909 and 1914 have fared worst. Eclipsed on arrival by the productions of Diaghilev's Ballets Russes, these ballets have long been overlooked by scholars, the majority of whom have maintained a steady focus on the Russian company. Indeed, with the exception of Lynn Garafola's monograph on Diaghilev's troupe, which draws informed comparisons between Russian and French balletic practice, scholarly reference to the Opéra's pre-war ballets is limited to the institutional histories of Léandre Vaillat, Olivier Merlin and Ivor Guest.[1] As a result of their perceived subsidiary status, the ballets *La Fête chez Thérèse*, *España*, *La Roussalka*, *Les Bacchantes*, *Suite de danses*, *Philotis* and *Hansli le bossu* exist only as visual and textual traces: design sketches, posed photographs, librettos, musical scores, press reviews and other anecdotal testimony lying dormant in the Bibliothèque-musée de l'Opéra, Paris.

I should like to attempt an awakening of sorts here. My aim, at least at the outset of this chapter, is to offer a sense of what pre-war ballet at the Opéra was like, from its visuals and structure to the interaction of music and drama. The surviving materials may also offer clues to the Opéra's aesthetic impulse, suggesting the extent to which the institution sought to respond to its contemporary situation. This final point is a serious one, given the volume and intensity of press calls, issuing from the early 1900s, for the development of a national ballet. As critics recalled, since the celebrated 'Romantic'

An early version of this chapter appeared in the *Journal of the Royal Musical Association*, 133/3 (November 2008), pp. 220–69; see www.informaworld.com. I am grateful to the journal's anonymous reviewers for their careful and considered comments.

[1] Lynn Garafola, *Diaghilev's Ballets Russes* (1989; repr. New York: Da Capo, 1998); Léandre Vaillat, *Ballets de l'Opéra de Paris* (Paris: Compagnie Française des Arts Graphiques, 1943); Olivier Merlin, *L'Opéra de Paris* (Fribourg: Hatier, 1975); and Ivor Guest, *Le Ballet de l'Opéra de Paris: trois siècles d'histoire et de tradition* (1976; repr. Paris: Flammarion, 2001). Guest offers a particularly comprehensive survey of the productions and goings-on at the Opéra, as well as a catalogue of its balletic repertory, principal dancers and ballet-masters.

decades of the 1830s and 40s, ballet at the Opéra – the hothouse of ballet Romanticism – had fallen into decline. Owing in part to the increasing 'feminization' of ballet as a social and artistic practice, and to the increasing emphasis on technique, ballet was downgraded to second-class status, to the rank of simple *divertissement* designed to showcase the resident *danseuses étoiles*.[2] (These *étoiles* – several of whom came from the Scuola di Ballo of La Scala in Milan – tended to flaunt their brilliant virtuosity at the expense of dramatic expression.) Adding to ballet's misfortune were three unfortunate cases of combustion. In 1862 the tulle skirt of the up-and-coming Emma Livry caught fire from a stage gaslight and consumed the dancer in flames; in 1894 a fire at a warehouse on Rue Richer destroyed the sets and costumes of all but two ballets in the Opéra's repertory; this was merely twenty-one years after the fire on Rue Le Peletier, which burnt the theatre to the ground, along with much of its production material.

With an impoverished repertory and declining standards, ballet at the Opéra, to quote a well-worn phrase, 'tomba en décadence'. Critics at the turn of the century bemoaned its indecipherability, the result not only of dancers' technical emphasis but of over-complicated plots and obscure gestural vocabularies. In a review of the Opéra's 1907 creation *Le Lac des aulnes*, critic Pierre Lalo criticized the ballet scenario:

Ne pourrait-on imaginer des actions plus élémentaires, et mieux faites pour la pantomime, dont la signification se laisserait apercevoir plus aisément? ... Le nombre des ballets intelligibles est excessivement petit.[3]

(Could we not imagine simpler action, better suited to pantomime, the meaning of which could be more easily perceived? ... The number of intelligible ballets is extremely small.)

Reviewing the ballet for *Le Monde musical*, editor André Mangeot described a similar 'incompréhensibilité':

Cet argument est tellement clair et si bien rédigé que trois lectures consécutives ne nous permettent pas d'en découvrir le sens.[4]

(This scenario is so clear and well formed that three consecutive readings were not enough to make sense of it.)

---

[2] For recent revisionist accounts of ballet Romanticism, see Lynn Garafola (ed.), *Rethinking the Sylph: New Perspectives on the Romantic Ballet* (Hanover, NH: University Press of New England, 1997).

[3] Pierre Lalo, 'La Musique', *Le Temps*, 3 December 1907; clipping, F-Po, Dossier d'œuvre, *Le Lac des aulnes*.

[4] André Mangeot, 'La Danse à l'Opéra et le ballet "Le Lac des aulnes"', *Le Monde musical*, 30 November 1907, pp. 331–2 at p. 331.

Mangeot also made the point about technique becoming an end in itself – an end, even, to the eminence of ballet as art. His musings over the definition of dance are worth quoting at length:

La danse est-elle, comme l'ont toujours voulu les artistes, LA BEAUTÉ DANS LE GESTE, ou bien, comme les professionnels de la danse et la grande masse du public se le figurent, L'AGILITÉ DANS LE MOUVEMENT?

Si la première définition est exacte, il est malheureusement vrai que les exercices de chorégraphie auxquels nous assistons à l'Opéra *ne sont pas de la danse*. Si, au contraire, nous acceptons la seconde définition, l'Opéra est la grande école de Terpsichore, car jamais mollets féminins ne connurent dextérité pareille à celle du corps de ballet de notre Académie nationale de musique et de danse.

Est-il besoin de dire que, sous cette dernière forme, la danse cesse d'être un art? C'est un exercice adroit, aux multiples contorsions, qui demande infiniment de travail, car il exige des membres inférieurs des mouvements et des positions anti-naturels, et l'on sait quelle peine il faut prendre pour violer la nature. Ces déformations engendrent inévitablement de la laideur, car la première condition de la beauté humaine est d'être conforme à la nature.[5]

(Is dance, as artists have always wished it, BEAUTY EMBODIED IN GESTURE, or, as dance professionals and the great majority of the public imagine, PHYSICAL AGILITY?

If the first definition is correct, it is a sad fact that the choreographic exercises we witness at the Opéra *are not dance*. If, on the contrary, we take the second definition, the Opéra is the grand school of Terpsichore, because female calves have never been as dexterous as those of the corps de ballet of our national academy of music and dance.

Is it necessary to say that, under this second definition, dance relinquishes its status as art? It is a skilful exercise, with multiple contortions that demand much practice, because of limbs that are not used to certain unnatural movements and positions, and because we know how much effort is needed to battle against nature. These deformations inevitably lead to ugliness, because the primary condition of human beauty is to conform to nature.)

Non-natural, non-dance, non-art: these harsh words from Mangeot under-line the perceived sterility and irrelevance of ballet at the Opéra. More than this, the words contrast vividly with those bandied about two years later in reviews of Diaghilev's Ballets Russes. The two companies, it seems, were polar opposites: one, a trite and tired residue of nineteenth-century ballet convention; the other, a fresh and frenetic band of exotic dancing 'Others'. As is well known, French critics luxuriated in the Russian troupe's perceived exoticism – at once 'subtil' and 'grisant' ('intoxicating'), 'sauvage' and

---

[5] *Ibid.*, p. 331.

'barbare' – as well as in the new brand of choreographic spectacle the Russians had to offer. But the Opéra and its ballets were not forgotten. A good deal of the journalistic ink expended on the Russian troupe was devoted to the instruction it could offer the national ballet. The Russians were 'les professeurs slaves', the French their 'bons élèves': 'l'enseignement des Ballets Russes' was a favourite journalistic topic.[6]

The press leaned first and foremost on decor, lamenting the Opéra's taste for realism and visual excess, whilst promoting the Russians' simpler and more suggestive style. According to the well-known critic and man-of-letters Camille Mauclair:

Le point le plus frappant de notre conception, c'est le désir obstiné de la vraisem-blance immédiate et du réalisme de détail: réalisme élégant, certes, admettant le caprice ornemental et la changeante féerie des éclairages, mais réalisme tout de même et quand même ... Le décor russe est compris au pur et simple point de vue de la peinture décorative dans sa mission essentielle: la suggestion émotive par le langage de la couleur, par le contraste chromatique ... Tout consiste dans la richesse et la hardiesse de la tonalité. L'accessoire est réduit au strict nécessaire. Le dessin des silhouettes est complètement exempt du souci des détails.[7]

(The most striking aspect of our conception is the obstinate desire for an immediate true-to-life-ness and for realism in all its detail: an elegant realism, to be sure, allowing for ornamental fancies and changing enchantments of lighting, but realism all the same and even so ... The essential aim of Russian decor follows the pure and simple point of view of decorative painting: emotive suggestion through the language of colour [and] chromatic contrast ... Everything consists of rich, bold tones. Props are restricted to what is necessary. Outlines are sketched without any concern for details.)

Also observing these differences between French and Russian decorative tendencies was Jean-Louis Vaudoyer. In a lengthy review for *La Revue de Paris*, Vaudoyer described the effect of decor on the spectator:

Les décors russes sont synthétiques, et, refusant de distraire l'œil par mille petits détails 'finis' avec soin, ils se contentent, par des alliances de deux ou trois couleurs ... de faire éprouver une impression très forte, et celle-ci permet au spectateur d'achever par l'imagination tout ce que des omissions aussi adroites laissent facilement deviner. Les décorateurs français, d'une habileté trop conscien-cieuse, font s'écrier au spectateur: 'Comme c'est cela!' Les Russes sont plus ambitieux

---

[6] For these terms, see Émile Vuillermoz, 'Les Ballets Russes', *Musica-Noël* (1912), pp. 255–7.

[7] Camille Mauclair, 'L'Enseignement de la saison russe', *La Revue*, 1 August 1910, pp. 350–60 at pp. 350–1.

et parviennent à nous faire dire: 'Nos rêves sont vaincus.' Onques avant eux le mensonge ne nous avait à ce point satisfaits et dupés.[8]

(Russian decor is synthetic, and, refusing to distract the eye with a thousand small, carefully 'finished' details, is happy, by the juxtaposition of two or three colours … to create a very strong impression, and this lets the spectator's imagination fill in those skilful omissions. French stage designers, too conscientious in their talent, make the spectator exclaim: 'That is how it is!' The Russians are more ambitious and succeed in making us say: 'Our dreams are defeated.' Never before them had illusion so contented and deceived us.)

According to this formulation, the Russians' economical use of stage props, along with their preference for vivid juxtapositions of colour, helped to offer spectators an imaginative licence, a free rein to conjure the stage world and indulge in personal fantasy. Audiences were thus assigned an active role; they were participants in the stage spectacle, necessary to its dramatic effect.[9]

Yet 'un cours de décoration' was not all the Russians had to offer. French critics also pointed to Russian choreography: not as something wholly original, but rather as an offshoot of the French 'classical' tradition exported to Russia in the late eighteenth century by a series of European (and, for the most part, French) choreographers.[10] The irony of this was not lost on the French. Critics found it absurd that, whilst their own choreographic practice had become stilted and stale, that of the Russians – really, of the continuing French tradition – was uniquely expressive and dramatic. Diaghilev's principals, in particular, were widely regarded as symbolically animate: Nijinsky was lauded not only for his virtuosic agility and weightlessness, but for the metaphysical condition he was thought to embody. In the words of Charles Méryel:

---

[8] Jean-Louis Vaudoyer, 'Variations sur les Ballets Russes', *La Revue de Paris*, 15 July 1910, pp. 333–52 at pp. 349–50.

[9] This idea of active spectatorship meshes neatly with a comment from Lucien Alphonse-Daudet. Writing in *Comœdia illustré*, the critic described the intimate relationship between audience and art kindled during Ballets-Russes performances: 'Nous ne sommes pas seulement spectateurs de ces danses, nous y jouons un rôle et c'est pourquoi elles nous bouleversent.' See his article '6e Saison des Ballets Russes au Châtelet', *Comœdia illustré*, 15 June 1911, pp. 575–8 at pp. 575–6.

[10] Mauclair, for example, writes: 'Nous avons été étonnés de reconnaître, dans la chorégraphie russe, les principe[s] de l'ancienne chorégraphie française, absolument oubliés aujourd'hui, importés en Russie à la fin du XVIIIe siècle et au début du XIXe, par nos maîtres de ballet.' See his 'L'Enseignement de la saison russe', p. 355. More recently, Richard Shead has offered an account of the heritage of the Russian ballet in his *Ballets Russes* (London: The Apple Press, 1989), pp. 10–13. Shead notes the line of Frenchmen – from Jean-Baptiste Landé, through Charles-Louis Didelot, to (most famously) Marius Petipa – who helped introduce European 'classical' dance to Russia.

Nijinsky semble, comme on l'a dit, se dérober aux lois de la pesanteur ... Nijinsky extériorise un élan intérieur ... La plupart jouent ou dansent avec leurs corps: Nijinsky danse aussi avec son âme.[11]

(Nijinsky, as we said of him, seems immune to the laws of gravity ... Nijinsky expresses an inner impulse ... Most play or dance with their bodies: Nijinsky dances also with his soul.)

Quite the opposite, the dancers of the Opéra – even the highly regarded Carlotta Zambelli – were rarely anything more than 'ravissante' or 'gracieuse'.[12] They were defined in general by the dexterity of their limbs, not by any inner significance or expressive intent.[13]

That French critics saw room for improvement at the Opéra is clear. André-E. Marty, writing in *Comœdia illustré*, summed up:

Que les Français, à l'exemple des Russes, secouent un peu cette torpeur où ils menacent de s'alanguir, qu'ils perdent le goût fade pour le joli, qu'ils prennent le parti de subordonner le décor à l'action ... qu'ils reviennent à leurs anciennes traditions en formant d'admirables danseurs; ils n'en perdront certes pas pour cela les admirables qualités classiques de goût et de mesure qui font leur gloire. Ils ne cesseront pas d'être eux-mêmes, mais le seront d'une façon plus large et plus vivante.[14]

---

[11] Charles Méryel, 'L'Adieu aux Ballets Russes', *Comœdia illustré*, 15 June 1912, pp. 749–55 at p. 750.

[12] Two press reports that describe Zambelli in such terms are Adolphe Jullien, 'Revue musicale', *Journal des débats*, 1 December 1907, and Henry Gauthier-Villars, *L'Écho de Paris*, 27 November 1902. (Gauthier-Villars is better known as Willy, the first husband of the novelist Colette.)

[13] On this point, the words of Mangeot are once again evocative. In his review article of *Le Lac des aulnes*, quoted earlier, Mangeot singles out Zambelli as the personification of the sterile, stilted and specifically French style of dancing he so deplored. More than this, he issued Zambelli with an invitation to submit her dancing to the science of 'la cinématographie' – a series of successive photographs that could capture the individual gestural components of her movements and thus endorse (or not) their essential 'beauté'. Zambelli's initial response was to send Mangeot her calling card ('Carlotta Zambelli, Mille remerciements'); according to Mangeot, this was tantamount to admitting defeat – admitting that her dancing could not withhold serious gestural analysis or the attention of the qualified artists (painters and sculptors) he planned to engage. Zambelli replied again, granting Mangeot a half-hour conversation in which she explained how the fluidity of her dancing denied the sort of 'décomposition' that Mangeot had in mind ('lorsqu'on veut l'arrêter sur une pose, ce n'est plus ça'). But Mangeot remained unconvinced: his conversation with Zambelli was pleasant enough (as was the dancer herself), but she could not really answer his questions about 'les lamentables traditions dont elle est la plus haute incarnation'. The dialogue between Mangeot and Zambelli can be found in the pages of *Le Monde musical*, 30 November, 15 December and 30 December 1907.

[14] André-E. Marty, 'Encore les Ballets Russes', *Comœdia illustré*, 15 August 1909, pp. 459–60 at p. 460. Vaudoyer closes his 1910 piece with something similar, expressing a hope that French choreography and stage design might follow the Russians' lead; see his 'Variations sur les Ballets Russes', p. 352.

(Let's hope that the French, following the example of the Russians, escape a little from this torpor in which they threaten to languish, that they lose the insipid taste for prettiness, that they resolve to subordinate decor to action … that they return to their old traditions by training admirable dancers. They will certainly not lose the admirable classical qualities of taste and moderation that characterize their glory. They will not stop being themselves, but rather be themselves to the full, and in a more animated manner.)

But what of Marty's prophecy? The question of the Russians' influence on the Opéra is complex and multi-layered. There was no full-scale capitulation to Russian practice – no overhaul of the national ballet, no franco-*Cléopâtre* or *Schéhérazade*. The latter, in fact, was an idea that Ivan Clustine, ballet-master from 1911 to 1914, found preposterous. Writing in the popular music journal *Musica*, Christmas 1912, Clustine declared:

Quant à préconiser une influence des ballets russes sur les ballets d'opéra, ce serait folie. Ces deux formes d'art, dont la genèse s'oppose entièrement, n'offrent aucun point commun dans la réalisation. Styliser *Coppélia* avec des costumes rutilants et au moyen de décors aux tonalités multiples produirait une impression cocasse. Il n'est pire sottise que de changer le cadre où évolue une œuvre. Que l'on essaie de jouer *Schéhérazade* en ne se conformant pas aux principes qui animent la réalisation de ce ballet, et l'on rompra toute unité d'art.[15]

(To recommend that the Ballets Russes influence the ballets of the Opéra would be madness. These two forms of art, the geneses of which are entirely opposed, have not one point in common concerning their method of production. To stylize *Coppélia* with gleaming costumes and multi-tonal decor would be laughable. There is nothing more foolish than to change the context in which an oeuvre develops. Performing *Schéhérazade* without conforming to the ballet's vital principles would destroy its artistic unity.)

Nonetheless, and despite Clustine's protestations, several features of the Opéra's post-1909 ballets, along with its institutional conventions and balletic policy, appeared to betray a Russian influence. The appointment of Clustine is a case in point. A Russian émigré previously engaged in Monte Carlo (and, before that, at the Bolshoi in Moscow), Clustine arrived in Paris to a flurry of press commentary on his nationality and choreographic agenda. His hiring was thought a direct attempt by the Opéra to imitate the Russian company; even he thought as much, maintaining, not without despondency, that inspiration too often came from the north:

---

[15] See Ivan Clustine, 'Ballets Russes et Ballets d'Opéra', *Musica-noël* (1912), p. 245.

Des gens bien informés – il en est toujours qui prétendent recéler la pensée des autres – affirmèrent que j'allais briser l'actuelle statue d'Euterpe. Une révolution éclatera! . . . Une révolution! méthode que l'on applique souvent au pays des tsars.[16]

(The well-informed – there are always some who claim to harbour the thoughts of others – claimed that I was going to crush the current statue of Euterpe. A revolution will break out! . . . A revolution! A method that people often apply in the country of the tsars.)

Clustine, although acknowledging his nationality with pride, harboured none of the revolutionary intentions that some thought an inevitable consequence of being Russian. He wanted, he argued, merely to rectify certain details: to promote the male *danseur* over the *danseuse travestie* (the female dancer dressed as a male and taking a male part); and to encourage the wearing of tutus only when dramatically appropriate.[17] Nonetheless, these details, like Clustine's appointment, were also thought imitative – further examples of the Opéra taking the lead from the Russian troupe. The Russians were known for abolishing conventional balletic hierarchy, foregrounding the *danseur* (and thus toppling the *danseuse étoile* from her pedestal) and doing away with cross-dressing. Their costume designs were equally notorious and often replaced the tutu with more dramatically suitable dress, including free-flowing tunics, harem pants and decorative body stockings.

As for the French ballets themselves, that seven works were produced in such close succession – *La Fête chez Thérèse* (1910), *España* (1911), *La Roussalka* (1911), *Les Bacchantes* (1912), *Suite de danses* (1913), *Philotis* (1914) and *Hansli le bossu* (1914) – was itself remarkable: not since the mid-nineteenth century had anything similar been accomplished. What is more, and according to Guest and Vaillat, several of the ballets invite comparison with Russian productions, particularly in terms of choreography and drama. Describing the inevitability of any Russian influence on the Opéra, Guest proposes a specific gestural equivalence between *Les Bacchantes*, from Greek mythology, and the Ballets Russes' *L'Après-midi d'un faune*: a similarity of poses in profile, seemingly inspired by bas-reliefs.[18]

---

[16] *Ibid.*

[17] As it happens, the fate of the tutu provoked something of an uproar in the popular press, several critics bewailing the garment's seeming demise. In response to an article entitled 'Est-ce la fin du tutu?', Clustine wrote specifically of his intentions, claiming that, whilst the tutu might be appropriate for a supernatural character, it was unbefitting of peasants and religious folk; see Louis Delluc, 'À propos du "tutu"', *Comœdia illustré* (n.d.); clipping, F-Po, Dossier d'auteur, Ivan Clustine.

[18] See Guest, *Le Ballet de l'Opéra de Paris*, p. 149. It seems likely that the gestural language of *Les Bacchantes* was also influenced by the bas-relief postures of *Cléopâtre* and *Narcisse*, as well as *Faune*.

He goes on to describe a second correspondence, evoking the Opéra's appropriation of Russian neo-Romanticism: *Suite de danses*, he writes, is a 'replica' of the Ballets Russes' *Les Sylphides*, first performed four years earlier (itself an adaptation of the Maryinsky's *Chopiniana* of 1907).[19] Both works evoke ballet's former Romanticism by means of tulle skirts, pointe slippers and a general etherealness; both are set in a moonlit park and to the music of Chopin; and both consist of a series of individual pieces strung together on a plot that is negligible in *Suite* and non-existent in *Les Sylphides*. Besides this neo-Romantic influence, there was an obvious infiltration of exotic subjects into the Opéra's output. Vaillat, though less concerned than Guest with the business of Russian teaching, implies as much, enquiring after the thematic contingency of *España*, with its titular exoticism, and of *La Roussalka*, which leans heavily on Slavic legend.[20]

But there is a gap in both Vaillat's and Guest's accounts. Neither historian notes any correspondence – gestural, dramatic or otherwise – between the Russian repertory and *La Fête chez Thérèse*: indeed, Vaillat's history locates *Thérèse* (1910) before the arrival of the Russian company in 1909. The sense of both accounts is that *Thérèse* was historically and temporally adrift, incongruous within a local balletic context and immune from contemporary influence. The bare bones of reception appear to support this, for whilst *Thérèse* received its premiere in 1910, archival sources suggest that plans for the production date back to 1907.

These circumstances – and the cohering idea of the ballet's incongruity – serve as the launch-pad for this chapter, which will explore the hows and whys of *Thérèse*'s very nature, comparing and contrasting the ballet with other contemporary works. Needless to say, this kind of study involves some sleight-of-hand. Choreographed by 'Mlle Stichel' (real name, Louise Manzini), based on a libretto by Catulle Mendès and with music by Reynaldo Hahn, *Thérèse* suffers from a lack of reliable documentation, particularly on its gestural aspect. There is no surviving choreographic record or stage manual, and reviews offer vague and atmospheric descriptions of the production rather than any detailed gestural analysis. The commentary offered here thus focuses less on choreography than on other balletic param-eters, those traceable through the surviving sources: Mendès's libretto, the original publication of which has survived, and Hahn's score – the annotated orchestral performing score (signed by the composer) and the piano reduc-tion housed in the Bibliothèque-musée de l'Opéra. Together, libretto and score suggest scenario, setting, character and structure, not to mention the role of music as a storytelling agent. They also offer clues, if only partial ones,

---

[19] *Ibid.*   [20] Vaillat, *Ballets de l'Opéra de Paris*, pp. 47–56.

to dance style and placement, suggesting how dance might be associated with plot, character and scene.

Pursuing these clues is central to my project – a close reading of *Thérèse*, its visuals, narrative, structure and music. I also hope to suggest something of the ballet's broader cultural resonance, inviting a review of the taxonomies by which histories of the contemporary dance scene are usually plotted and a reassessment of the dominant historiographical strategy itself.

Backward glances: scene and narrative

The stage was festooned with long dresses. Some were elaborate, bell-shaped creations, worn by characters with fancy coiffures and fans; others were made from muslin or gingham, accessorized with pinafores and bonnets; still more were in the making, half-stitched cuttings of satin, silk, gauze and tarlatan lying on a table, pored over by eager assemblers.

This was the setting of *Thérèse*, Act One: a fashion designer's studio, with seamstresses attending to their clients' demands, offering garments for try-on sessions and rhapsodizing on the tried-on. The dresses of course are a clue to the studio scene. The animate ones, filled with performing bodies, help differentiate between character and class, customer and employee; the inanimate suggest industry or work, as well as the article of trade. But both types, animate and inanimate, betray something beyond a local dramatic scene; for these were not dresses of a style or taste to suit 1910s Paris. Instead, they were vestiges from a bygone age, material residue of a former fashion that, along with other scenic elements, signalled a time other than the present day. In the words of critic F. Mobisson:

La mise en scène de *La Fête chez Thérèse* [est] un véritable enchantement … Le décor, le mobilier, les accessoires, les costumes, d'une rigoureuse exactitude, sont une reconstitution fort plaisante du style Louis-Philippe.[21]

(The *mise en scène* of *La Fête chez Thérèse* [is] truly enchanting … The decor, the furniture, the accessories, the costumes, rigorously exact, are a most pleasant reconstruction of the Louis-Philippe style.)

Louis-Philippe had reigned some seventy years earlier, in a period characterized by ostensible liberalism and reform, along with a marked historical consciousness: the king famously converted the château at Versailles into a

---

[21] F. Mobisson, *Le Journal* (n.d.); clipping, F-Po, B 717 (a collection of press cuttings about *Thérèse*, mostly dating from the weeks surrounding the ballet's premiere).

museum dedicated 'à toutes les gloires de la France'.[22] Indeed, there is something of the museum about *Thérèse*'s Act One scene. Besides the quasi-authentic props (vases, dressing tables, curtains) and costumes, the stage was peppered with real-life remains. At Mendès's request, portraits of some of the most famous French ladies of the day hung on the studio walls, reflected by mirrors and lit with a vibrant gold light. The writer Émile de Girardin, the duchesse d'Abrantès, the dancer Carlotta Grisi, the actresses Virginie Déjazet, Marie Dorval and 'Rachel' (Élisabeth Rachel Félix): these icons of the July Monarchy came to life in full material finery. They were all-consuming, inescapable; the studio was a sort of iridescent shrine.

So much was noted by the press. Journalistic nods to the scene – 'exquis', 'charmant', 'ingénieux' and, most important, 'très français' – were rife. *Thérèse*, on a visual surface at least, recalled French history, perhaps even in a manner similar to Louis-Philippe's recycled chateau. Indeed, just as the ballet's visuals appealed to a national heritage, its plot evoked a specifically balletic one.

Here is a short synopsis:

Seamstresses at work in Madame Palmyre's studio are interrupted by their respective suitors. A scene of romancing ensues, but is cut short by the arrival of clients come to try on their outfits for Duchess Thérèse's forthcoming ball. Their suitors disappear behind folding screens; the seamstresses welcome the customers, a party which includes dancers from the Opéra, as well as Duchess Thérèse herself. Suddenly, a folding screen falls to the ground: Théodore, a suitor in hiding, has accidentally knocked it over in an attempt to get a better view of Thérèse. Enraged that a man has witnessed her undress, Thérèse storms out of the studio, followed by an apologetic Palmyre. Théodore remains, enraptured by Thérèse, ignoring his once-beloved seamstress Mimi and her protestations of love. He kisses a glove left by the duchess as his jilted lover breaks down in tears.

Act Two stages the 'fête' of the ballet's title: masked revellers entertain Thérèse and her guests with scenes of diegetic dancing, music and general buffoonery; Théodore, uninvited and disguised as a cavalier, pursues Thérèse. But Mimi has also sneaked in. Cornering Thérèse, she begs the duchess to relinquish her new suitor. Touched by the young girl's sincerity, Thérèse dismisses Théodore, though not without blowing

---

[22] The seminal account of Louis-Philippe's conversion of the chateau from royal residence to 'musée national d'histoire' is Pierre Francastel, *La Création du musée historique de Versailles et la transformation du palais, 1832–1848* (Paris: Les Presses Modernes, 1930). For more on the king's preferred, some would say politicized, version of the past, see Michael Marrinan, *Painting Politics for Louis-Philippe: Art and Ideology in Orleanist France* (New Haven, CT, and London: Yale University Press, 1988), and Petra ten-Doesschate Chu and Gabriel P. Weisberg (eds.), *The Popularization of Images: Visual Culture under the July Monarchy* (Princeton University Press, 1994).

him a final kiss. Dejected, Théodore returns to his former lover, who waits with open arms. The revellers indulge in a final dance.

What is traditional about this? According to Opéra director André Messager, not a lot: 'Ce qui nous séduisit, c'est que *La Fête chez Thérèse* est un ballet d'un genre tout nouveau à l'Opéra, c'est une chose intime, évoquant la vie et les costumes de 1840' (What attracted us is that *La Fête chez Thérèse* represents a new type of ballet for the Opéra; it has something intimate about it, evoking the life and costumes of 1840).[23] 'Intimate', certainly: *Thérèse* tells of a personal affair of the heart, a domestic intrigue set against a picturesque backdrop of (in Act One) an interior workplace and (in Act Two) a private party. But 'a brand new genre'? *Thérèse* betrays little of the Russian-inspired exoticism or abstract poeticism that infiltrates contemporary works; and its local, anecdotal history seems out of place amongst the mythological settings and themes favoured by the Opéra. (Eight of the eleven ballets commissioned by the Opéra between 1900 and 1914 were based on legend.[24]) Yet the ballet was not wholly anomalous. The historical setting, historically authentic backdrop, opulent staging, elaborate plot, domestic intrigue and plot formulae (suspense, social contrast, cause-and-effect incidents): all these features invite comparison with the *ballet-pantomime* – the self-standing dramatic genre, combining dance and mime, that featured heavily at the Opéra during the July Monarchy, the period depicted in *Thérèse*.

Much is known of this double-barrelled species, thanks in large part to the work of Marian Smith.[25] A few parallels with *Thérèse* are particularly worthy of note. Perhaps the most vivid concerns the centrality of a love story and certain amorous plot situations: a man's love for and pursuit of a woman of higher social standing (in *Thérèse*, Théodore's desire for the duchess); a love triangle or scene of romantic crisis at the end of the first act (Mimi's

---

[23] Clipping from *L'Écho de Paris* (n.d.); F-Po, B 717.

[24] *Bacchus*, premiered on 26 November 1902, was about the god of wine and his romance with an Indian princess betrothed to the king; *La Ronde des saisons*, 25 December 1905, was based on a Gascon legend in which Oriel, a sprite, beguiled the young Tancrède; *Le Lac des aulnes*, 25 November 1907, was inspired by Goethe's 'Erlkönig'; *España*, 3 May 1911, was an exotic fable about Spanish dancers; *La Roussalka*, 8 December 1911, was based on a Russian myth (and a poem by Pushkin) in which a woman, having drowned herself when separated from her lover, returns as a water spirit to claim him; *Les Bacchantes*, 30 October 1912, was loosely inspired by *The Bacchae* of Euripides and told of conflict between Bacchus and the Theban king; *Philotis*, 18 February 1914, was about a wealthy, love-struck dancer from Corinth battling against the will of Apollo; and *Hansli le bossu*, 22 June 1914, followed an Alsatian folk tale about a hunchback. The three non-mythological commissions were *Danses de jadis et de naguère* (Dances of old and of late), *Thérèse* and *Suite de danses*. The ballets *Javotte* and *Namouna* were also staged at the Opéra during this period, but were recreations.

[25] Marian Smith, *Ballet and Opera in the Age of 'Giselle'* (Princeton University Press, 2000).

desperation over her beloved's newfound love interest); a woman's attraction to a man, disguised, whose name and identity she does not know (Thérèse's fondness for the masked Théodore).[26] This last situation leads to an additional parallel, in that *Thérèse* also follows the standard *ballet-pantomime* in its staging of a masked ball. (The popularity of ball scenes in *ballet-pantomimes* of the July Monarchy is thought to result from their scenographic potential and narrative verisimilitude: the scenes provided a rationale for stage dancing and thus alleviated librettists' concern for dramatic realism.[27]) There is also the matter of dramatic mood. The *ballet-pantomime*, Smith argues, was light-hearted and lightweight entertainment; ballet itself was considered inappropriate as a medium for conveying political and religious content, and more suited to romantic themes, happy endings and 'soothing', pastoral backdrops.[28] *Thérèse* offers a similar 'calm': the ballet reconciles the on–off seamstress/suitor relationship amongst the celebratory festivities of a ball, denying any sombre connotations or sense of struggle.

What are we to make of these similarities? What do they reveal of *Thérèse*, its creative methods, motivations and general historical aura?[29] My next section, on the ballet's structure and stylistic shifts, will cast light on these questions with specific reference to Hahn's score.

Backbone: the score

On a most basic level, a musical score can reveal a ballet's structural divisions, its succession of 'numbers' or seamless, through-composed form. But a score can also indicate movement – by means not only of the mimetic and cartoon-like synchronization of contour, punctuation and rhythm (known as 'mickey-mousing'), but of a more general coincidence of musical style and

---

[26] Details of the July Monarchy *ballet-pantomimes* that foreground such romantic themes can be found in Smith's exhaustive table of 'plot situations' characteristic of the genre; *ibid.*, pp. 26–7.

[27] Smith discusses the issue of verisimilitude, noting librettists' 'acute sense of what was proper and improper subject-matter for the ballet-pantomime'; *ibid.*, p. 66.

[28] *Ibid.*, pp. 71–2. To account for this lighter tone, Smith points to the public's perceived connection between ballet, the body and sex. According to Smith, the overt objectification and sexualization of the *danseuse*, both on stage and off, steered ballet towards amorous themes, private realms and seductive impulses.

[29] It is important to note a potential red herring: that *Thérèse* was in fact labelled 'ballet-pantomime en deux actes'. Whilst this generic designation seems to confirm the above-mentioned parallels, in fact it lays a false trail. Several ballets of the period were labelled 'ballet-pantomime' (including *Le Lac des aulnes*, *La Roussalka* and *Les Bacchantes*), though most lacked any of the dramatic characteristics of the 1840s genre. From period press reports on ballet and its definition, one may discern that the label as used in the early twentieth century referred not to any appropriative or retrospective impulse, but rather to a ballet's narrative bent: 'pantomime' merely signified the presence of action over 'pure danse'.

movement style. In *Thérèse*, two musical styles prevail: one is characterized by periodic phrasing, rhythmically distinct themes (often repeated, occasionally in different keys), solo obbligato textures, on-the-beat and metrically regular bass-lines, punctuated chordal endings or endings softer in dynamic and articulation, suggesting the winding-down of stage movement and the dispersal of dancing groups (see Example 2.1[30]); the other is through-composed, changing continually in phrasing, metre, theme and key (see Example 2.2, of which more later). The former corresponds to scenes of dance – often set dances, extraneous to the plot and entitled 'danse' or some more precise descriptor ('valse', 'menuet'). Here, metrical and phraseological stability tends to anchor dance movements to a codified aural pattern; easy-on-the-ear melodic material encourages a focus on the moving body. The latter style signifies scenes of mime: annotations include stage directions and, occasionally, words to be mimed by the dancers. This style follows the unfolding of drama on stage, as well as the shifting nuances of character and emotion.

An oscillation of these two styles in a ballet score of 1910 was not exceptional. Although the Ballets Russes, in their first season of 1909, had tended to dance to *musique pure* (music not written for dance), ballet at the Opéra was almost always accompanied by music of bipartite categorization: discrete and formulaic 'numbers' contrasted with passages of wandering affect. Yet what stands out in *Thérèse* is the concentration of each style – hence the concentration of dance and mime, even the concentration of 'story'. In brief, of the Opéra's ballets premiered between 1909 and 1914, *Thérèse* had the greatest proportion of through-composed music – that is, music to accompany mime. Just over half (52 per cent, by my reckoning) of Hahn's score was devoted to music for miming, compared to roughly two-fifths of Lucien Lambert's *La Roussalka*, one-fifth of Alfred Bruneau's *Les Bacchantes*, and none of the orchestrated Chopin that accompanied *Suite de danses*.[31] Moreover, in their own ways, *La Roussalka*, *Les Bacchantes* and *Suite de danses* all promoted dance: *Suite de danses*, as the title suggests, comprised a succession of dances with no intervening mime; *La Roussalka* featured

---

[30] The *contredanse*, indicated in Example 2.1, developed from the English country dance introduced at the French court in the 1680s; including circle, square and long-ways formations, it became popular in urban society throughout the eighteenth century and into the nineteenth, until ousted from the floor by the quadrilles and round dances of the waltz and polka.

[31] I arrived at these fractions with reference to the published piano reductions of each ballet (in the absence of annotated autograph scores, *répétiteurs* and recordings): I simply added the number of bars of set dance in each score, and, assuming the remainder (with the exception of the scene-setting passages at the beginning of each act) to be action music, calculated the proportions accordingly. My calculations are admittedly approximate.

Example 2.1 Hahn, *La Fête chez Thérèse*, Act One, scene 2, 'La Contredanse des grisettes'.

Example 2.1 (cont.)

Example 2.1 (cont.)

characters, the Roussalki water spirits, whose supernatural movements resembled 'classical' gestures; and *Les Bacchantes* offered an act-length sequence of diegetic dances performed as part of Bacchus's spiritual rite. This last ballet, in fact, appears less a mimed musical drama with dancing than a danced work with a modicum of miming. Of the twenty-one 'numbers', only four are labelled 'pantomime': 'story' is subordinated to the dancing spectacle, is almost entirely submerged.

One might wonder whether this narrative evanescence relates to changing dance practices elsewhere (the evolution of 'modern' dance, the famously non-narrative *Les Sylphides*) or to the now infamous literary conceptions of dance as a non-figurative 'Idée', an abstract sign without signified.[32] But this would be to stray from the topic at hand. *Thérèse*, clearly, was devoted to storytelling: it offered roughly equal amounts of 'ballet' (set dance) and pantomime, thus devoting roughly equal time to virtuosic display and to action. Yet if this structural composition marked a point of departure from

32 The writings of Stéphane Mallarmé are especially well known; see his 'Ballets' (1886), *Crayonné au théâtre*; repr. in *Œuvres complètes*, ed. G. Jean-Aubry and Henri Mondor (Paris: Gallimard, 1945), pp. 303–7.

Example 2.2 Hahn, *La Fête chez Thérèse*, Act One, scene 5, 'Pantomime'.

Example 2.2 (cont.)

Example 2.2 (cont.)

Et toi tu es un pauvre poète sans gloire!

Elle ne t'aimera jamais.

Lent
Mais il persiste dans son rêve.

Moins lent
Et moi? moi? Tu ne t'inquiètes

pas de moi! De moi qui t'aime! que tu as prise! que tu as aimée!

Moderato
Il se détourne et s'éloigne vers le fond.

Elle veut le retenir.   L'air somnambulique, il l'écarte doucement, il va vers le milieu du théâtre. Il ramasse un gant que la DUCHESSE

Example 2.2 (cont.)

Example 2.2 (cont.)

contemporary practice, it harked back to the 1840s genre introduced earlier. *Thérèse*, it appears, is a literal *ballet-pantomime*, a formal equivalent of the genre typified by its titular split of dance and mime.[33]

Back-chat: music and drama

Another angle from which to consider *Thérèse*'s score and its historical significance involves the coincidence of music and dramatic expression. Exploring the role of ballet music, needless to say, is a complicated business. There is little context for discussion, little archival material and little sense of how music closely allied with dance might sound, might *mean*. Nonetheless, the inevitable complications may be less severe with *Thérèse*: even as the ballet escapes gestural reconstruction, its scenes of pantomime, complete with stage directions and dialogue to be mimed, hint at the relation between music and the drama unfolding on stage.

One such scene has been mentioned already: the episode from the end of Act One in which Théodore, mesmerized by the sight of the duchess in déshabillé, snubs Mimi and her amorous declarations (Example 2.2). In this

---

[33] Smith notes the proportions of *Giselle*, perhaps the most famous *ballet-pantomime* of the 1840s: fifty-four minutes of mime to sixty minutes of dance; see her *Ballet and Opera in the Age of 'Giselle'*, p. 175.

episode, two distinct musical figurations are obvious, at least in the opening thirty-seven bars. The first comprises off-beat semiquavers in duple time, oscillating thirds (at the start of each entry) and simple, top-heavy textures. The second, in a slower tempo and compound time, is textually thicker and more lyrical, and consists mainly of conjunct (and often chromatic) melodic motion. These two styles alternate throughout the scene: moreover, they do so in line with text and character. According to annotations in the score, the frenzied semiquavers mark an exclamation, question or action by Mimi; the more expressive music accompanies Théodore.

There is, then, a clear sense of musical dialogue, of characters linked to musical styles – styles that are themselves dramatically suggestive. Mimi's off-beat snatches depict not only the agitation of her outbursts, but the aural impression of outbursting: the on-the-beat rests break the musical flow, creating short bursts of instrumental flurry; the undulating contours, widening intervals and occasional syncopation approach the inflections of speech, giving the music a 'talking' quality. (In Mimi's first entry, the number of musical snatches equals the number of phrase she is to 'speak'/mime: 'verbal'/gestural and musical phrases line up.) As for Théodore, whilst his music lacks that ventriloquistic tendency (he is largely silent, after all), it helps communicate his mood. Not only is the soupy lyricism appropriate to his wistful, dream-like state, but it tends towards the two identifying themes of Thérèse, the subject of his reveries. The first of these themes – which both recur throughout the ballet – appears in bar 12 in an inner voice: this is a lilting melody, rising in contour and seemingly heading towards A major, until its interruption five bars later by an implied diminished seventh (on D♯) over a bass E. This last chord, which seems to highlight Mimi's disturbance of Théodore's reverie, is left unresolved as the tonality shifts to C♯ minor for Mimi's next 'speech'. The second identifying theme, beginning in bar 22, is an upper-voice modified-triplet figure, the final chord of which (a dominant ninth on A♭) also fails to resolve: Mimi's fast notes recur (for the third time) in the next bar, again wrenching the tonality towards an unrelated minor key.

Théodore's music thus conjures not only his dramatic mood, but the focus of his thoughts; Mimi's music reflects her disposition as well as her mode of address. This loading of the score with narrative content – with metaphorical and real-time 'voices', aural reminiscences of character and other pictographic traces – continues throughout the scene: Mimi's gesture to Thérèse's portrait in an attempt to convince Théodore of the duchess's noble status is accompanied by one of Thérèse's identifying themes in a heavily articulated, chordal and fanfare-like guise (bar 46); Mimi's collapse, following her pursuit of a departing Théodore, is synchronized to a low timpani roll breaking out of a rising chromatic line over four octaves higher (bar 74); and Mimi's solitary crying at the end of the scene is attended by a sparse orchestral texture and a staccato melody played *pianissimo* by solo oboe and piano (bar 78). This last moment was singled out as one of the ballet's highlights by critic Édouard Risler:

> La scène – une page de poète – où Mimi . . . 'pleure doucement'. Je ne connais guère d'impression plus triste que ces quelques notes . . . auxquelles se mêle, comme une orgue de Barbarie lointaine, le son grêle du piano.[34]

(The scene – a poet's page – in which Mimi . . . 'cries softly'. I hardly know of a sadder impression than these few notes . . . blending with the shrill sound of the piano, like a distant barrel organ.)

Risler's words are worth noting; clearly, the critic was impressed by the music's seeming poeticism, its ability to bring silent, moving images to life. He noted as much earlier in his review:

> Le meilleur livret ne vit que par la musique qui l'anime, et celle de Reynaldo Hahn l'anime d'une vie qui lui assure une perpétuelle jeunesse . . . chaque page contenait une idée.[35]

(The best libretto lives only by means of the music that animates it, and that of Reynaldo Hahn animates with a life that assures the libretto a perpetual youth . . . each page contains an idea.)

Others spoke similarly of the music's dramatic resonance. Robert de Montesquiou went so far as to describe the score as an active force, coaxing the characters into movement:

> D'un bout à l'autre de ces deux actes, elle [la musique] a fait tourbillonner, avec une inlassable vélocité et un charme non moindre, des modistes, des duchesses, des gigolos en complets de casimir, des Gilles aux taffetas luisants.[36]

(From start to finish, the music, with relentless speed and no less charm, makes milliners, duchesses, gigolos in cashmere suits and Gilles in gleaming taffeta all swirl round.)

André Rigaud summed up:

> Elle [la musique] est si étroitement liée à la poësie du sujet qu'elle est le sujet lui-même, l'esprit, la grâce, le charme . . . C'est à elle qu'on doit de voir tout ce qui est peint sur la toile et aussi tout ce qui n'y est pas.[37]

---

[34] Édouard Risler, review of *Thérèse*, untitled (n.d.); clipping, F-Po, B 717. [35] *Ibid.*

[36] Robert de Montesquiou, 'Une collaboration entre Devéria et Lancret à propos de *La Fête chez Thérèse*' (n.d.); clipping, F-Po, B 717.

[37] André Rigaud, 'La Fête chez Thérèse à l'Opéra' (n.d.); clipping, F-Po, B 717.

(The music is so closely linked to the poetry of the subject that it is the subject itself, spirit, grace, charm ... It is through the music that we see all that is painted on the scenic canvas and also all that is not there.)

These comments endorse the impression of carefully wrought musical-dramatic effects; but they also strike a peculiar note. In the context of early twentieth-century ballet criticism, commendations of music's dramatic effectiveness were scarce. For the most part, reviewers described French ballet music in unexceptional terms, often lamenting a perceived superficiality or surface gloss. According to Pierre Lalo, for example, Henri Maréchal's score for *Le Lac des aulnes* followed the action precisely, but without energy, vivacity or life:

Est-elle [la musique] mauvaise? Non point. Est-elle bonne? Non plus. Elle est correcte, elle est consciencieuse, elle est sage, elle est modérée. Elle s'efforce honnêtement de suivre l'action, d'en exprimer avec exactitude les péripéties. Elle est d'un musicien qui connaît son métier ... et tout cela serait parfait, si seulement cette musique était en vie. Le malheur, c'est qu'elle ne vit point du tout.[38]

(Is it [the music] bad? No. Is it good? No. It is proper, conscientious, restrained and moderate. It endeavours to follow the action closely, to express its events exactly. It is by a musician who knows his trade ... and all that would be perfect, if only this music was alive. The misfortune is that the music is not at all alive.)

Five years later, critic Julien Torchet invoked a similar mediocrity in Alfred Bruneau's score for *Les Bacchantes*, noting that the music would add nothing to Bruneau's reputation.[39] Another critic even suggested a reason for Bruneau's troubles:

Il existe entre la Musique et la Danse, ou plutôt entre les Compositeurs et les Danseurs, un malentendu, que le ballet des Bacchantes ne parviendra pas encore à dissiper. Ce malentendu provient de ce que, à l'Opéra plus encore que sur d'autres scènes, la Danse ignore la Musique et la Musique ignore la Danse.[40]

---

[38] Pierre Lalo, *Le Temps*, 3 December 1907; clipping, F-Po, Dossier d'œuvre, *Le Lac des aulnes*. Curiously, the sort of musical superficiality criticized by Lalo had previously been considered necessary to a successful ballet score. An article in *Le Voltaire* (8 March 1882) maintained that ballet composers should think only on the most superficial of musical levels. (Even more curious, this comment was made in response to a score for the ballet *Namouna* composed by Pierre Lalo's father Édouard. The music of the more senior Lalo was considered 'neuve', 'originale' and 'personnelle' – and thus far from the requisite 'superficielle'.)

[39] Julien Torchet, *Hommes du jour*, November 1912; clipping, F-Po, Dossier d'œuvre, *Les Bacchantes*.

[40] André Mangeot, *Le Monde musical*, 30 October 1912; clipping, F-Po, Dossier d'œuvre, *Les Bacchantes*.

(There exists between Music and Dance, or rather between Composers and Dancers, a misunderstanding that the ballet of Bacchantes will not yet succeed in clearing up. This misunderstanding is a result of the fact that, at the Opéra more than at other theatres, Dance ignores Music and Music ignores Dance.)

Here, of course, we are some distance from the lauded pictoriality of *Thérèse*. Shared amongst the above quotations is a sense of ballet music's arbitrariness, a sense that runs contrary to earlier comments about *Thérèse*'s musical poetry and animation. The ballet's incongruity in a contemporary context comes to the fore once again, inviting us to compare Hahn's score with a couple of others.

Comparing scores

Let us begin with Maréchal's *Le Lac des aulnes* and a scene, chosen almost at random, in which a magician's daughter, Lulla, attempts to introduce her father to a sprite, Elfen, visible only to Lulla herself (see Examples 2.3a and 2.3b). A first point to note is the repetition of mime music at separate dramatic moments. Consider, for example, the G major motif of the 'Largo assai' (Example 2.3a, bar 2), used to accompany Lulla's examination of Elfen. This motif recurs (albeit altered melodically) a few moments later (bar 8) when, following her father's disavowal of the sprite's existence, Lulla begins to play with Elfen; it is heard again, doubled at the octave, in the 'Largo maestoso' (Example 2.3b, bar 1). Such a musical recurrence may seem of only minor importance, perhaps reflecting an imperative of musical economy rather than any musical-dramatic coherence. Nonetheless, it may also alert us to a potential non-pictoriality about the music (what does it mean that the same motif accompanies actions of bodily inspection, play and dance?), and, more important, to a kinship between music for mime and music for dance. This is a second point to note: that mime music tends to borrow from dance, and vice versa. The motif of the 'Largo assai' is exemplary. Even on its first 'mimetic' appearance, this music has something dance-like about it, owing to those undulating flourishes, a general melodic expressivity and, not least, a lilting, waltz-like feel. (The $\frac{12}{8}$ time signature, taken slowly, is likely to suggest a triple metre.) When the motif recurs at the 'Largo maestoso' it is granted full-scale waltz treatment: the entire mimed passage of the 'Largo assai' is arranged as a set dance, 'ironed' into a regular, periodic structure, complete with fanfare-like accompaniment.

  This blurring of styles may be significant: because there are plenty of occasions in the ballet when a similar motivic continuity is apparent (or else

Example 2.3a Maréchal, *Le Lac des aulnes*, Act One, 'Largo assai'.

occasions when mime music approaches dance, if not becoming the subject of a danced scene itself); and because this blurring contrasts acutely with the musical specificity of *Thérèse*. An initial comparison of Maréchal's and Hahn's scores suggests a marked disparity of dramatic effect. Whilst Hahn's music tends to be shaped by the immediate needs of text and action, belonging firmly in the diegesis, Maréchal's participates less directly in the diegetic goings-on (here I disagree with Lalo, quoted earlier). The latter

Example 2.3b Maréchal, *Le Lac des aulnes*, Act One, 'Largo maestoso'.

remains less a *raconteur* than a scenic cloth suggestive more of a general style than a specific substance – a cloth stitched from idiomatic snippets, gesturing to a mode of performance.

As for *Les Bacchantes*, what of its supposed 'misunderstanding' between 'Dance' and 'Music'? Turning to the first 'Pantomime' scene of only thirteen bars, one finds a consistency of metre, a thick, chordal texture, regular harmonic progressions, question-and-answer phrases and a rounded form, with introductory staccato octaves and concluding sustained chords

Example 2.4 Bruneau, *Les Bacchantes*, Act One, 'Pantomime'.

(Example 2.4). These features may well be dramatically suggestive: the chorale-like texture may evoke the ballet's religious overtones, whilst the *très lent* tempo, the plodding rhythms and heavy, semiquaver articulation may conjure Bacchus's nobility of character. But more intimate, moment-by-moment effects are absent. There is no 'speech' music (*à la* Mimi in *Thérèse*) and no local musical-dramatic synchronicity; 'voice' and 'words' are submerged. Indeed, this idea finds literal realization in a handful of passages from the ballet in which characters sing. Whilst one might expect these sung sections to help advance the action, to state plainly the words to be mimed, they tend to do the opposite. Singing occurs not in scenes of pantomime, but scenes of dance; vocal lines offer personal reflections on the stage goings-on rather than narrative exposition. Moreover, in the final sung passage (the penultimate number of the ballet), the singing voice is used purely for its sonic effect. There are no words at all, but merely the tuned murmurings of characters.

This 'neutralization' of musical narrative could certainly generate further discussion – of the neutralization of narrative itself (mentioned earlier) and the development of more subtle means of musical characterization. For the present, though, it will be sufficient to register the contrast – between, on the one hand, *Les Bacchantes* and *Le Lac des aulnes* and, on the other, *Thérèse*. The last offers a musical-dramatic intimacy, a planned and patterned synchronization, that suggests little in the way of similarity with the other ballets of the period. Yet, and perhaps unsurprisingly, this synchronization may be reminiscent of an older balletic tradition: *Thérèse* draws from the same stock of musical-dramatic crutches as the 1840s *ballet-pantomime*.[41] As Smith describes in her study of the genre, composers went to great lengths to tell a story, to provide a literal and transparent musical text made up not only of identifying themes and familiar signifiers for mood, feeling and geographic location, but of specifically balletic devices, notably the instrumental recitative.[42] This device, designed to imitate the speech rhythms and contours of words to be mimed (written in libretti), features prominently in *Thérèse*. Mimi's music, for example, constructs a straightforward signifying system that parallels verbal language: the music appears to 'talk', to 'envoice' the silent dancing character.

A second musical device favoured by *ballet-pantomime* composers was also employed by Hahn: his score is notable for its borrowings, especially from music with familiar connotative value – music thus able to directly facilitate spectators' understanding of the plot.[43] One of these borrowings may be of particular dramatic significance. Prior to the dress consultations of Act One, the seamstresses spot a familiar face amongst the clientèle; it is Carlotta Grisi, beloved *étoile* of the Opéra. Gathering around the ballerina,

---

[41] This idea has an interesting footnote. Of the three scores for *Thérèse* housed in the Bibliothèque-musée de l'Opéra, two reveal a number of cuts that, to judge from handwritten scrawls and adhesive tape, were made after the ballet's premiere (and presumably realized on the ballet's recreation at the Opéra in 1921). A couple of the cuts are from scene-setting music: the opening of Act Two, as the curtain goes up on Thérèse's garden; and the end of Act Two, scene 2, an atmospheric passage entitled 'Clair de lune'. A couple more are of passages from set dances, including sixteen bars from the Act Two 'Menuet'. But most of the cuts are from action scenes. One is particularly conspicuous: a passage from Act Two, scene 3, in which Mimi's identifying theme (the piano melody heard to accompany her tears at the end of Act One) signals, according to Mendès's directions, the character's dramatic presence on stage. It is of course tempting to wonder whether these cuts reflect a larger objective, perhaps a culling of musical mimeticism in line with 1920s trends.

[42] Smith, *Ballet and Opera in the Age of 'Giselle'*, pp. 97–123.

[43] See *ibid.*, pp. 101–10. Smith includes a detailed list of the borrowed extracts in *ballet-pantomime* scores from 1777 to 1845 (pp. 104–7).

the seamstresses request a private performance. Grisi acquiesces, performing the waltz from *Giselle* to original music by Adolphe Adam. The seamstresses burst into applause.

From an interpretive standpoint, this scene offers a crowning stroke. *Thérèse* not only participates in an act of borrowing typical of the *ballet-pantomime*; it borrows from one of the most illustrious *ballet-pantomimes* of all. In other words, and to pull together the several strands of these pages, *Thérèse* thematizes the genre – literally, in its quotation of *Giselle* – whilst simultaneously offering a structural, narrative and musical restoration. What is more, following the seamstresses' applause, Grisi teaches the *Giselle* waltz to Mimi, and the seamstress goes on to repeat the dance in full. This repetition not only highlights the historical signifier; the dramatized didacticism extends off stage and towards the spectators in the theatre. The audience also receives instruction in the ways of the waltz, reminded once again of Grisi, of *Giselle* and of those illustrious days of ballet at the Opéra.

It is but a small step from here to a 'cultural-political' reading of the ballet, one that speculates about motivation, agenda and reception. *Thérèse*'s references to the *ballet-pantomime* may be configured as tactics of edification, designed to moralize on a national balletic history; the ballet itself may be an exercise in self-promotion, a product of an Opéra seeking roots in its past, historicizing its own history as a means of self-glorification. Indeed, in its references to the 1840s, *Thérèse* evoked an era when ballet – its technique, terminology, aesthetics, practitioners and products – was explicitly French. The *ballet-pantomime*, as noted earlier, was an exemplary French species, created and developed by French practitioners; although it gained acceptance on many European stages (in Milan, Stuttgart and Vienna), its home was the Paris Opéra.

Of course, this 'cultural-political' argument might be made firmer and more compelling by recourse to the historical context of early twentieth-century ballet – to the 'décadence' at the Opéra, not to mention the success of the Ballets Russes. One might ponder the fact that, just as the Russians captivated Paris with their exotic dancing and decor, the national company withdrew into the traditions that enfolded it. The historical coincidence of *Thérèse* and the Russian seasons, then, may encourage us to think again about old oppositions: oppositions between companies and the men at their helm, but also between creative aesthetics, dramatic models and musical styles.

There is an additional opposition to consider, one that may signal the complexity of visual and musical signifiers, as well as the possibility of historical cross-currents. To explain, I shall turn to another of Hahn's musical borrowings.

Back to reality? A counter-narrative

After her turn as Giselle, and her warm reception by Palmyre's workers, Carlotta Grisi singles out the prettiest: 'Toi, qui es-tu, petite? Tu es la plus jolie!' The seamstress (played by Carlotta Zambelli) replies with the following mimed 'speech':

Mimi Pinson est une blonde,
Une blonde que l'on connaît.
Elle n'a qu'une robe au monde,
Landerirette,
Et qu'un bonnet.
(Mimi Pinson is a blonde,
A blonde whom we know.
She has only one dress in the world,
Landerirette,
And only one bonnet.)

The words are not those of Palmyre's apprentice; the accompanying music is not that of Hahn. Quoted here is a well-known poem by Alfred de Musset, to music by Frédéric Bérat – a poem that confirms the identity of the seamstress as the blonde-haired grisette of 1840s Parisian subculture, a certain Mademoiselle Pinson (see Example 2.5).[44] What is offered here, then, and on a most basic level of character, is another reference to the period of *Thérèse*'s assumed heritage, a reference 'realized' through one of its most iconic characters: the Mimi of Musset, of Henri Murger, Puccini and Leoncavallo.[45]

   Yet Mendès's grisette shares few characteristics with her historical ancestors: with Musset's thoughtful, insouciant heroine; with Murger's pert, wilful coquette (and Leoncavallo's similarly drawn gold-digging flirt); and with Puccini's fragile muse.[46] The Mimi of *Thérèse* – incidentally, the real

---

[44] De Musset's poem, first published in 1845, is included in his anthology *Poésies nouvelles* (1851; repr. Paris: Gilbert, 1962), pp. 161–2.

[45] I should note a further, equally glaring backward glance to the mid-nineteenth century: the ballet's title draws on a poem by Victor Hugo (included in *Les Contemplations*, published in 1856) as the pictorial basis for Act Two.

[46] An insightful account of Mimi Pinson's literary and stage characteristics can be found in Allan W. Atlas, 'Mimi's Death: Mourning in Puccini and Leoncavallo', *Journal of Musicology*, 14/1 (1996), pp. 52–79. Other studies that explore Mimi and her Bohemian heritage include Jerrold Seigel, *Bohemian Paris: Culture, Politics, and the Boundaries of Bourgeois Life, 1830–1930* (New York: Viking, 1986); Arthur Groos and Roger Parker (eds.), *Giacomo Puccini, 'La bohème'* (Cambridge University Press, 1986); and Jürgen Maehder, 'Paris-Bilder: Zur Transformation von Henry Murgers Roman in den Bohème-Opern Puccinis und Leoncavallos', *Jahrbuch für Opernforschung*, 2 (1986), pp. 109–76.

Example 2.5 Hahn, *La Fête chez Thérèse*, Act One, scene 3, 'La Chanson de Mimi Pinson'.

protagonist of the ballet – is a different creation: confident and self-assured, she demonstrates a mature initiative, winning back her lover through practical pleas and, unusually, surviving the ordeal. One might even describe her narrative portrayal as forgiving. Not only does Mimi forgive her lover's wandering affections, but we, the audience, tend to forgive her more irksome characteristics: her spectacular balletic prowess (she learns the *Giselle* waltz in record time, trumping Grisi's version with her own, six times the length); the aggressive, if sincere, language of her plea to Thérèse ('Oh! Don't love him! Tell him not to love you! Give him back to me!'); and her nagging interrogation of Théodore at the end of Act One.

Mendès may have modelled this balletic Mimi, if not on the character's historical ancestors, then on her seamstress sisters of 1910: the 'Mimi Pinsons' of Gustave Charpentier's Parisian night school, the Conservatoire Populaire de Mimi Pinson, founded by the composer in 1902. These namesakes – young, underprivileged working women (mainly shop-girls and seamstresses) – were offered classes by Charpentier and his cadre of distinguished colleagues in piano, popular song, dance, pantomime, declamation and, interestingly, fencing. By January 1910, roughly five hundred 'Mimi Pinsons' attended the school on the Élysée des Beaux-Arts, performing in public concerts at the Tuileries, the Place des Vosges and the Place de la Nation, and even attending national events (such as the unveiling in the Paris suburb of Suresnes of Émile Derré's bust of Zola). The students became symbols of social advancement and equality; Charpentier's school, to quote scholar Mary Ellen Poole, represented 'the last gasp of Fourierist "art for the masses" as a didactic, morally uplifting, and pleasure-giving force'.[47]

Mimi, too, may represent an ideal of social parity – an upward mobility that resonates with Charpentier's institution. In a manner not dissimilar from that of the composer's best students, Mimi triumphs over her domestic and social circumstances. More specifically, she triumphs over Thérèse: as one critic noted of the ballet, 'C'est le triomphe de la grisette sur la grande dame.'[48] (Incidentally, this triumph owes to a musical coercion: Mimi's identifying theme, granted an extra-diegetic quality, is literally 'heard' by Théodore and Thérèse during their passion, prompting the duchess, out of sympathy, to return Théodore to the seamstress.) Thérèse herself loses her lover, her clothes and even her dignity. Humiliated over Théodore's presence during her undressing in Act One, scene 3, she continues to dance in only a petticoat. Critic Robert de Montesquiou was appalled: characters of noble rank rarely danced on stage (owing to librettists' concerns for verisimilitude), let alone in their underwear.[49]

As well as this broadly socialist resonance, the character of Mimi may also evoke contemporary politics of gender and identity. On this subject, Hahn's score is once again evocative, in terms of both the amount of material allotted to Mimi and this music's linguistic authority. The mime scene between Mimi and Théodore examined earlier will help illustrate (Example 2.2). Clearly, there is a marked disparity between the quantity of music assigned to each character (Mimi receives roughly twice as many bars as Théodore) – a disparity that might simply reflect Théodore's dreamy, faraway state and Mimi's desperate resolve. But Mimi's music is by far the more idiomatic, as well as the more rhetorically persuasive. She has a distinct and distinctly recognizable identifying theme (the Bérat melody), as well as characteristic semiquaver 'chatter' – 'chatter' that, often beginning with a tonal wrench (suggesting the relentlessness of her discourse), overwhelms Théodore's mimetic attempts. Théodore's music, on the other hand, is hazy and vacuous. Here and earlier in the ballet, he is granted no identifying theme and tends

[47] Mary Ellen Poole, 'Gustave Charpentier and the Conservatoire Populaire de Mimi Pinson', *19th-Century Music*, 20/3 (1997), pp. 231–52 at p. 231.

[48] *Journal des débats*, 20 February 1910; clipping, F-Po, B 717.

[49] Montesquiou, 'Une collaboration entre Devéria et Lancret à propos de *La Fête chez Thérèse*'; clipping, F-Po, B 717.

instead merely to borrow music from one of his women. He seems disinclined to articulate himself clearly or individually, to enter into dialogue or to address the audience in monologues; he seems disinclined to 'talk' at all.

So much is evident – and the ensuing gender implications equally so: Mimi represents feminine authority, assertiveness, even aggression; Théodore embodies masculine submissiveness and docility. These gendered representations, which inverted the essential divisions of bourgeois life, are characteristic not only of the ballet in question, but of the early 1900s, a period that witnessed the rise of feminism and feminist periodicals, easier access for women to higher education and professional careers, a declining birth-rate and new divorce laws.[50] This general historical condition shored up the image of the *femme nouvelle* (the bourgeois 'she-man'), a woman newly visible and equal to men (in social and professional station, as well as physical presence), independent and educated, and keen to campaign for her rights. One example of such a woman may be Mlle Stichel, the Opéra's ballet-master and the choreographer of *Thérèse*. Previously engaged at the Châtelet, Paris, and the Théâtre de Monte-Carlo, Stichel was one of few women to occupy the much-vaunted position.[51] She was also one of few to contest her authorial rights, taking legal action against the Opéra in a bid for an equal share (with librettist and composer) of *Thérèse*'s royalties and authorship. The bid, pleaded in front of the Tribunal Civil de la Seine on 9 February 1911, was successful, Stichel claiming victory for choreographers – and for women – nationwide.[52]

A second example may be Mimi herself. The character – her actions, her fate and not least her music – may be representative, a theatrical incarnation of the social and gendered ideals of bourgeois life. Even her costume is suggestive. To rewind to the dresses with which the ballet began: all the dresses on display had long skirts, the length being historically authentic in suggesting 1840s fashion (see Figure 2.1). That Mimi's skirt was long, though, was something of an irregularity. As Zambelli described in an interview with *Le Miroir*:

Ce fut une belle affaire. Les chroniqueurs d'alors s'en emparèrent. Les vieux abonnés étaient stupéfaits et déconcertés. Une robe longue à la place du tutu! ... Une danseuse dont on ne voyait pas les jambes! ... C'était la révolution![53]

---

[50] On the French feminist movement, see Karen Offen, 'Depopulation, Nationalism, and Feminism in *Fin-de-Siècle* France', *American Historical Review*, 89/3 (1984), pp. 648–76; and Debora L. Silverman, '*Amazone, Femme Nouvelle*, and the Threat to the Bourgeois Family', in her *Art Nouveau in Fin-de-Siècle France: Politics, Psychology and Style* (Berkeley and Los Angeles: University of California Press, 1989), pp. 63–74.

[51] Stichel's tenure, which followed that of Clustine, lasted only a year.

[52] The lawsuit was reported extensively in *Gazette des tribunaux*, 4 March 1911.

[53] Quoted in André Arnyvelde, 'Carlotta Zambelli: l'étoile de la danse classique', *Le Miroir* (n.d.); clipping, F-Po, Dossier d'artiste, Carlotta Zambelli.

Figure 2.1 Zambelli as Mimi Pinson, *La Fête chez Thérèse* (1910).

(It was a fine business. The columnists of the time seized hold of it. The old subscribers were stupefied and disconcerted. A long dress instead of a tutu! ... A dancer whose legs one could not see! ... It was a revolution!)

Zambelli went on to describe how one male spectator failed to recognize her backstage following the premiere and made the mistake of asking her name.

Je gardai mon sérieux et lui répondis:
– Zambelli.
   Le vieil abonné eut un sursaut de surprise. Il s'excusa, un peu confus ... Il ne m'avait pas reconnue ... Il ne pouvait pas me reconnaître: la robe longue, songez, monsieur, la robe longue![54]

(I kept a straight face and replied:
– Zambelli.
   The old subscriber gave a start with surprise. He excused himself, a little confused ... He had not recognized me ... He could not recognize me: the long dress, think, Monsieur, the long dress!)

Functioning as a protective shield, the skirt was not only exceptional on a balletic body more accustomed to knee-length (and above) gauze; it screened the body itself, concealing Zambelli's identity – especially her sexual identity as an object of the male gaze. Yet the skirt also lent the dancer, and the character she played, some of the physical modesty and sobriety associated with the image of the *femme nouvelle*, an image that overturned the traditional type of decorative, eroticized femininity. This new, desexualized image even struck a chord with the dancer's offstage social status and reputation. As Zambelli made plain in an article for the journal *Je sais tout*, the Opéra's *étoiles* of the early twentieth century were far from the sexual trophies of the mid-nineteenth; they were rarely offered the lavish gifts, salaries and attention received by their historical counterparts. Instead, the Opéra's brightest stars thought of themselves as mere civil servants, self-made working girls working hard to make a living. Like Mimi herself.[55]

Backing up (conclusion)

Considered together, these ideas project a striking image of *Thérèse* and its resonance with contemporary culture – with the French feminist movement, with social reform and even with the practical matter of dancers' social status. The 'contemporary' should be underlined, for all this discourse on 'real life' *c.*1910 leads us far from the original historical signifier – the French *ballet-pantomime* of the 1840s. A new line of argument emerges, one that may well

---

[54] *Ibid.*
[55] Carlotta Zambelli, 'Danseuses d'hier et d'aujourd'hui', *Je sais tout*, 15 November 1907, pp. 535–42.

be of signal importance to our understanding of the institutional project of the Opéra. Talk of didacticism, for example, might refocus on social instruction, on the amelioration of the female working class; previous notions of nationalism and nostalgia might cede to contemporary ideals of womanhood and the equality of classes and sexes.

Yet these two historical signifiers – the one retrospective, the other specific to the belle époque – can in fact coalesce: in other words, the contemporaneous currency of the ballet can endorse its generic heritage. As Marian Smith explains, the *ballet-pantomime* was prone to a mirroring of social relations, particularly gendered ones. Plots tended to uphold notions of masculine power and feminine submissiveness, to teach object lessons in social and sexual relations.[56] *Thérèse*, then, fits the bill. Like the *ballet-pantomime* of the 1840s, the ballet leans heavily on contemporary gender ideology. Only now, of course, this ideology has been inverted, the image of the decorative and eroticized ballerina replaced by that of the long-skirted Mimi, merely one of a crowd.

This argument – almost too convenient – should not make for a miserable conclusion. The position of *Thérèse* within an institutional and historical context throws up an important question about the relationship discussed at the start of this chapter – between the Paris Opéra and the Ballets Russes. Both companies were active in a period of intense debate about ballet, tradition and influence, a period that saw ballet-makers strive for self-preservation, self-aggrandizement and the wholesale capitalization on what was then a new and prominent public and critical interest. The Ballets Russes are often considered in this context. Historians have long described – and celebrated – the troupe's innovative aesthetic, its relation to tradition and its 'uncanny' awareness of contemporary trends and tastes. But what would it mean to discern these same characteristics in the French ballet, the official and supposedly 'conservative' company? What if *Thérèse* was as self-conscious and strategic as the Russian offerings? The broadness of the ballet's frame of reference, the number of onstage/offstage analogies, the multiply-allusive and iconic characterization, the composite score: these features may be contingent not only on a pre-established generic mould, but on a contemporary artistic climate in which ballet, for the first time in a good few decades, was actively seeking to make itself relevant, to communicate with a newfound audience.

These ideas run deep into the complexities of the historical scene, as well as the historiographical assumptions of 'innovation' and 'Otherness' that

---

[56] Smith, *Ballet and Opera in the Age of 'Giselle'*, pp. 70–1.

saturate the scholarly literature. In airing the ideas here, I hope simply to encourage a more wide-angled view of early twentieth-century ballet. For if the usual story of the period glorifies (foreign) individuals and initiatives, then revisionism might value continuities and cohabitation, might consider the French and the Russians (the self and the 'Other') in the same frame.

3 ❧ Nijinsky's *Faune* revisited

As far as hackneyed subjects go, at least for scholars of music and dance, Nijinsky's *L'Après-midi d'un faune* may be exemplary. Performed by the Ballets Russes, and premiered at Paris's Châtelet theatre on 29 May 1912, the ballet has earned a place amongst twentieth-century *scandales*, associated with stories of sex and secrecy that have acquired almost mythic proportions. To recount popular conjecture: Nijinsky stumbled upon ideas for *Faune* during a visit to the Louvre, when he stood up friend and collaborator Léon Bakst in favour of some Egyptian reliefs; rehearsals for the ballet – all 120 of them – were conducted behind closed doors so as not to upset principal choreographer Michel Fokine (jealous of Nijinsky's rising status); a commotion erupted at the premiere, owing largely to a final and supposedly masturbatory gesture from Nijinsky as faun; Diaghilev ordered the ballet to be repeated immediately; Gaston Calmette, the editor of *Le Figaro*, wrote a front-page article denouncing 'des vils mouvements de bestialité érotique et des gestes de lourde impudeur' (vile, bestially erotic movements and thoroughly shameless gestures); in defence, Auguste Rodin penned a positive piece for *Le Matin*; Calmette was further enraged, berating Rodin's own artistic tendencies and even his private circumstances – namely, his housing in Paris's Hôtel Biron at the tax-payer's expense.[1]

An accumulation of picture books, photo albums and not-quite-academic texts has recounted this history, rhapsodizing on matters of genesis and reception, even drawing comparisons (in terms of ensuing insurrection) with Nijinsky's later choreographic offering *Le Sacre du printemps*.[2] Clearly, this

This chapter is an expanded version of a paper given at the 'Diaghilev Symposium' held at Columbia University, April 2009, and, in revised form, at the conference 'Music and Representation', Merton College, Oxford, March 2010. Thanks to Boris Gasparov, Lynn Garafola and Joshua Walden for invitations.

[1] See Gaston Calmette, 'Un faux pas', *Le Figaro*, 30 May 1912, p. 1; Auguste Rodin, 'La Rénovation de la danse', *Le Matin*, 30 May 1912, p. 1; and Calmette, 'À propos d'un faune', *Le Figaro*, 31 May 1912, p. 1. According to some reports, Rodin did not write the article in *Le Matin*, but merely signed it; the author is thought to be French writer, art critic and collector Claude Roger-Marx.

[2] Of the secondary literature on the ballet, Jean-Michel Nectoux's edited volume *Nijinsky: 'Prélude à l'Après-midi d'un faune'* (London: Thames and Hudson, 1990) offers a particularly valuable resource, comprising reports on the ballet from the period press (including those by Calmette and Rodin) as well as essays by recent critics. Other studies to recount *Faune*'s history, in variously

body of literature has helped nourish and sustain the ballet, along with its perceived status as a 'special case'. But scholars of music and dance have also contributed. Comments on the relation between Nijinsky's choreography and Debussy's 1894 symphonic poem, used as musical accompaniment, have tended to emphasize the peculiar, the irrational and the unorthodox. According to the standard scholarly wisdom, *Faune* offers one of the first examples of a dissonant – theorists might call it 'anempathetic' – relation between music and visuals. To quote Stephanie Jordan, the ballet represents a 'dual experience', a 'dissociation of sensibilities' between an 'impressionistic' music and an 'angular', 'staccato' choreography.[3] Veteran dance writer Robert Greskovic has described something similar: 'The flattened, angular postures and moves of Nijinsky's choreography passed through the music's lush atmosphere like ships through a fog. Instead of directly acknowledging Debussy's score, Nijinsky worked artfully against it.'[4] This deliberate contradiction, according to theatre historian Hanna Järvinen, contributed to the ballet's essential 'modernism': 'Th[e] possibility for a new kind of danced expression, even when accused of forcing the dancing bodies into "unnatural" forms that did not suit the flowing musical score, was what made the work modernist; the experience of formal difference was what made it memorable for both performers and spectators.'[5]

Repeated again and again in the literature, this line of argument is difficult to shake from the imagination. Indeed, there is plenty of evidence in support – evidence, at least, of the choreographic rigidity and 'unnaturalness' described by scholars. The ballet's primary visual source – the photographic collection of Baron Adolf de Meyer, comprising posed shots of characters from *Faune* taken in a London studio – is exemplary. Figures 3.1 and 3.2 are from de Meyer's collection: the former shows the faun (Nijinsky) in a crouched position with bent elbows, wrists, knees and ankles; the latter, of the faun and chief nymph (Lubov Tchernicheva), juxtaposes sharp angles (crossed arms, turned heads, a bent knee and foot) with an intense and athletic straightness (fingers, palms, Nijinsky's left arm and torso).

colourful terms, include Richard Buckle, *Nijinsky* (London: Weidenfeld and Nicolson, 1971) and *Diaghilev* (London: Weidenfeld and Nicolson, 1979); Lynn Garafola, *Diaghilev's Ballets Russes* (1989; repr. New York: Da Capo, 1998); and Kevin Kopelson, *The Queer Afterlife of Vaslav Nijinsky* (Stanford University Press, 1997).

[3] Stephanie Jordan, 'Debussy, the Dance, and the *Faune*', in James Briscoe (ed.), *Debussy in Performance* (New Haven, CT, and London: Yale University Press, 1999), pp. 119–34.

[4] Robert Greskovic, *Ballet 101: A Complete Guide to Learning and Loving the Ballet* (1998; rev. edn Milwaukee, WI: Limelight Editions, 2005), p. 56.

[5] Hanna Järvinen, 'Dancing without Space: On Nijinsky's *L'Après-midi d'un faune* (1912)', *Dance Research*, 27/1 (2009), pp. 28–64 at p. 30.

Figure 3.1 Nijinsky as faun, crouching (1912); photographer, Baron Adolf de Meyer.

This stylized coincidence of Euclidean forms – straight lines, criss-crosses, sharp angles – also emerges from the secondary visual source: the film reconstruction of the ballet, based on Nijinsky's choreographic score.[6] The dancers move across a foreshortened stage, moving in profile and by means of the most basic of steps – simple footfalls, runs, pivots and turns. Their angular postures are striking (especially when 'held' for what seems like several

---

[6] The reconstruction, performed by the Julliard Dance Ensemble, was directed by dance expert Ann Hutchinson Guest. Guest exhumed Nijinsky's choreographic score (dating from 1915) from the British Library, London, where it had been deposited by Romola Nijinsky on her husband's death in 1950. In collaboration with dance scholar Claudia Jeschke, Guest managed to decipher Nijinsky's unique notational system, going on to translate the score into the more conventional Labanotation. Then followed the film reconstruction (1991) and a book charting the reconstructive process, aptly titled *Nijinsky's 'Faune' Restored* (Philadelphia, PA: Gordon and Breach, 1991). Admittedly, some scholars have taken issue with the reconstruction, questioning its authenticity in relation to the memory-based versions of the ballet.

Figure 3.2 Nijinsky as faun, crossing arms with chief nymph (1912); photographer, Baron Adolf de Meyer.

seconds) and serve to highlight the twin places (the two-dimensionality) of the visual scene. But equally striking is Debussy's music, its legato phrases, restrained dynamics, conjunct melodies, gentle articulations, expressive timbres and seamless, sutured forms.

It is not difficult to imagine the incongruity of impression, not to mention the 'terror' felt by Debussy at the dress rehearsal. In a 1914 interview for an Italian newspaper, the composer raged:

Imagine if you can the discrepancy between a sinuous, soothing, flexible musical line on the one hand, and on the other a performance whose characters move like those on Greek or Etruscan vases, ungracefully, rigidly, as though their every gestures were constricted by the laws of plane geometry. So profound a dissonance can know no resolution![7]

Press accounts of the ballet's premiere pushed a similar line, most in sympathy with the composer.[8] According to Pierre Lalo in his regular column for *Le Temps*: 'tous les éléments décoratifs, plastiques et chorégraphiques sont en contradiction absolue avec le caractère poétique et musical de leur sujet' (all the decorative, plastic and choreographic elements contrast wholly with the poetic and musical character of their subject).[9] André Mangeot, editor of *Le Monde musical*, explained:

Vous savez que le *Prélude* de Debussy est d'un contour extrêmement arrondi. Flûtes, hautbois, cors et chanterelles y dessinent, aussi bien au premier plan, que comme fond de décor, des lignes courbes et sinueuses, souples, fluides, amoureuses et languissantes. Rien n'y est anguleux, ni saccadé. Or la représentation graphique de M. Nijinski est exclusivement anguleuse et saccadée. Elle est toute en coudes pointus, en gestes brefs, en lignes brisées, en un mot elle est le contraire de la musique dont elle s'accompagne.[10]

(It is known that the contour of Debussy's *Prélude* is extremely smooth. Flutes, oboes, horns and strings map out curved, sinuous, supple, fluid, loving and languid lines, as much in the foreground as in the background scenery. Nothing is angular or jerky. Now, Nijinsky's graphic representation is exclusively angular and jerky. It is performed throughout with sharp elbows, short gestures and broken lines; in brief it is the opposite of the music that it accompanies.)

Mangeot maintained that Nijinsky had misunderstood and mistreated Debussy, that the ballet amounted to 'une véritable trahison' (a veritable act of treachery). This idea generated its own debate, one that tapped into

[7] Debussy, interview in *La Tribuna*, 23 February 1914; quoted in Jordan, 'Debussy, the Dance, and the *Faune*', pp. 125–6. Incidentally, similarities between the postures of *Faune*'s characters and those depicted on classical Greek vases have been noted by a number of commentators; Nectoux, for example, offers some compelling illustrations in his *Nijinsky: 'Prélude à l'Après-midi d'un faune'*, pp. 20–3. Buckle proposes an alternative frame of reference for Nijinsky's choreographic design, pointing to the Egyptian paintings and reliefs that Nijinsky may have encountered in the Louvre; see his *Diaghilev*, p. 185. I have a different idea, one that shall be explained towards the end of this chapter.

[8] Also see the memoirs of Marie Rambert, *Quicksilver* (London: Macmillan, 1972), p. 54; and a review by Maurice Ravel, 'Nijinsky comme maître de ballet' (no date), in Arbie Orenstein (ed.), *A Ravel Reader: Correspondence, Articles, Interviews* (New York: Dover, 2003), pp. 404–5.

[9] Pierre Lalo, 'La Musique', *Le Temps*, 11 June 1912, p. 3. Lalo went on to argue that Nijinsky's *Faune* was not the only production of the Ballets Russes to offer incongruous music and visuals.

[10] André Mangeot, 'Les Ballets Russes: Le *Prélude à l'Après-midi d'un Faune* de Debussy maltraité par Nijinski', *Le Monde musical*, 15 June 1912, p. 182. Critics noted a similar disjunction – between stilted, mechanical gestures and subtle, flowing music – in *Jeux*, choreographed by Nijinsky to a newly commissioned score by Debussy.

contemporary anxieties about dancing to non-dance music (*musique pure*) and about the nature and extent of a 'primitive' influence on French culture (more on this in the following chapter).[11]

Yet amongst the mass of critical reception is a smattering of remarks that should give us pause. Here, and perhaps most compelling, is Louis Schneider in an article for *Le Théâtre*, June 1912:

Nijinsky a adopté l'épisode chorégraphique de l'œuvre de Debussy avec une sincérité absolue, après avoir longuement médité sur le sujet et s'être imprégné de l'atmosphère du tableau peint par le compositeur . . . Nijinsky obtient . . . une fusion plus intime, plus parfaite, une cohésion plus directe entre les divers éléments de la musique et les mouvements du corps qui les commentent.[12]

(Nijinsky adopted his choreography from Debussy's music with absolute sincerity, after having pondered the subject for a long time and soaked up the atmosphere of the scene painted by the composer . . . Nijinsky obtained . . . a more intimate, more perfect fusion, a more direct cohesion between the various aspects of the music and the bodily movements that commented on it.)

'Absolute sincerity', 'perfect fusion', 'direct cohesion': what are we to make of these descriptions? Some readers may dismiss Schneider straight off, particularly as his version of events departs from the usual story (from Nijinsky's wife Romola) in which the choreographer turns to Debussy's piece as a last resort – certainly not pondering its subject or soaking up its scene.[13] Then there is Schneider's vagueness and lack of specifics: he shies away from specifying the 'various aspects' of the ballet that formed the 'intimate' link. But the commentary is intriguing. Schneider does not deny the choreographic angularity, let alone how this angularity might be at odds with the music; but, and even so, he recognizes some special expressive quality about the ballet. Indeed, he goes further, outlining a balletic synthesis, a blending of sight and sound that was intimate, direct and sincere.

Schneider was not alone in this alternative thinking. Reviewing the ballet for the theatrical daily *Comœdia*, Louis Vuillemin maintained: 'Pour moi, j'avoue n'avoir jamais joui pareillement d'une si parfaite union de la pantomime et de la musique, de la si complète joie de l'œil et de l'oreille.'[14]

---

[11] According to Émile Vuillermoz, concern for Nijinsky's tampering with *Faune* arose prior to the production: 'L'idée qu'un des chers barbares moscovites allait toucher au précieux prélude debussyste était secrètement désagréable'; 'La Grande Saison de Paris', *Revue musicale S.I.M.*, 8/6 (1912), pp. 62–8 at p. 66.

[12] Louis Schneider, 'Les Ballets Russes', *Le Théâtre*, I June 1912, pp. 4–9 at p. 8.

[13] In her 1933 biography, Romola also noted her husband's admission that 'the musical movement would not be the same as his own plastic expression'; *Nijinsky* (London: Victor Gollancz, 1933), p. 125.

[14] Louis Vuillemin, 'Troisième série des Ballets Russes', *Comœdia*, 30 May 1912, p. 2.

(As for myself, I confess to having never enjoyed so much a perfect union of pantomime and music, such a complete joy to the eye and the ear.) Then there was Debussy. In a letter of 1913 written to Nijinsky following a successful run of *Faune* in London, Debussy proclaimed the choreographer a 'genius', thanking him for adding 'a new dimension of beauty' to his music, and complementing the English on having 'understood' it.[15] As a historical source, and in view of Debussy's other comment about 'unresolvable dissonance', this one may be sarcastic – a vestige perhaps of the composer's journalistic flippancy. But as a remark it is curious, provocative even. Some thirty years later, American dance critic Edwin Denby echoed Debussy's praise. Describing Nijinsky's 'musical intelligence' as of 'the highest order', Denby also implicated some other dimension about the ballet, one that transcended the musical surface: 'this was the first ballet choreography set clearly not to the measures and periods, but to the expressive flow of the music, to its musical sense.'[16]

The gift of these comments should be clear: they write a counter-narrative to the conventional line, conjuring impressions that extend beyond and behind the cliché of regrettable dissonance. The mention of 'beauty' and 'fusion', moreover, may inspire an alternative reading, may be taken as index of a new realm of possibility about the ballet – to quote Schneider, 'une région tout à fait inexploitée dans l'art de la chorégraphie'.[17] My initial thoughts may be worth outlining here. Something, I think, is happening to the means of balletic illusionism in *Faune*: to the ways in which sounds and images are called upon to function, to generate structural coherence, to implicate space and time, to create drama and expression, to *mean*. And this something, not solely a matter of stylistic and structural incongruence, has to do with how the choreography conceptualizes Debussy's score: as sonic backcloth, diegetic appendage, temporal yardstick, aesthetic object.

There is more. This music–choreographic relation, I argue, casts a revealing light on the ballet's initiatory modernism – something that is usually conceived in purely visual terms (according to Lynn Garafola, in terms of the two-dimensional design and stylized gestures) or else in terms of the 'formal difference' (to quote Järvinen once again) between music and dance.[18]

---

[15] Although the original letter, as far as I can make out, is lost, its content was reported in *The Daily Mail*, 21 February 1913; also see Buckle, *Diaghilev*, p. 244.

[16] Edwin Denby, 'Notes on Nijinsky Photographs' (1943); repr. in *Dance Writings* (New York: Knopf, 1986), pp. 495–501 at p. 498. Dancer Lydia Sokolova, from the original cast, voiced a similar idea. In her memoirs of 1960, Sokolova described how the dancers 'had to be musical': 'it was necessary to relax and hear the music as a whole; it had to trickle through your consciousness, and the sensation approached the divine'. See Lydia Sokolova, *Dancing for Diaghilev: The Memoirs of Lydia Sokolova*, ed. Richard Buckle (London: John Murray, 1960), p. 40.

[17] Schneider, 'Les Ballets Russes', p. 9.

[18] See Garafola, *Diaghilev's Ballets Russes*, p. 58 and Järvinen, 'Dancing without Space', p. 30.

My ideas as presented here – ideas that rely centrally on Debussy's score, the film reconstruction and de Meyer's photographs (all of which can be identified within the original choreography) – suggest an alternative interpretive paradigm, a ballet modernism that challenged not only the established 'rules' of stage representation, but the representational mandate of the accompanying music.

This music, of course, has generated a substantial literature of its own; scholars from across the musicological establishment have variously argued and explained Debussy's debt to his source text, Mallarmé's infamous *éclogue*. Amongst the recent literature, David Code's 2001 article 'Hearing Debussy Reading Mallarmé' offers a particularly compelling analysis, arguing for an affinity of compositional syntax and 'sonorous poetry'.[19] Leaning heavily on the music's often overlooked lyricism and rhetorical intensity, Code describes how both *Prélude* and *éclogue* articulate 'a moment on the cusp of modernism', a moment 'that hovers between nineteenth- and twentieth-century modes of musical thought'.[20] This 'moment' may be important here. Watching Nijinsky hearing Debussy reading Mallarmé, as we could envisage it, inspires a further reflexive turn in the argument. For Nijinsky's choreography embodies that same modernist moment, that 'point of no return' from which traditional representational logic is distilled, dismantled and, to quote Code, 'acknowledged as arbitrary'.[21]

My objective here is to reflect on these ideas, to submit them to a series of refinements that should serve to open up a new site of critical engagement with *Faune*, its gestures and music. As will become clear, my study is essentially interpretive in nature, rather than an argument about intention or authorship. Nonetheless, it will circle around the cultural, artistic and intellectual dynamics of the period, poised at the turning point of early twentieth-century modernism.

Synopsis

We can start with a simple excursion through the ballet and with a simple question in mind: what does Nijinsky's choreography 'do' to Debussy's score? A first point emerges in the opening bars (see Example 3.1). As the flute solo commences, the faun is alone on stage, lying on a rocky outcrop in some wooded wilderness. He has a flute, a frontally held one, and remains in

---

[19] David J. Code, 'Hearing Debussy Reading Mallarmé: Music *après Wagner* in the *Prélude à l'après-midi d'un faune*', *Journal of the American Musicological Society*, 54/3 (2001), pp. 493–554.
[20] *Ibid.*, p. 542 and p. 548.   [21] *Ibid.*, p. 548.

Example 3.1 Debussy, *Prélude à l'après-midi d'un faune*, bs 1–4.

a playing position throughout the solo; he moves the instrument away from his mouth as the solo ends, then moves it back as the solo repeats (see Figure 3.3). The effect is obvious: by pretending to play, the faun locates Debussy's music within the diegesis, creating the illusion of musical literalism or sound effect. This effect continues at the third solo (Example 3.2, beginning b. 21) as the faun repositions himself on the rock, again holding his instrument in place for the duration. His staticism and almost cataleptic rigidity is conspicuous: staring straight ahead, he pays no attention to the nymphs who enter during the solo; he is seemingly transfixed by the sounds of his flute.

Next, and as the solo clarinet commences an altogether livelier melody, the faun turns towards the nymphs, all seven of whom are lined in a row along the front of the stage (Example 3.3, b. 31). The chief nymph, in the middle of the row and set slightly forward, unpins a veil from her outfit before letting it fall. The other six nymphs stand facing forward with heads

Figure 3.3 Nijinsky as faun, with flute (1912); photographer, Baron Adolf de Meyer.

turned sideways; in pairs, and in succession, they fling out their arms, elbows bent at right angles. These arm movements – abrupt and almost robotic – are synchronized to the crotchet pulse; gesture and music line up with clockwork precision (Example 3.3, bs 32–33). The movements then repeat, as the music itself repeats: the clarinet replays its solo (a minor third higher); the chief nymph loses another veil; and her companions continue jerking their arms (Example 3.3, b. 34).

As for the orchestration of this passage, the nymphs appear prominent to the sounds of the oboe and clarinet, whilst the faun takes centre stage as the flute emerges from the orchestra. Debussy's music is thus accorded timbral significance, and along traditionally gendered lines: man's association with the flute, and woman's with reed instruments, goes back at least to the classical tales of Pan, his 'syrinx' and the mythological sirens.[22] Nijinsky's

---

[22] For more on these associations, see John G. Landels, *Music in Ancient Greece and Rome* (London: Routledge, 1999); and Leofranc Holford-Strevens, 'Sirens in Antiquity and the Middle Ages', in Lynda Phyllis Austern and Inna Naroditskaya (eds.), *Music of the Sirens* (Bloomington: Indiana University Press, 2006), pp. 16–51.

Example 3.2 Debussy, *Prélude à l'après-midi d'un faune*, bs 21–22.

choreography appears to foreground these associations. For example, and fast-forwarding to b. 79, as the flute solo recommences, the faun is alone on stage; nymphs enter with angular postures to an animated oboe solo with trill, *sforzando* and staccato notes (Example 3.4, b. 83). At the oboe version of the flute solo (Example 3.5, b. 86) the faun is alone again, but he is now carrying one of the chief nymph's veils. The instrumental switch (from flute to oboe) may be dramatically appropriate: as the faun is consumed by

Example 3.3 Debussy, *Prélude à l'après-midi d'un faune*, bs 30–34.

Example 3.3 (cont.)

Example 3.3 (cont.)

Example 3.4 Debussy, *Prélude à l'après-midi d'un faune*, bs 79–83.

Example 3.4 (cont.)

Example 3.4 (cont.)

Example 3.5 Debussy, *Prélude à l'après-midi d'un faune*, bs 86–88.

thoughts of his female fancy, his music is consumed by her double-reed timbre.

Returning to the audio-visual synopsis: following the nymphs' entrance and the dropping of veils, there is a passage of group interest (from b. 37): the nymphs continue to move along the front of the stage, the chief offering a series of poses along her own linear trajectory; the faun joins the nymphs, watches their footwork, copies them slightly and then scares them away – all except the chief. There are some striking moments here: the chief nymph drops a veil at b. 53; the faun abruptly changes direction at b. 48; he places his foot down, slowly and with deliberation, at b. 51 (see Example 3.6). The ponderousness of this last step prepares for the central duet, as the faun gradually draws closer to the nymph, eyes fixed upon her. At b. 55, and as

Example 3.6 Debussy, *Prélude à l'après-midi d'un faune*, bs 45–53.

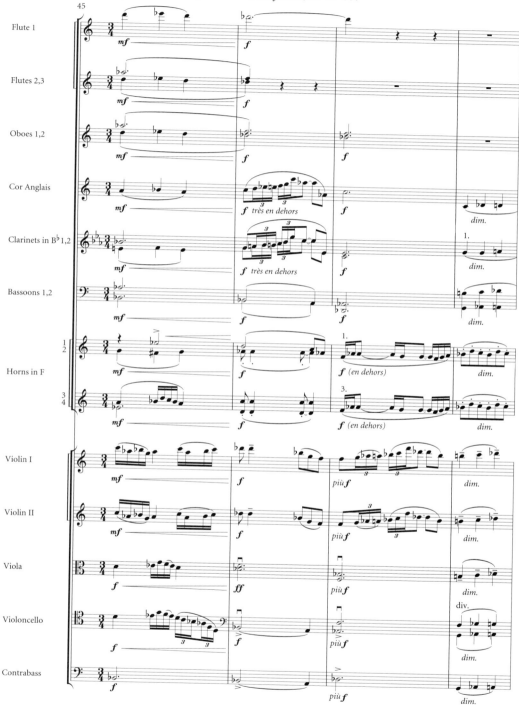

Example 3.6 (cont.)

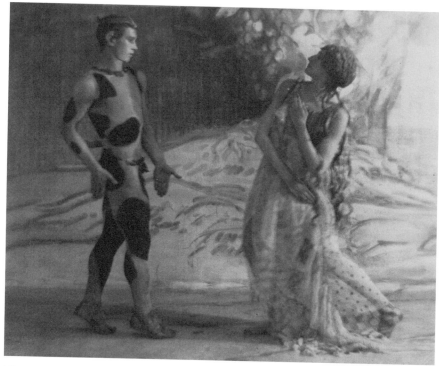

Figure 3.4 Nijinsky as faun, with chief nymph (1912); photographer, Baron Adolf de Meyer.

Debussy's D♭ major theme commences in the unison winds, both faun and nymph turn to face each other and hold their posture (Figure 3.4 and Example 3.7). The impression is reminiscent of the opening of the ballet, when the faun lay still playing his flute. On both occasions, bodily stasis suggests some sort of cerebral absorption: that music can be expressive, can be worth listening to; simpler still, that music *can* be listened to, even within the diegesis. (More on this later.)

The duet continues: the faun kicks a leg backward, abruptly and impatiently, then he jumps across the stage; the chief nymph bows, rises, arches her back, then thrusts her arms forward before following the faun. Next another freeze: at b. 63 (Example 3.7), as the D♭ theme is repeated in the strings, faun and nymph repeat their 'held' posture (now on the other side of the stage). Then follows a series of smaller repetitions, each matching musical and gestural phrases: bs 67–68 and bs 69–70; b. 71 and b. 72 (Example 3.7). One by one the nymphs exit the stage, before returning, along with a chirpy oboe solo (Example 3.4, b. 83), to collect a missing veil. But the faun has claimed it. To the familiar sound of the flute, and with veil in arms, the faun

Example 3.7 Debussy, *Prélude à l'après-midi d'un faune*, bs 54–73.

Example 3.7 (cont.)

Example 3.7 (cont.)

Example 3.7 (cont.)

Example 3.7 (cont.)

Example 3.7 (cont.)

Figure 3.5 Nijinsky as faun, veil in arms (1912); photographer, Baron Adolf de Meyer.

walks back to his rocky lair (Figure 3.5). After laying the veil on the ground, he lowers himself on top of it. A first 'ting' on the cymbals signals a moment of climax (b. 108): the faun raises his torso in ecstasy, then lies on his front (Figure 3.6 and Example 3.8).

Illusionism

I have described the music and visuals here in a way calculated to fortify their coordinations, to make plain the couplings of metre, phrase, timbre and character that persist throughout the ballet – if not throughout the scholarly literature. But what is striking, at least from my perspective, is less the persistence of these effects than their blatancy. The coordinations are not only literal; they are too, too, literal. The noise of the cymbals as the faun

Figure 3.6 Nijinsky as faun, final posture (1912); photographer, Baron Adolf de Meyer.

experiences climax; the synchronized footfalls and abrupt changes of direction; the flinging of arms to the crotchet pulse; the duration of time for which postures are held, particularly at the D♭ major theme: these examples have a grossness or crudeness about them that suggests some creative exercise in the over-evident. Not to mention the generic. When the ballet's music and choreography acknowledge their simultaneity, they do so by means of surface devices – 'synch' points, sequences, identifying themes and sonorities – that could hardly be more common or garden.

There is, of course, a sting. Each and every one of these devices is defused by moments more abstruse – and more plentiful. To put this simply: if particular footsteps are marked individually, are coordinated to the musical metre, then the majority are haphazard, falling in a no man's land between beats; if characters seem on occasion to play up to instrumental timbres, to find some sonorous corollary, then in the main they do not, entering and exiting the stage to sounds associated with someone else; if a particular dramatic gesture is synchronized with prominent percussion, so too are much less vivid movements; and if stage movement seems at times to follow

Example 3.8 Debussy, *Prélude à l'après-midi d'un faune*, bs 106–10.

the musical phrase, then for the most part it drifts off-course, following its own sense of structural logic. At base, then, there exists a play between obviousness and obscurity: in audio-visual terms, between consonance and dissonance, parallelism and counterpoint.

More specific examples may help explain, and for these we can turn back to the opening of the ballet and the various dramatizations of the flute solo. As mentioned earlier, the solo begins as diegetic: it emanates, we assume, from the instrument held by the faun. At the second solo (b. 11), the same effect is implied, as the faun still has the look of playing. But watch carefully. After three bars, and with three notes left to play, the faun moves the flute from his lips. The flautist in the pit continues, but the sounds are instantly dislocated from their presumed source, now without ground in the material reality of the diegesis.

What is going on here? A first thought might assume some creative homage on Nijinsky's part: that the choreographer wanted to return the Mallarméan sense of mystery to the faun's flute, a sense that any real-time miming was bound to deny.[23] A second idea might be that the fugitive sounds – those final 'acousmatic' notes of the solo – render suspect the credibility of the diegesis, not to mention that of its characters; they imply that some other thing or being might be just out of sight, might have assumed control of what is played and heard. Confusions about sonic origin and significance ricochet throughout the ballet. For example, during the final flute solo at b. 94, when the faun strolls back to his lair with veil in arms, there is no flute-prop in sight; the music is wholly non-diegetic, detached from the literal and the manifest. The previous oboe version of the theme (Example 3.5, b. 86) may be similarly disembodied. Although earlier I entertained a dramatic reading of this passage, suggesting that the oboe instrumentation might betray the subject of the faun's thoughts (the chief nymph), this reading is less than compelling, for the lining up of character and timbre is itself inconsistent throughout the ballet.

With these points and pitfalls in mind, perhaps all that can be inferred from the staging of the flute solo is a basic trajectory: from straightforward sound effect, through musical–spatial disorientation, to the opposite of musical literalism, this being music of invisible origin, of lost connotations and strange symbolism. *Faune*, it seems, dramatizes music's indeterminacy; the ballet tests the limits of musical signifiers, strains their significance,

---

[23] As is well known, Mallarmé chose the flute as a musical and poetic symbol for infinite, interminable meaning: to quote Carolyn Abbate, for 'all that cannot be thought, said, or remembered'; see Abbate, 'Debussy's Phantom Sounds', *In Search of Opera* (Princeton University Press, 2001), pp. 145–84 at p. 146.

makes them redundant. First, we are presented with a simple and blatant synthesis, one that harnesses music to dance and to character. But then the three embark upon an antagonistic interplay. The audience is confused: beckoned towards one interpretation after another, but denied each, we are sent wandering again, towards new and ever more difficult discriminations.

Contemporaneity

It is possible to step back and acknowledge a sense of terra cognita. The freer and freer play of the signifier, the groundswell of local irrationalities, the generation of impossible objects: these are hallmarks of the modernist project. *Faune*, like any other experiment in modernist art, sought to overturn the established mechanics of Western illusionism, to lead its audience away from the comforts of verisimilitude and mimesis, and towards new orders of perception and experience. Moreover, and in keeping with modernist aesthetics, the ballet issued a challenge to conventional expectations of functionality, setting up a distinction between on the one hand the representational, pictorial and mimetic and on the other the illogical, elusive and even the arbitrary.

A specific comparison between the ballet and contemporary modernism may be worth isolating, for it emerges from the primary source-material: an article by Charles Tenroc, published prior to the ballet's premiere in 1912, entitled 'Nijinsky va faire dans *L'Après-midi d'un faune* des essais de chorégraphie cubiste'.[24] Recent scholars have embraced this source, substantiating stray comments by Tenroc and Nijinsky himself with reference to *Faune*'s visual and choreographic design. According to Järvinen, for example, the stage space was constructed along the same specific – and specifically geometric – lines as the Cubist picture space. The dancers' profiled stance, the lack of painted horizon, the foreshortened stage, the absence of shadow effects, the asymmetrical groupings and the linear trajectory of movement: all helped 'flatten' the visual scene, fusing the dancers with their background, denying their voluminous bodily form.[25]

But this may only scratch the surface. Cubism sought to expose illusionism's bag of tricks, to turn conventional pictorial devices against the kind of bourgeois perception they had served – a perception that envisaged the canvas as a comprehensive and secure spatial totality. A classic example is Picasso's *The Architect's Table* (Figure 3.7, 1912). Clearly, the painting no longer deals in conventional representational modes, for the real-life objects

---

[24] Charles Tenroc, 'Nijinsky va faire dans *L'Après-midi d'un faune* des essais de chorégraphie cubiste', *Comeodia*, 18 April 1912, p. 4.

[25] Järvinen, 'Dancing without Space', p. 49. Also see Jordan, 'Debussy, the Dance, and the *Faune*', p. 130.

Figure 3.7 Picasso, *The Architect's Table* (1912).

that crop up on the canvas – a knife, a lemon squeezer, a sugar strainer, the calling card of American writer Gertrude Stein – are abstracted from their real-life context. But these visual indicators still look to be describing, to be referring to things of the world. The point is that their function – their descriptive function – has been obscured.[26]

---

[26] My understanding of Cubism owes to the following: Richard R. Bretell, *Modern Art, 1851–1929: Capitalism and Representation* (Oxford University Press, 1999); Mark Antliff and Patricia Leighten, *Cubism and Culture* (London: Thames and Hudson, 2001); David Cottington, *Cubism and its Histories* (Manchester University Press, 2004); Jonathan P. Harris, *Writing Back to Modern Art* (London: Routledge, 2005); and T. J. Clark, *Farewell to an Idea: Episodes from a History of Modernism* (New Haven, CT, and London: Yale University Press, 1999), pp. 169–223.

Is this – or at least something analogous – not what happens in *Faune*? Let us agree, first of all, that both ballet and painting are marked by the formal disposition of old, traditional signifiers and strange new ones: in other words, by the juxtaposition of obviousness and obscurity commented on already. Think of the ballet's synch points, its audio-visual sequences and identifying themes; how each of these almost banal devices is overridden by peculiar audio-visual mismatches. Look at Figure 3.7. The painting is cluttered with interjected tokens, each familiar and mundane; but it is also cluttered with fragments of planes and broken lines, with effects of lighting and spacing that conflict with a conventional language of painterly representation. Moreover, by obscuring signifiers and confusing perspectives, both ballet and painting betray the redundancy of the interpretive encounter. To return to my earlier comment about Nijinsky confounding his audience: *Faune* and our Cubist case intimate the arbitrariness of the signifier, the irrelevance of metaphor. They suggest that the search for meaning and significance, at least according to conventional paradigms, may well be futile. There is no straightforward passage into the symbolic space in which either painting or ballet functions dramatically or expressively. There is perhaps no symbolic space at all.[27]

The point at issue here – that meaning and interpretation may no longer be the point – is one that a handful of recent scholars have been keen to embrace. For example, T. J. Clark, in his seminal monograph *Farewell to an Idea: Episodes from a History of Modernism*, suggests the sort of attention that the Cubist canvas appears to provoke. His response to *The Architect's Table* goes like this:

Run your hand over the architect's table … hang on to the knife by its handle. Of course, we shall not be able to hang on (that is also the point), but we are expected to be stubborn. Look for the lemon squeezer and the sugar strainer: be prepared never to find them, or not in any form they have taken before: learn by all means to make the best of that obscurity, and finally to revel in it.[28]

This is not an interpretive reading seeking to divine the metaphorical potential of the painting. This is a series of directives to the spectator. As Clark would have it, Picasso's canvas calls for an immediate, non-contemplative viewing experience; it calls its viewer to engage in surface, sensuous effects – not to scrutinize for symbolic meanings or social

---

[27] With this point in mind, the name Gertrude Stein (visible on Picasso's canvas, towards the bottom right) takes on particular significance, for Stein's characteristic literary style also flaunted the irrelevance and redundancy of the conventional search for meaning; see Judith Ryan, *The Vanishing Subject: Early Psychology and Literary Modernism* (University of Chicago Press, 1991), pp. 89–99.

[28] Clark, *Farewell to an Idea*, p. 184.

contingencies. Hans Ulrich Gumbrecht offers something similar – not on Cubism specifically but on the centrality of tactile visuality and sensory impressions to modern art. In an essay of 2005, Gumbrecht suggests how the high modernist moment of the early twentieth century witnessed a cultural shift from the production of 'meaning' to that of 'presence': 'to a rediscovery of the sensual qualities of what had until then been exclusively seen as the signifiers'.[29] A good deal of art from this period, Gumbrecht implies, assumed a corporeal immediacy that eradicated any trace of intellectual reflection, of the traditional Kantian ideal of detached contemplation. Authors Jonathan Crary and Lynda Nead have argued this same point, describing how early attempts at moving images, as well as modern technologies of vision (such as the stereoscope), offered the viewer 'a newly corporealized immediacy of sensations'.[30] A new model of spectatorship, they propose, came into being, as embodiment and aesthetic pleasure became topics of intellectual debate.

Bringing these ideas together, one might acknowledge the contemporaneity of *Faune*, of its confusions and contradictions, its seemingly irrational signifying system. The ballet defeats conventional interpretation like many a modernist artwork; its repertoire of signifiers leads in one direction, then another, never disclosing any internal rationale. This very irrationality, though, may prompt the viewer to embrace a new and different mode of audio-viewing, one that also resonates within a contemporary context of cultural aesthetics and painterly practices. *Faune*, like *The Architect's Table*, issues a set of instructions to its audience:

Listen to the flute solo, see how it is mimed by the animal-man on stage; see how he lies, transfixed by his sounds; then look at his abrupt, angular gestures. Notice how the flute sounds unravel, how they drift from the instrument into some mysterious, unknown territory. Be prepared never to find their source, never to resolve their function. Learn to revel in the music nonetheless, to respond to it instinctively.

The second half of this chapter runs with this idea.

---

[29] Hans Ulrich Gumbrecht, 'Production of Presence, Interspersed with Absence: A Modernist View on Music, Libretti, and Staging', trans. Matthew Tiews, in Karol Berger and Anthony Newcomb (eds.), *Music and the Aesthetics of Modernity* (Cambridge, MA: Harvard University Press, 2005), pp. 343–55 at p. 355. Also see his *The Production of Presence: What Meaning Cannot Convey* (Stanford University Press, 2004).

[30] See Jonathan Crary, *Techniques of the Observer: On Vision and Modernity in the Nineteenth Century* (Cambridge, MA: The MIT Press, 1992); and Lynda Nead, *The Haunted Gallery: Painting, Photography and Film c.1900* (New Haven, CT, and London: Yale University Press, 2007), quotation at p. 179.

The audio-visual contract

Before going further, it may be useful to flag the terms with which the ballet has been described (here and elsewhere); for, if we examine these terms at all closely, it becomes clear that they betray certain assumptions – a 'perceptual strategy', if you like – about how music and dance should work together. Put simply, we tend to envisage organicism as interpretive metaphor: that musical contours should determine bodily ones; that musical phrasing should match gestural phrasing; that rests are to be respected by pauses in the choreography; that rhythm is transparent to both eye and ear; that musical dynamic should impact muscular tension; and that *legato* melodic motion dictates *legato* physical motion. To be sure, this analogic mode of understanding is not uncommon: present-day spectators experience theatrical phenomena after indoctrination in Romantic, pseudo-Wagnerian aesthetics – after years of thinking about music and visuals as mutually contingent.[31] And, certainly, it *was* not uncommon: the late nineteenth and early twentieth centuries witnessed a number of pedagogic and theoretical attempts to codify the relation between music and movement, as dance-practitioners and men-of-letters entered a debate about possible correspondences between the arts.[32] Nonetheless, and as mentioned above, the period also witnessed the emergence of new models of spectatorship, ones that implicated the formulation and evaluation of aesthetic response. Might these new models make room for a perceptual viewpoint that nurtures the ambiguities and irrationalities of the modern artwork?

[31] According to film theorist Mary Ann Doane, the spectatorial habit of striving for unity betrays a psychological desire to maintain a centred, unified subjectivity. Theatrical effects of unity and cohesion, Doane argues, bring about narcissistic pleasure, 'grounded by the spectator's fantasmatic relation to his/her own body'; see Doane, 'The Voice in the Cinema: The Articulation of Body and Space', *Yale French Studies*, 60/1 (1980), pp. 33–50 at p. 34. Spectators' (and critics') tendency to invoke benchmark unity may also function to repress an awareness of the material heterogeneity and divided agency of the theatrical apparatus, papering over a constitutional lack of unity.

[32] In this context, the writings of Jean d'Udine (real name, Albert Cozanet) are particularly noteworthy. D'Udine, a follower of the renowned Swiss pedagogue Émile Jaques-Dalcroze, maintained the significance of synaesthesia in art – in poetry, painting, architecture, and especially music and dance. Drawing on the system of musical education developed by Dalcroze ('la gymnastique rythmique', designed to develop rhythmic sensitivity in musicians), as well as the biological theories of Frenchman Félix Le Dantec, d'Udine proposed a parallelism between music and movement that exalted their shared basis in 'les mouvements de l'âme' (movements of the soul). D'Udine's monograph *L'Art et le geste* (Paris: Félix Alcan, 1910) offers a comprehensive survey of his ideas; his other writings include *L'Orchestration des couleurs, analyse, classification et synthèse mathématiques des sensations colorées* (Paris: A. Joanin, 1903); *Traité complet de géométrie rythmique* (Paris: Heugel, 1926); and a biography of Gluck (Paris: H. Laurens, 1906).

The question asked earlier can be asked again: what does Nijinsky's choreography 'do' to Debussy's music? A simple answer now would posit the music as coercive. Throughout much of the ballet, the characters' jerky movements and angular poses, as well as their linear trajectories and frontal positioning, convey an undertow of the mechanical. Moreover, at various moments of synchronization, the music sounds like an animating force, giving impetus to bodies on stage. We might think of these bodies as dynamos through which inductive musical impulses pass; equally, we might envisage unconscious automatons, rhythmicized bodily movements driven by submission to musical metre, pulse and structure.[33]

A second aspect of this coercion relates to those moments in the ballet when characters appear transfixed by music – by its sonorous and sensuous reality. Two moments are outstanding: the start of the ballet, when the faun is absorbed by the sounds of the flute, oblivious to the entrance of the nymphs; and the D♭ major theme (Example 3.7), during which faun and nymph are riveted to the spot, seemingly engrossed in Debussy's score. On both these occasions, stage gesture (or rather a lack of it) sets the music apart as an object of attention, one that is seemingly experienced by characters on stage.[34] Moreover, this 'object' functions as a massive suture. Taking the foreground, it spills out from the orchestral pit and envelops the diegesis; it carries the characters into a metadiegetic sublime – a place where dramatic time is dilated and dramatic meaning suspended. To put this another way, the choreography at these moments does not intimate that music carries messages. It intimates that music simply *carries*. The beautiful, gushy, over-ripe, clichéd, Romantic, *bel canto* theme inveigles the characters into a sensual immediacy betrayed by their exaggerated stillness – a stillness that in turn betrays music's infamous power to enthral.[35]

---

[33] These ideas – of the performer as a 'human motor' or an automated 'dancing machine' – are discussed and contextualized by Felicia McCarren in her *Dancing Machines: Choreographies of the Age of Mechanical Reproduction* (Stanford University Press, 2003). McCarren focuses on the status and significance of dance within an early twentieth-century 'culture of the machine'.

[34] *Faune*'s several 'static' moments were singled out by Michel Fokine; see his *Memoirs of a Ballet Master*, ed. Anatole Chujoy, trans. Vitale Fokine (London: Constable, 1961), p. 209. According to Lynn Garafola, they betray the influence of Russian theatre director Vsevolod Meyerhold; see her *Diaghilev's Ballets Russes*, pp. 53–5. Järvinen points also to the conventions of the 'tableau chorégraphique'; see 'Dancing without Space', p. 46.

[35] The sense of my argument here meshes neatly with current musicological enthusiasm for musical performance and phenomenology: to lean on Carolyn Abbate, for the 'drastic' moments when the 'irreversible experience' of playing or listening comes to our attention; see Abbate, 'Music: Drastic or Gnostic?', *Critical Inquiry*, 30/3 (2004), pp. 505–36. And yet I suspect there may be more to my ideas than this disciplinary baggage. What I suggest here stems not from autobiographical example, but rather from the behaviour of the characters on stage.

A web of affinity

All this is interesting speculation and may give us pause, may suggest an aura of significance around *Faune* that transcends the usual interpretive frame. At this point, then, I hope to have suggested that the ballet might be worth watching again, and watching without the careful attention to what does or doesn't synchronize convincingly. But this need not be the end of the matter. The ideas above bring *Faune* into direct discussion with a number of historical contexts that deserve mention here.

First is a similarity between the terms of the above musical reading – 'enthralling', 'arresting', 'engrossing' – and those used by critics from the 1890s. To recall: Raymond Bonheur, artist, friend of Debussy and dedicatee of *Faune*, described the 'dazzled sensation' he experienced when the composer played his sketches; writer Raphaël Cor spoke of 'novelty' and 'enchantment', how Debussy's piece 'works on you like a narcotic'; Austrian music critic Ernst Decsey noted the 'hypnotic' sound of the opening flute solo; and conductor Gustave Robert admitted to being 'completely seduced, ravished, captured' at a rehearsal of Debussy's piece.[36] Of course, the specifics of these comments – exactly what 'captured' Robert or 'dazzled' Bonheur – are unknown, and thus sweeping generalizations about musical effect may be unwise. But the sense of aural wonder emerges clearly, and is clearly in tune with the ideas above. One could make the argument that Nijinsky's ballet thematizes a spectatorial response to Debussy's score: that what we see on stage is a composing-out, in visual and physical terms, of what the experience of listening to Debussy's music might look like. The 'listening to' is important. The characters on stage are susceptible to music as a live, sonorous event; they are as 'completely seduced' by Debussy's score as the composer's earliest critics.

A second context also concerns the music itself. A comparison of Debussy's published orchestral score and the *version pré-orchestrale* (a short-score manuscript, published by the Robert Owen Lehman Foundation in 1963) reveals a number of revisions made by the composer that appear to enhance the 'arresting' and 'hypnotic' qualities noted by

---

[36] Citations can be found in William W. Austin (ed.), Norton Critical Score, *Claude Debussy: Prelude to 'The Afternoon of a Faun'* (London: Norton, 1970), pp. 156, 161, 157, 138 and 139; and Brian Hart, '"Le Cas Debussy": Reviews and Polemics about the Composer's "New Manner"', in Jane F. Fulcher (ed.), *Debussy and His World* (Princeton University Press, 2001), pp. 363–82 at p. 371. Several press reviews of *Faune* from the early 1900s indulge in similar terminology: I think particularly of Amédée Boutarel's piece for *Le Ménestrel*, 22 November 1903, in which Debussy's music is described as 'seductive'; Marcel Orban's review for *Le Courrier musical*, 1 April 1913, which features the same adjective; and René Brancour's column in *Le Ménestrel*, 15 March 1913, which praises *Faune*'s 'mysterious and subtle murmurs'.

critics. Take the D♭ major theme (Example 3.7). In the early version, the first four bars are divided into (four) one-bar phrases; in the published score, they become (two) two-bar phrases. The former would seem reminiscent of the minuet, its one-bar phrases and prominent downbeats helping orient the listener metrically and melodically. The latter, in contrast, tends to transcend the dance-like impression, substituting shorter phrases with ones that seem to stretch and strain, to dissolve metric boundaries. These distended phrases conjure a sense of lyrical vastness that is not only peculiar but peculiarly beguiling. Debussy seems to tease the listener, to invite us to follow the unfolding melody, to hold our breath in anticipation of a break between phrases. The woodwind scoring (another revision of Debussy's) adds to this sense of entrancement, for it verges on the unidiomatic. One might argue, and performers might agree, that the woodwind parts are difficult to play in tune, to play *piano*, to play in unison, and to play as marked, with a *crescendo* on the approach to the theme's third bar through a descending leap of a minor sixth to each instrument's lower range (Example 3.7, b. 56). The two-bar phrases might even aggravate the situation, prolonging the instrumentalists' breath, straining their respiratory technique, whilst further enticing the listener. Similar impressions are evoked by the opening flute solo, also subject to revision by the composer (Example 3.1). The last three notes of the solo, originally articulated separately, were later encompassed within the piece's third phrase. A small point maybe, but by extending the phrase Debussy further reels the listener in – and, of course, frustrates the performer.[37] (The solo is well known for its respiratory demands and remains one of the most difficult passages of the flute's orchestral repertoire.)

Clearly, one can't argue for any specific intention on Debussy's part, or for any determining influence the composer may have had on choreographic and critical visions. But one can argue for the range of reference – for the web of affinity between musical revisions, critics' comments and *Faune*'s choreographic design. A third and final reference – to the (seemingly unlikely) field of psycho-physiological science – will extend the imagination even further. Here is a briefly sketched background.

From (roughly) the 1870s to the early 1900s the nascent discipline of psycho-physiology sought to analyse and establish the relation between the surface of the body and its basic anatomical and neuro-psychological

---

[37] To better appreciate the aural effect of the long opening phrase, readers may wish to compare recordings of *Faune* in which the flute solo is played in one and two breaths. Suggested recordings include Gabriel Pierné conducting the Orchestre des Concerts Colonne (1930; reissued on Malibran-Music CDRG 140), in which the flautist breathes in b. 3; and Walther Straram conducting the Orchestre des Concerts Straram (1930; reissued on VAIA 1074), with flute legend Marcel Moyse illustrating his lauded respiratory technique.

processes. Experiments on the physical effect of various external and internal stimuli resulted in theories of stimulus-response, linking specific gestures and postures to states of pleasure, pain and terror, as well as to the instinctive mechanics of the body's 'lower' faculties. Leading psycho-physiologist Charles Féré proposed that all stimuli generated an augmentation of muscular force measurable on a device called a dynamometer – designed to respond to the pressure exerted by the hand grip of a human subject. Féré's dynamometric findings implied the existence of an unconscious bodily function – something automatic, instinctive, almost primitive – whilst maintaining the potency of all sensory stimuli.[38]

Including music. Turn-of-the-century psycho-physiology explored the corporeal effects of music as much as it did those of visions, feelings or smells. Foremost amongst experimental accounts were the writings of French theorist Albert de Rochas, in which the author described his experiments with musical stimuli and the human body. Leaning on the work of psychologists Jules Héricourt, Prosper Despine and Aldred Warthin, Rochas revealed how specific musical notes provoked specific gestural forms – particularly in subjects with an acute sensory awareness:

Des expériences que j'ai poursuivies pendant plusieurs années ont montré que chez certains sujets dont la sensibilité a été hyperesthésiée ... la musique agit sur les centres moteurs de manière à provoquer des expressions faciales et des gestes ... [L]'audition des diverses notes de la gamme détermine la contraction de muscles spéciaux pour chaque note. Ainsi la tonique fait remuer les pieds; la tierce, le bassin; la quarte et la quinte, les bras et les mains; la sensible, les lèvres et les yeux.[39]

(Experiments that I have conducted for several years have shown that with certain subjects, those excessively sensitized ... music acts on their motor faculties and provokes facial expressions and gestures ... Different notes of the scale determine different muscular contractions. To illustrate, the tonic makes the feet move; the third, the pelvis; the fourth and fifth, the arms and hands; the leading note, the lips and the eyes.)

Rochas's thesis – essentially, of symptomatic gesture – was endorsed by a number of contemporary observers. Philosopher Albert Bazaillas, for

---

[38] Charles Féré, *Sensation et mouvement* (Paris: Alcan, 1887). On Féré, his research into 'dynamogeny' and his influence on late nineteenth-century scientific thought, see Diane F. Sadoff, *Sciences of the Flesh: Representing Body and Subject in Psychoanalysis* (Stanford University Press, 1998), pp. 91–100; and Jonathan Crary, *Suspensions of Perception: Attention, Spectacle and Modern Culture* (Cambridge, MA: The MIT Press, 1999), pp. 165–77.

[39] The quotation is from a paper given by Rochas – titled 'L'Origine physiologique des arts de la musique et de la danse' – at the Congrès de Grenoble, 1904. His main argument – about music's stimulatory effect – echoes that of his monograph *Les Sentiments, la musique et le geste* (Grenoble: H. Falque and F. Perrin, 1900). The monograph examines the physical responses of humans (and animals) to musical stimuli.

example, in a 1908 monograph on music and the unconscious, spoke similarly of 'les dispositions physiques causées par la mélodie et le rythme' (the physical effects of melody and rhythm).[40] Although Bazaillas noted none of the specific alignments described by Rochas, he maintained the general principle of musical coercion: 'l'existence de sensations fonctionnelles, de phénomènes circulatoires et respiratoires, parfois même spasmodiques, de courants viscéraux, causés par les impressions auditives et par leur organisation systématique' (the existence of sensory functions, of circulatory, respiratory and even spasmodic phenomena, and of visceral currents, caused by auditory sensations and their systematic organization).[41] Several years earlier, Ange-Ernest-Amédée Ferrand, writing in the *Bulletin de l'Académie de Médecine*, had trumpeted this same effect, claiming motor, muscular and nervous significance for all sonic stimuli. Ferrand, interestingly, had a specific aim in mind. His article was an early attempt at music therapy; he suggested how music, more than a simple domestic or social distraction, might help stimulate and enhance both physical and mental awareness.[42]

How easy would it be to relate these scientific studies to my ideas in this chapter, to advance a shared psycho-physiological grounding in music's real-time effect? Spelling things out clearly, I might suggest that Nijinsky and his characters responded to Debussy's music in a manner similar to that of the sensitized human subjects studied by Rochas and his colleagues: in short, that they responded instinctively, almost involuntarily.[43] On both the theatrical and medical stages, it seems, music could function as some sort of generative mechanism, as a potent, sonorous force able to act on the corporeal unconscious, to stimulate – even, to stylize – physical motion.

But something is missing from this account: an adequate sense of how and why the dancers in *Faune* responded to Debussy's music in the manner in which they did – with flung-out arms and gestural angularity. The scientific context may again help explain. Of particular significance is a method of psycho-physiology practised by Jean Martin Charcot, clinician at Paris's Salpêtrière hospital in the late nineteenth century. As is well known, Charcot's experimental activities promoted an inherent connection between the physical and the psychological. Hypnosis provided a practical tool; at his

---

[40] Albert Bazaillas, *Musique et inconscience: introduction à la psychologie de l'inconscient* (Paris: Alcan, 1908), p. 155.

[41] *Ibid.*, p. 156.

[42] Ange-Ernest-Amédée Ferrand, 'Essais de psycho-physiologie sur la musique', in *Bulletin de l'Académie de Médecine* (Paris: Librairie de l'Académie de Médecine, 1895). Ferrand sums up (p. 25): 'La musique peut donc être rapprochée des plus profonds modificateurs de l'activité du système nerveux, et par conséquent, mériterait de prendre rang dans la thérapeutique.'

[43] Garafola also raises the issue of instinct in her discussion of the ballet, but in a specifically sexual context; see her *Diaghilev's Ballets Russes*, p. 58.

weekly lectures, open to 'le Tout-Paris' (writers, artists and critics, as well as scientists and physicians), Charcot exhibited real-life subjects in order to demonstrate the physical capacity and corporeal substance of unconscious sensitivities. According to one observer, 'some of them [Charcot's patients] smelt with delight a bottle of ammonia when told it was rose water, others would eat a piece of charcoal when presented to them as chocolate'.[44] With his enigmatic style and slow pronunciation, Charcot acquired the trappings of a theatrical showman; hypnotism acquired contemporary currency in both academic and popular arenas.[45]

What I should like to suggest about Charcot and his 'theatre' turns on the business of physical embodiment: the postural effects of hypnosis – 'written' on the body of the patient, caught on camera by the photographic service of the Salpêtrière, captured in plaster by the hospital's Museum of Casts, and disseminated in the clinical publication *Nouvelle Iconographie de la Salpêtrière*.[46] Examined at all closely, photographs of Charcot's patients bear a marked resemblance to those, taken by Baron de Meyer, of characters from *Faune*. Consider, for example, Figure 3.8, a plaster cast of the upper body of a patient at the Salpêtrière; and Figure 3.9, one of de Meyer's shots of Nijinsky as faun. The similarities should be clear: in both photographs, the right arm is rigid and bent at almost 90 degrees (though hands are held differently). Figure 3.10, a photograph of a Salpêtrière patient suffering from lethargy and catalepsy, is also suggestive, particularly when compared to Figure 3.2 (described earlier), a shot by de Meyer of the faun and chief nymph. Note the similar arm positioning of the photographed women: both raise their left arm along a (roughly) horizontal line from the shoulder; elbows are bent; lower arms are raised; palms face forward. Then there is the 'backward' posture (known as the *arc de cercle*) of the hypnotized female

---

[44] See Axel Munthe (a Swedish physician), *The Story of San Michele* (London: John Murray, 1930), p. 296.

[45] For more on Charcot and his experimental research at the Salpêtrière, see Georges Guillain, *J.-M. Charcot (1825–1893): sa vie, son œuvre* (Paris: Masson, 1955); Christopher G. Goetz, *Charcot the Clinician: The Tuesday Lessons* (New York: Raven Press, 1987); Yannick Ripa, *Women and Madness: The Incarceration of Women in Nineteenth-Century France*, trans. Catherine du Pelous Menagé (Minneapolis: University of Minnesota Press, 1990); Christopher G. Goetz, Michel Bonduelle and Toby Gelfand, *Charcot: Constructing Neurology* (Oxford University Press, 1995); and Elisabeth Bronfen, *The Knotted Subject: Hysteria and its Discontents* (Princeton University Press, 1998). Catherine Hindson links the essential theatricality of the Salpêtrière with the dance aesthetics of Jane Avril in her *Female Performance Practice on the Fin-de-Siècle Popular Stages of London and Paris* (Manchester University Press, 2007), pp. 88–112.

[46] The *Nouvelle Iconographie de la Salpêtrière* ran from 1888 and numbered twenty-eight volumes. Photographs taken under the auspices of clinical knowledge were also published in the *Iconographie photographique de la Salpêtrière*, a three-volume publication by clinician Désiré-Magloire Bourneville and photographer Paul Régnard (Paris: Progrès Médical/Delahaye et Lecrosnier, 1875–80).

Figure 3.8 Plaster cast of the upper body of a Salpêtrière patient (date unknown).

patient captured in an 1887 painting by André Brouillet, a reproduction of which is shown here as Figure 3.11. The scene is one of Charcot's weekly lectures: the clinician is standing in the centre-right, the patient on his left; a female nurse is ready to catch the patient should she fall. The patient's backward bend creates an unnatural asymmetry – one that is roughly comparable to a characteristic 'backward' posture of the chief nymph in *Faune*, illustrated in Figure 3.12.

These examples are only a small selection of the available visual evidence, but they are representative. Time and again during the ballet, characters gesticulate in a manner not dissimilar from that of Charcot's hypnotized subjects. The shared sense of rigidity – of motor impotence – is compelling: Charcot himself spoke of muscular contracture, describing the involuntary

Figure 3.9 Nijinsky as faun, with bent right arm (1912); photographer, Baron Adolf de Meyer.

and unpredictable rigidity of his patients' limbs.[47] Equally significant are the moments of exaggerated stillness, those that in fact enabled photography. *Faune*'s postural 'freezes' have already been discussed; those of Charcot's patients, according to the neurologist, turned the body into an 'expressive statue, a motionless model'.[48]

---

[47] Jean Martin Charcot, *Œuvres complètes*, 9 vols. (Paris: Progrès Médical/Lecrosnier et Babé, 1886–9), vol. IX, p. 447.

[48] Jean Martin Charcot and Paul Richer, 'Note on Certain Facts of Cerebral Automatism Observed in Hysteria during the Cataleptic Period of Hypnotism', *Journal of Nervous and Mental Disease*, 10 (1883), pp. 1–13 at p. 9. (The authors refer to a patient whose facial muscles had been electrically stimulated.)

Figure 3.10 Planche XVI (Hémi-léthargie et hémi-catalepsie), *Iconographie photographique de la Salpêtrière*, vol. III (1880).

There is of course a larger point here, for as well as casting an interesting light on *Faune*'s choreographic design, these visual correlations bear centrally on my reading of Debussy's music. To argue that the ballet's characters move like hypnotized subjects – under the influence of an external stimulus – is to imagine the music as that stimulus: the means of generating the acute angles, the taut muscles and jerky movements. Nijinsky's *Faune* thus presents Debussy's score as a hypnotic attraction. The music functions like a hypnotist's voice, galvanizing onstage bodies, generating corporeal effects. The choreography is pure symptom.

Figure 3.11 Brouillet, *Une Leçon clinique à la Salpêtrière* (1887).

Disciplinary resistance (conclusion)

It would perhaps be dangerous to lean too heavily on this scientific context in conclusion. Mapping the details of an interaction between musical and medical theatres would inevitably amount to an enormous interdisciplinary undertaking, one that may hinge on the availability of visual evidence, as well as the complexities of visual analysis. But there is certainly much to ponder. As Felicia McCarren has argued, meanings attached to the performing body from the *fin de siècle* were intimately embroiled with contemporary medical theories. Medicine, McCarren writes, became a 'major cultural index' by which the body's physical responses were measured and understood, both on and off the stage.[49] Indeed, cross-cultural histories of the period have proposed an intricate and complex system of exchange between aesthetic, social and psychological domains. Jane Wood has explored the 'pathologization' of Victorian literature, describing how novelists variously engaged

---

[49] Felicia McCarren, *Dance Pathologies: Performance, Poetics, Medicine* (Stanford University Press, 1998), p. 167.

Figure 3.12 Nymph bending backwards (1912); photographer, Baron Adolf de Meyer.

medical vocabulary, ideology and discourse; Dorothy Ross has traced links between the psychological and social sciences; Lawrence Rainey has argued for a specifically Futurist psycho-cultural homology; and Mark Micale has speculated on a broader 'psychologization' of *fin-de-siècle* culture, describing both the diffusion of psychological ideas and the receptivity of historical minds as symptomatic of Euro-American modernism.[50]

---

[50] Jane Wood, *Passion and Pathology in Victorian Fiction* (Oxford University Press, 2001); Dorothy Ross (ed.), *Modernist Impulses in the Human Sciences, 1870–1930* (Baltimore, MD: The Johns

Whether Nijinsky's *Faune* can be subsumed within this contemporary climate, whether the cross-cultural project can extend in a new and specifically balletic direction – these matters require further study. There is also the question of influence: the extent to which Nijinsky's conceptualization of music in *Faune*, and his specific choreographic vocabulary, had an impact on his next ballet, the infamous *Sacre du printemps*. But here, in conclusion, it will be useful to return to the business of audio-visual relations, to refocus on the cumulative effect of the music–choreographic ideas of these several pages.

On the simplest level, this chapter offers a gentle warning: that we can close off potentially significant critical avenues if we indulge in an audio-visual analysis that is staunchly analogical, that automatically and habitually privileges a set of shared stylistic and structural coordinates between the musical and the physical. From the perspective of these coordinates, the music and dancing of *Faune* may appear incongruous. But, considered alongside contemporary artistic methods that overlook the notion of parallelism as benchmark, the ballet is curiously cohesive. Nijinsky's choreography is perfectly attuned to Debussy's score: not, to press the point one last time, to its internal genetics, but rather to its material, sonorous condition.

To some extent, then, *Faune* resists musicology, resists its interpretive methods and assumptions, its tendency to make meaning settle. The impossibility of a stable interpretation – even, of a stable interpretive viewpoint – calls into question the mechanics of audio-viewing, and calls us to reflect on the circumstances that lead to the production and privileging of certain forms of critical enquiry and not others. This is the rub, yet also the reward. Whilst defying our conventional interpretive logic, *Faune* offers an immanent self-critique that instigates and directs a new enquiry that reaches beyond the conjunct/disjunct dyad, beyond the stylistic and structural coordinates. To put this another way, the ballet contains the seeds of its own understanding: not as a bestially erotic, anti-musical travesty, but as modern aesthetic experience embodied on stage.

Hopkins University Press, 1994); Lawrence Rainey, 'Taking Dictation: Collage Poetics, Pathology and Politics', *Modernism/Modernity*, 5/2 (1998), pp. 123–53; and Mark Micale (ed.), *The Mind of Modernism: Medicine, Psychology, and the Cultural Arts in Europe and America, 1880–1940* (Stanford University Press, 2004).

　　# Metaphors of invasion: the Ballets Russes and the French press

Having pushed so far in this 'alternative' study of the Ballets Russes, it is time to examine the reception of the troupe in the French press: the large-circulation daily newspapers and the smaller-scale, specialist journals. Comments from the press, of course, have already been cited, primarily for the information they furnish about productions and performers, or else for the lines of investigation they suggest. But here these comments themselves – and the broader sphere of journalistic criticism – become my primary focus.

Why? Not only because of recent disciplinary initiatives: in particular, the emergence and development of 'reception studies' as a means of revitalizing musicological enquiry. There is also a suspicion that, in the case of the Ballets Russes, press articles and reviews have not yet been sufficiently addressed. The following pages, then, invite us to look afresh at the source-material, to think about the content, nature and significance of what was published. More than this, I am interested in the historical, intellectual and aesthetic conditions on which press criticism was inevitably contingent: in other words, the assumptions, agendas and political forces behind critics' points of view.

Admittedly, I have an agenda of my own, one that relates in no small measure to our habitual view of the Russian company, outlined in the first chapter of this book. Acclaiming the company's 'radical' departures from choreographic conventions, celebrating their 'revolutionary' productions, we tend to envisage the Ballets Russes with an enthusiasm bordering on infatuation: the company, it seems, can do no wrong – and did no wrong in the belle époque. Yet close attention to the press discourse surrounding the troupe reveals an alternative perspective. If studied at all seriously, and through a lens wiped clean of a centenary's praise and privilege, this discourse promises an antidote to the standard rhetoric and reasoning, that which still seduces writers and readers today.

Puff

Some background is needed, for this standard line of thinking in fact originated within the press: in particular, within *Comœdia illustré*, a journal quoted more than once in this book already. An offshoot of the daily news-paper *Comœdia*, itself devoted to Paris's theatrical scene, *Comœdia illustré* was a glossy, full-colour and fortnightly supplement aimed at the well-to-do of Parisian society.[1] Featuring advertisements for restaurants and banks, as well as for perfumes, soaps and diet drugs, the magazine offered readers whet-the-appetite accounts of Paris's most prestigious theatrical events. These accounts took multimedia form. The team at *Comœdia illustré* pioneered the use of photojournalism, mixing text, sketches and costume designs with photographic portraits. As a result, and as editor Gaston de Pawlowski declared in the inaugural edition, the magazine could boast a visual allure that regular publications, including *Comœdia*, could not.[2] If there was ever a 'performative' journalistic discourse – one that could reflect and recreate the theatrical experience – it was this.

As for this discourse, here is Marguerite Casalonga, bidding farewell to the Russian troupe after its second season in Paris.

Ils sont partis, les oiseaux de rêve, les charmeurs de légendes, les subtils et vibrants danseurs. Finies, leurs rondes colorées, leurs bacchanales rythmées, leurs voluptueux gestes et leurs eurythmies ensorcelantes; évanouis, les splendides décors de simple richesse, et de coloris vibrants, qui créèrent l'atmosphère féerique à leurs envolées gracieuses, à leurs pointes agiles et trépidantes, à leurs courbes séduisantes, savam-ment réglées. Leurs légendes nous ont laissé, avec les sonorités de leur musique d'Orient, si adéquate à leurs ballets, un parfum d'une insistance particulière, un charme de couleur et d'accents indéfinissables.[3]

(They have left, the birds of dreams, the enchanters of legends, the fine and vibrant dancers. Their animated round dances, rhythmic bacchanals, sensuous gestures and bewitching eurhythmics have finished. Their sumptuous but simple decor of vivid colours, which created the magical atmosphere for their gracious lifts, their agile and thrilling pointe-work, their seductive and skilful bends, have receded. Their legends have left us, with the sonorities of their Oriental music so appropriate to their ballets, a particularly pungent perfume, a charm of indefinable colour and accent.)

With an embarrassment of adjectives, Casalonga swoons over the Russian company – the expressiveness and sensuality of its dancing, the opulence of colour, the exoticism of music. Her words seem to spill forth, to convey not only the perceived magnificence of the Russian productions, but their seduc-tive, enchanting energy. Hence the emphasis on dreams, legends, mystery

---

[1] *Comœdia illustré* ran from 1908 to 1936.
[2] Gaston de Pawlowski, 'La Cadette', *Comœdia illustré*, 15 December 1908, no page numbers.
[3] Marguerite Casalonga, 'Adieux . . . (Ballets Russes)', *Comœdia illustré*, 15 July 1910, pp. 595–8 at p. 595. Incidentally, the Ballets Russes were variously described in the press as a flock of birds, a swarm of bees and guests at a wild party.

and magic: the sense of the other-worldly defines the Ballets Russes, lending force to the power of their 'parfum' – their exotic, intangible essence – over the spectator.

French novelist and critic Lucien Alphonse-Daudet, in a 1911 preview, was equally enraptured. Indeed, the critic seems almost to keel over with praise: beginning his article with an admission that would appear to foreclose any lengthy exposition ('Tout a été dit sur les ballet russes'), Alphonse-Daudet indulges in the sounds, colours and decor of the Russian productions, not to mention their choreography ('quels gestes! et quelles attitudes!').[4] This choreography was not simply dramatic or descriptive; it embodied the most fundamental of human sentiments: 'l'amour et la haine, la joie et la fureur, l'exaltation et la lassitude, l'espoir et la déception' (love and hate, joy and fury, exaltation and exhaustion, hope and deceit).[5] The critic goes on to describe the spectator's active role in the productions, invoking a kinship between those on and off stage:

À nous de donner un sens plus personnel à ces allégories préfiguratives qui s'adapteront à nos pensées et à nos désirs au point d'en devenir la représentation, la cristallisation véritable. Nous ne sommes pas seulement spectateurs de ces danses, nous y jouons un rôle et c'est pourquoi elles nous bouleversent. Non contents d'assister à leur divine turbulence, nous nous y mêlons, nous confions à leurs rythmes notre cœur qu'ils dévastent, nous mesurons à la sagesse de leurs pas, à la souple étreinte de leurs enlacements et à la frénésie de leurs tourbillons nos sorts et nos souvenirs. Les paroles et les échos de ces tragédies muettes, nous en sommes les récitants et les répercuteurs, nous les soumettons à notre étoile et à notre volonté, et souvent nous ne reconnaissons pas nos voix, ennoblies et magnifiées par l'harmonie qui les soutient.[6]

(It is to us to find a personal resonance to these prefigurative allegories, which will adapt themselves to our thoughts and our desires, becoming the true representation of them. We are not merely spectators of these dances, we play a role in them and this

---

[4] Lucien Alphonse-Daudet, '6me Saison des Ballets Russes au Châtelet', *Comœdia illustré*, 15 June 1911, pp. 575–8 at p. 575: 'Tout a été dit sur les ballets russes qui, depuis quelques années, sont le nouveau signe zodiacal de notre solstice d'été, et cependant quelque chose peut être dit encore, puisque l'enthousiasme est un champ aux javelles éternellement renaissantes où chacun moissonne son bouquet privilégié. Je n'essayerai pas ici de décrire plastiquement les somptuosités cadencées et balancées d'une si noble eurythmie qu'ont résumées cette année sur nos murs parisiens les affiches de Jean Cocteau: Mlle Karsavina, rapide et touchante, pâmée comme un lis blanc sous le charme de sa propre odeur, et Vaslaw Nijinsky dont le bras retourné ainsi que le pétale d'une rose, imbriqué autour de sa tête, répand sur la ville le parfum de la fleur primordiale; après ce jeune et grand poète qui fut l'un de leurs plus éloquents intronisateurs et veut être aussi leur habile imagier, après MM. Blanche et Vaudoyer, d'autres encore, j'en serais incapable. Ce que je voudrais essayer d'expliquer, c'est l'émotion profonde qui se dégage de ces danses, et tout ce qu'elles continuent à susciter en nous de pathétique, même lorsque leurs feux se sont éteints et que leurs féeries se sont évanouies.'

[5] *Ibid.*, p. 575.   [6] *Ibid.*, pp. 575–6.

is why they bowl us over. Not satisfied to simply watch their divine antics, we become embroiled, we entrust our ravished heart to their rhythms, we match the precision of their steps, the supple embrace of their intertwining and the frenzy of their turns to our fate and our memories. We recite the words, we reflect the reverberations of these silent tragedies; we submit them to our fortune and our will, and often we do not recognize our voices, ennobled and magnified by the harmony that supports them.)

What emerges from this couple of examples? Certainly, little of substance, of raw, factual information on the performers and productions in question.[7] Yet there are recurring themes: the exotic and the otherworldly; the profundity of choreographic expression; the spectator's seduction by the stage spectacle. These themes reappear in almost all accounts of the troupe published in *Comœdia illustré*, as well as in many other journals (such as *Musica, Le Ménestrel*).[8] As noted earlier, they have proved remarkably pervasive across the scholarly literature: Nancy Van Norman Baer, for example, devotes an entire volume to *The Art of Enchantment: Diaghilev's Ballets Russes*.[9] Clearly, authors then and now have sought to make explicit their thrill and fascination before the troupe, to submit not only to the special theatricality and glamour of the Russian spectacles, but to the discursive style and sensationalism of the accompanying journalistic commentary.

To confront this irresistibility – to wrestle free from the seductive force of both company and criticism – may be to interrogate the ideological and aesthetic premises upon which articles and reviews were constructed. As Mary E. Davis has shown in her searching account of the Ballets Russes and the fashion industry, journalistic writing was heavily laden with agenda: in particular, with a promotional spin from which both the

---

[7] Robert Brussel attempted to justify critics' silence on the stage goings-on, maintaining the inappropriateness of the established choreographic vocabulary for descriptions of the 'unreal' visual scenes: 'Le spectacle ravissant que constituent les évolutions de ces danseuses, de ces danseurs, n'est point aisé à dépeindre. User de la terminologie consacrée semblerait vain et déplaisant pour d'aussi irréelles images.' See Brussel, 'La Saison russe', *Le Figaro*, 20 May 1910, p. 5. It seems likely, however, that critics lacked the choreographic expertise necessary to record the ephemeral impressions of dance (most were trained in music or theatre criticism) and thus gravitated towards a more reflective mode of discourse as a matter of necessity; Valérien Svétlov comments on contemporary critical tendencies in his *Le Ballet contemporain*, trans. Michel Dimitri Calvocoressi (Paris: Brunhoff, 1912), p. 106.

[8] See, for example, Louis Delluc, 'Les Ballets Russes en 1912', *Comœdia illustré*, 15 May 1912, pp. 655–7 at p. 655: 'Ne sont-ils pas tout le printemps, ces héros, ces héroïnes, voués à l'éternelle légèreté, qui semblent inventés par un Botticelli extraordinaire, dans l'élan d'une exaltation lyrique? Leurs pas, leurs danses, leurs rôles se réclament de la brise et de la lumière, ou bien ils créent eux-mêmes, par l'impétuosité spirituelle de leur art, par la ligne de leurs beautés, la couleur exaspérée dont ils sont revêtus, une lumière nouvelle et des soufflés volés à la brise des féeries.'

[9] Nancy Van Norman Baer (ed.), *The Art of Enchantment: Diaghilev's Ballets Russes* (San Francisco, CA: Universe Books, 1989).

Russian company and the publication in question could benefit.[10] *Comœdia illustré* offers a case in point. The magazine, Davis writes, gravitated towards Diaghilev and his troupe from their first days in Paris; the Ballets Russes offered exactly the sort of sexy and sumptuous subject-matter that the magazine sought to endorse.[11] From 1910, the two became further entwined, as the Paris Opéra (home to the company's second season) invited the magazine's editorial team to produce special souvenir programmes – deluxe booklets, decorated with gold, featuring synopses of the ballets, reproductions of designs by Léon Bakst and photo-essays on the star performers. *Comœdia illustré* continued to produce these programmes, and to publish special supplements, into the 1920s; the magazine became known for its inside access to the ballet company, whilst the company received continual promotion from one of Paris's leading and most colourful publications.[12] (Figure 4.1 shows the front cover of *Comœdia illustré*'s 1911 special edition, with Russian dancer Natalia Trouhanova in costume as the title character of the ballet *La Péri*. Priced at one franc, and heavily tipped in gold, this edition was twice the normal cost of the magazine. Incidentally, souvenir programmes from the period – at two francs – were even more expensive.)

That this mutually beneficial and unashamedly commercial relationship might have influenced the nature and tone of what was written inside the magazine seems more than likely. Insisting on the cultural cachet of the troupe, especially its exotic-erotic allure, *Comœdia illustré* could not help but boast the Russians' extravagance and special elusivity, and by means of prose style that was itself extravagant and elusive. Puff pieces counted for a lot. And contributors knew this, as Maurice de Brunhoff admitted in 1922, describing how the magazine was compelled to devote significant ink, often in haste, to Diaghilev and his team.[13] Brunhoff's colleague Marguerite Casalonga, quoted earlier, also realized the potential of the magazine's

---

[10] Mary E. Davis, *Ballets Russes Style: Diaghilev's Dancers and Paris Fashion* (London: Reaktion Books, 2010), pp. 23–60. Historian Émilien Carassus suggests that the proliferation of 'articles élogieux, parfois délirants' (laudatory, almost delirious articles) may also betray the influence of a nascent culture of 'snobisme'; see his *Le Snobisme et les lettres françaises de Paul Bourget à Marcel Proust, 1884–1914* (Paris: Armand Colin, 1966), pp. 364–9. For contemporary accounts of *snobisme*, see Alfred de Tarde, 'Chroniques de quinzaine', *Le Parthénon*, 5 March 1914, pp. 282–92; and Claude d'Habloville, 'Le Snobisme', *Revue générale*, 5/6 (June 1914), pp. 801–13.

[11] Davis, *Ballets Russes Style*, p. 27.

[12] For more on the souvenir programmes, see Beverly Hart's contribution to Jane Pritchard (ed.), *Diaghilev and the Golden Age of the Ballets Russes, 1909–1929* (London: Victoria and Albert Museum, 2010), pp. 124–5. As Hart notes, the visual appeal and sumptuosity of the programmes betrayed the influence of Maurice de Brunhoff – art director for *Comœdia illustré* and co-founder of *Vogue*.

[13] Quoted in Davis, *Ballets Russes Style*, p. 47.

3ᵉ ANNÉE. — Nᵒ 18.   NUMÉRO SPÉCIAL, PRIX : 1 franc   15 Juin 1911.

Mlle TROUHANOVA, dans le costume créé par Léon Bakst

Figure 4.1 *Comœdia illustré*, front cover, special edition (1911).

Russian association. Better known to her readers as 'Vanina' (a reference to the aristocratic heroine of a Stendhal story), Casalonga reported on the intersections between theatrical costuming and high couture, as well as on the fashions worn by females in Diaghilev's audience. Her modus operandi was to conflate exegesis and advertisement;[14] she appropriated the Ballets

---

[14] According to Calvocoressi, this conflation – in his words, 'une confusion entre les rubriques rédactionnelles et la publicité' – was commonplace within contemporary criticism; see his 'De La Critique musicale', *Revue française de musique*, 1 February 1913, pp. 317–30 at p. 327.

Russes as a cultural commodity, an essential ingredient of a fashionable lifestyle, and one that could generate interest and income across the commercial sphere.[15]

Confronting the press

How are we to deal with 'insider' accounts of this kind? As Katharine Ellis argues, for scholars engaged in reception studies, journalistic bias is 'quite simply, an occupational hazard'.[16] Clearly, there are no simple solutions, no easy ways to unlock the significance of articles and reviews, separating the independent criticism from the possible puff. Scholars, first and foremost, should acknowledge the complex cultural and intellectual forces tied up with press accounts, and acknowledge also that the meaning and significance of historical characters and events can be championed, contested, then distilled into a dominant viewpoint over a period of time.[17]

The contested aspect of this trajectory is that which I should like to address. With reference to a range of sources, this chapter suggests that the Ballets Russes were the subject of intense press debate, not only a touchstone of sophistication and style, but a locus of anxiety. This idea itself is not new. Pockets of anti-Ballets-Russes criticism, particularly those related to the infamous first nights of *Le Sacre du printemps* and *L'Après-midi d'un faune*, will be familiar.[18] Indeed, scholars have gone some way to explaining what, exactly, provoked the protests: in the case of *Le Sacre*, it was the Nijinsky choreography (Stravinsky's score seems to have passed relatively unnoticed, drowned out, according to several commentators, by jeers from the audience); as for *Faune*, and as explained in the previous chapter of this book, audiences reacted to the perceived incongruity between music and gesture, as well as the supposed lasciviousness of Nijinsky's faun. Yet even a cursory perusal of the Paris reviews obliges us to peg the problematics that underpin and undercut these individual reception histories, ones that also feed in and out of wider strains of cultural influence. As the forthcoming pages will make plain, the Russians' reception within the French press could not avoid debates about cultural politics: about the delimitation of boundaries, the preservation of identity and the nature of relational engagements.

---

[15] See Davis, *Ballets Russes Style*, pp. 40–5.

[16] Katharine Ellis, *Interpreting the Musical Past: Early Music in Nineteenth-Century France* (Oxford University Press, 2005), p. xvii.

[17] *Ibid.*, pp. xiii–xxii.

[18] Additionally, readers may be aware of the hostility with which Diaghilev and his troupe were often regarded in their home nation.

The Ballets Russes, at base, became a metaphor for invasion, an external force that could engulf and control, could penetrate the membrane of French society, culture and even art itself. The first few sections of this chapter will explore the most obvious aspect of this invasion, that which relates to the company's foreign presence in Paris. Following these, yet still following the press, I shall conceptualize the Russian invasion in specifically creative and compositional terms, diagnosing a model of selfhood or identity that maps onto both historical characters and works of art.

Cosmopolitics

'Les Ballets russes sont devenus une institution nationale', proclaimed critic Gaston Carraud in a review of the 1912 production *Le Dieu bleu*.[19] The Russian company – 'l'objet des toutes les conversations' – had so captivated the French audience that French, to the French, it had become.[20] Another critic spoke specifically of Diaghilev:

Serge de Diaghilew [*sic*] est devenu un parisien parisiennant tout en restant russe . . . russifiant. Chaque printemps il nous ramène des danseurs et le spectacle de ces ballets presque toujours admirables, jouit de l'engouement de l'élite du monde musical.[21]

(Sergey Diaghilev has become a Parisian amongst Parisians all the while remaining the most Russian of Russians. Each spring he brings us dancers and ballet spectacles that are almost always admirable, enjoying the craze of the musical elite.)

Through a kind of ethnic osmosis, the impresario had managed to ingratiate himself with Parisians, to cultivate specifically Parisian ways and means, yet also to remain distinctively Russian.[22] With his band of dancers, his backstage crew and artistic associates in tow, Diaghilev lived in Paris (at least during the summer), where he wined and dined influential French critics (in particular, Michel Calvocoressi and Robert Brussel), enjoyed the company of Parisians (Jean Cocteau, Misia Sert) and worked alongside prominent French businessmen (the Comtesse Greffulhe, Gabriel Astruc). Yet he continued to look

---

[19] Gaston Carraud, *La Liberté* (1912); clipping, F-Po, B 717 (a collection of press cuttings about the Russian ballet *Le Dieu bleu*).

[20] See 'Cerdannes', 'La Saison Russe a l'Opéra', *Comœdia illustré*, 1 June 1910, pp. 485–8 at p. 485.

[21] Unauthored clipping (1912); F-Po, B 717.

[22] For evidence of a similar osmosis, one might think of Giacomo Meyerbeer. Born in Germany and trained in Italy (hence the Italian form of his first name), Meyerbeer lived much of his life in Paris, where he played a decisive role in the development not only of French music but of an operatic genre that would serve as an international model.

upon his homeland with pride and patriotism, boasting of his desire to disseminate Russian culture across Europe. Moreover, to the French, the impresario and his French-named ensemble embodied the essence of *l'âme russe* – its exoticism, primitivism, child-like innocence and tribal communalism.[23] Ironically, the more the Ballets Russes impressed upon French culture and society, the more Russian they were considered. Frenchness and Russianness increased in tandem.[24]

As did fascination and fear. Witness to the rising popularity of the troupe and its increasing visibility within contemporary culture (symptomatic, in no small part, of the propagandist genius of Diaghilev), critics spoke regularly of 'enchantement', 'bouleversement' and 'fantaisie'. Yet they also invoked metaphors of invasion, describing the company's Parisian presence in terms of 'assaut' (onslaught) and 'conquête' (conquest). Terms such as these – understood both literally and metaphorically – cropped up throughout the press, including the fanatical prose of *Comœdia illustré*. According to the pseudonymous critic Mill Cessan, June 1910:

Les uns et les autres nous ont étonnés, ravis, conquis. Ils sont venus l'an dernier, troupe d'oiseaux lointains et passagers: Paris les adopta d'emblée, par un mouvement d'enthousiasme dont nul ne songea à s'étonner.[25]

(The one and the other astonished us, delighted us, won us over. They came last year, this passing troupe of birds from faraway: Paris adopted them straightaway, with an enthusiasm that no one found surprising.)

Merely one year later, also in *Comœdia illustré*, André-E. Marty maintained that Paris was no longer playing host to its international visitors: the capital was being invaded by them, becoming their exclusive property.[26]

For readers of *Comœdia illustré*, news of this Russian take-over may well have been read with excitement; the same readers likely bought Ballets-

---

[23] A more comprehensive account of the 'Russian soul', its cultural construction and attributes, is forthcoming in this chapter.

[24] Richard Taruskin makes a similar point with respect to the compositional development of Igor Stravinsky, describing how the intensified folklorism (read, Russianness) of the composer's pre-war ballets reflected a deliberate attempt on the part of the Ballets Russes to extend their international reach; see Taruskin, *Stravinsky and the Russian Traditions: A Biography of the Works through 'Mavra'*, 2 vols. (Berkeley and Los Angeles: University of California Press, 1996), vol. I, pp. 647–9.

[25] Mill Cessan, 'La Saison russe', *Comœdia illustré*, 15 June 1910, no page numbers; special supplement on the Ballets Russes.

[26] André-E. Marty, *Comœdia illustré*, 1 May 1911; quoted in Davis, *Ballets Russes Style*, p. 51. Not only Paris was at stake. As Diaghilev recalled, with the troupe's performance at Covent Garden, London (for the coronation gala of King George V), 'the Russian Ballet conquered the whole world'; quoted in Modris Eksteins, *Rites of Spring: The Great War and the Birth of the Modern Age* (Boston, MA: Houghton Mifflin, 1989), pp. 26–7.

Russes perfumes ('Le Parfum des Jardins d'Armide', 'Prince Igor') and clothing (*Schéhérazade*-style pantaloons, a corset called 'La Sylphide'), bought into the hoopla that heightened the troupe's fashionability within contemporary social circles. Nonetheless, for others reading and writing in the press, the prominence and popularity of 'les chers barbares russes' inflamed contemporary debates about *cosmopolitisme*.[27]

As is well known, the cosmopolitan aspect of Parisian life was never more pronounced than during the pre-war years of the belle époque. Riding high on the successes of two Expositions Universelles (1889 and 1900, the latter attracting a record-breaking number of visitors), the French capital was a world-leader in all things progressive and modern.[28] Specialist magazines – *Le Cosmopolite* (published in Paris, London and New York), *Cosmopolis* (Paris, London, New York, Vienna, Amsterdam, St Petersburg), *L'Information cosmopolite*, *Revue artistique cosmopolite*, *Le Financier cosmopolite* and *La Vie cosmopolite* – informed Parisians of news from around the world, as well as boasting of the city, its arts and culture, to readers at home and abroad.[29] To these readers, cosmopolitanism connoted modernity, urbanity, privilege, elitism and commercial savviness, as well as global influence and interest.[30] Paris was the focal-point for the present, as well as the perceived capital of the future. A commercial emporium, financial centre, tourist destination, colonial base, safe haven for exiled drifters and home to more foreigners than any other city, it was a nexus

---

[27] The term has become something of a buzzword within the burgeoning literature on globalization (embracing capitalism and consumption, international law, politics and human rights, and the early twentieth-century sociology of Georg Simmel): see, for example, Carol A. Breckenridge, Sheldon Pollock and Homi Bhabha (eds.), *Cosmopolitanism* (Durham, NC: Duke University Press, 2002); Steven Vertovec and Robin Cohen (eds.), *Conceiving Cosmopolitanism* (Oxford University Press, 2003) and Robert Fine, *Cosmopolitanism* (London: Routledge, 2007). As for historical accounts, there are a few innovative if isolated studies: Julia Prewitt Brown, *Cosmopolitan Criticism: Oscar Wilde's Philosophy of Art* (Charlottesville: University of Virginia Press, 1997); Jennifer Schiff Berman, *Modernist Fiction, Cosmopolitanism, and the Politics of Community* (Cambridge University Press, 2001); and Michael Stanislawski, *Zionism and the Fin de Siècle: Cosmopolitanism and Nationalism from Nordau to Jabotinsky* (Berkeley and Los Angeles: University of California Press, 2001). Tom Genrich, *Authentic Fictions: Cosmopolitan Writing of the Troisième République, 1908–1940* (New York: Peter Lang, 2004), offers an invaluable account of the early twentieth-century French usage of the term.

[28] The 1900 Exposition Universelle attracted almost fifty-one million visitors (more than the entire population of France), a record that was not beaten until Osaka, 1970. For more on the two exhibitions, their vaunting of both national progress and international fraternity, see Pascal Ory, *Les Expositions universelles de Paris* (Paris: Ramsay, 1982); and Jean-Pierre Rioux, *Chronique d'une fin de siècle: France, 1889–1900* (Paris: Seuil, 1991).

[29] See Tanya Agathocleous, *Urban Realism and the Cosmopolitan Imagination in the Nineteenth Century* (Cambridge University Press, 2010), pp. 53–68.

[30] According to A. de Tayac, writing in *Le Cosmopolite*, 1 October 1888 (p. 1), *cosmopolitisme* – 'la loi de l'avenir' – was an inevitable consequence of modern technological developments (transport, electricity, the telephone), all of which appeared to be making the world smaller and more accessible.

for the circulation of capital, commodities and people.[31] Thanks in no small part to the innovations of the Impressionists and Post-Impressionists (their so-called 'painting of modern life'), the capital had also become the site and subject of modern art. Paris lived off its own self-image, attracting international artists keen to witness cutting-edge art-in-the-making.[32]

Besides this burgeoning culture of visual art (which included film, photography and sculpture, as well as the new and distinctly modern art of poster design), the French capital enjoyed a vibrant and diverse theatrical scene, regularly showcasing ensembles and individual performers from across the globe. In his regular column for the daily newspaper *Le Temps*, in May 1912, Pierre Lalo joked:

La Grande-Saison de Paris: elle a commencé par une tragédie belge; elle a continué par des ballets russes; pendant ce temps, des chanteurs italiens occupent l'Opéra, et l'on voit au Vaudeville une pantomime allemande.[33]

(The Grande-Saison de Paris: it began with a Belgian tragedy; it continued with the Ballets Russes; during this period, Italian singers occupy the Opéra, and the Vaudeville is showing a German pantomime.)

Reporting on the 1913 summer season for *Le Monde artiste*, Gédéon Tallemant – in an article aptly titled 'Cosmopolis' – added a note of sarcasm:

Les Russes sont au Théâtre des Champs-Élysées. Maurice Maeterlinck, poète belge d'expression française triomphe au Châtelet avec un nouveau chef-d'œuvre, *Marie-Magdeleine*. L'Opéra donne la Tétralogie de l'Allemand génial Richard Wagner. Le divin d'Annunzio, poète italien, va nous offrir la primeur de sa *Pisanelle* au Châtelet et voilà que le Gymnase, qui joue encore la délicieuse *Demoiselle de magasin*, pièce belge de MM. Fonson et Wicheler, va prêter sa coquette salle à une troupe polonaise d'ailleurs remarquable, qui, sous le titre de Théâtre national polonais de Léopol, va donner une série de représentations en langue polsk. C'est ce qu'on appelle avec raison la *Saison de Paris*.[34]

(The Russians are at the Théâtre des Champs-Élysées. Maurice Maeterlinck, the francophone Belgian poet, triumphs at the Châtelet with a new masterpiece,

---

[31] For rich and readable accounts of the city, see Johannes Willms, *Paris, Capital of Europe: From the Revolution to the Belle Époque*, trans. Eveline L. Kanes (New York: Holmes and Meier, 1997); Patrice Higonnet, *Paris, Capital of the World* (Cambridge, MA: Harvard University Press, 2002); Alistair Horne, *Seven Ages of Paris: Portrait of a City* (London: Macmillan, 2002); and Colin Jones, *Paris: Biography of a City* (London: Allen Lane, 2004).

[32] See T. J. Clark, *The Painting of Modern Life: Paris in the Art of Manet and his Followers* (New York: Knopf, 1984).

[33] Pierre Lalo, 'La Musique', *Le Temps*, 28 May 1912, p. 3.

[34] Gédéon Tallemant, 'Cosmopolis', *Le Monde artiste*, 31 May 1913, p. 348. Also see La Dame au Masque, 'La Grande Saison Française', *La Critique indépendante*, 15 June 1913, p. 2.

Marie-Magdeleine. The Opéra stages the Tetralogy of the great German Richard Wagner. The divine Italian poet d'Annunzio is going to show for the first time his *Pisanelle* at the Châtelet and now the Gymnase, which is still showing the delicious *Demoiselle de magasin*, a Belgian play by MM. Fonson and Wicheler, is going to lend its charming theatre to a Polish troupe, remarkable for that matter, which, under the title of the Polish National Theatre of Léopol, is going to offer a series of performances in the Polish language. This is what we rightly call the *Saison de Paris*.)

Yet not all critics took the matter lightly. In a 1912 essay headed 'Paris aux Parisiens', also for *Le Monde artiste*, Maurice Lefèvre declared the matter of Paris's cosmopolitanism one of no small importance. He added:

Ne pensez-vous pas qu'il est temps qu'on rende Paris à ses véritables propriétaires? . . . Ne pensez-vous pas que l'exagération de ce cosmopolitisme intensif est quelque chose d'anormal et de gênant comme une maladie parasitaire? . . . Nous sommes, en ce moment, embourbés dans le cosmopolitisme à outrance . . . Il suffit de faire un retour sur nous-mêmes et de nous demander si nos hôtes ne sont pas en train de devenir nos maîtres.[35]

(Do you not think it's time to give Paris back to its true owners? . . . Do you not think that the amplification of this intensive cosmopolitanism is abnormal and a nuisance, like a parasitic illness? . . . At the moment we are excessively bogged down in cosmopolitanism . . . We need to do some soul-searching and ask whether our guests are not about to become our masters.)

Émile Vuillermoz had certainly done his. Soul-searching, recalling his original infatuation with the Ballets Russes yet describing his current frustration, Vuillermoz regretted 'cette période de cosmopolitanisme [*sic*] exaspéré'.[36] Writing in 1914, and applauding the recent production of two new French works at Paris's principal lyric theatres (*Scemo* at the Opéra and *Marouf, savetier du Caire* at the Opéra-Comique), the critic expressed a hope that

[35] Maurice Lefèvre, 'Paris aux Parisiens', *Le Monde artiste*, 11 May 1912, pp. 291–2 at p. 291. Also invoking Parisian cosmopolitanism ('le baggage cosmopolite'), Jacques-Émile Blanche described the city as 'une vaste gare centrale d'Europe' – a connection point and temporary stop-over, but no longer a cultural arbiter to the world; see his end-of-year review, 'Un Bilan artistique de 1913', *La Revue de Paris*, 15 November 1913, pp. 270–84 at p. 275 and p. 279.

[36] Émile Vuillermoz, 'L'Actualité', *Revue musicale S.I.M.*, 1 June 1914, p. 55. Incidentally, this same regret had surfaced seven years earlier in response to the French premiere of Richard Strauss's opera *Salome*. To quote critic Arthur Pougin, 'Semaine théâtrale', *Le Ménestrel*, 11 March 1907, pp. 146–8 at p. 146: '[O]n put craindre un instant que l'infortunée *Salomé* allait rester en route, lorsque heureusement se trouva tout à point la Société des grandes auditions musicales *de France* [*sic*], dont la spécialité est surtout de s'occuper de musique étrangère.' Pougin continued to note the forthcoming concerts of Russian music to be held in Paris (Diaghilev's first musical endeavour in the capital): 'Et maintenant que la Société des grandes auditions musicales *de France* [*sic*] nous a fait entendre de la musique anglaise, de la musique italienne, de la musique allemande, et qu'elle va nous offrir de la musique russe, est-ce qu'elle ne pourrait pas songer un peu à la musique française?'

some sort of equilibrium would soon be restored to the Parisian theatrical scene – an equilibrium that had long been overlooked. He added a prediction: 'Cette année, d'ailleurs, la revanche de nos théâtres de musique sera plus complète encore' (This year, moreover, the revenge of our music theatres will be yet more complete).[37]

Vuillermoz's optimism may well have been misplaced: French theatres were forced to close in August 1914 owing to the outbreak of war. But his concern for an encroaching cosmopolitanism – and for the dangerous influx of foreigners – was acute. And not new. Back in 1898, writer, journalist and man of politics Maurice Barrès had spoken angrily of a French political policy that was 'trop cosmopolite', one that had given rise to the disproportionate number of foreigners living and working within French frontiers.[38] In a political manifesto, and in words that would anticipate those of Lefèvre, above, Barrès described a parasitic invasion:

Aux sommets de la société comme au fond des provinces, dans l'ordre de la moralité comme dans l'ordre matériel, dans le monde commercial, industriel, agricole, et jusque sur les chantiers où il fait concurrence aux ouvriers français, l'étranger, comme un parasite, nous empoisonne.[39]

(In the top ranks of society, as in the heart of the provinces, in the moral and in the material sphere, in commerce, industry, agriculture, and even in building sites where he competes with French workers, the foreigner is poisoning us like a parasite.)

Nine years earlier, awaiting the opening of the 1889 Exposition Universelle, Edmond de Goncourt had also made caustic comment on the influx and influence of foreigners:

Des pagodes, des minarets, des moucharabys, tout un faux Orient en carton. Pas un monument rappelant notre architecture française. On sent que cette exposition va être l'exposition du *rastaquouérisme*. Du reste à Paris, dans le Paris d'aujourd'hui, oui, le Parisien, la Parisienne, ça commence à devenir un être rare . . . Au fond Paris n'est plus Paris, c'est une sorte de ville libre, où tous les voleurs de la terre qui ont fait leur fortune dans les affaires, viennent mal manger, et coucher contre de la chair qui se dit parisienne.[40]

---

[37] Vuillermoz, 'L'Actualité', p. 55. Debates about French theatres and their promotion of non-French works were of course longstanding, the Opéra itself regarded as a cosmopolitan institution. Yet Vuillermoz may be right to note an intensity of cosmopolitanism at the time; as my next chapter reveals, French opera was going through a period of crisis, owing partly to the influence of various foreign forms of the genre.

[38] Maurice Barrès, 'Le Programme de Nancy' (1898); in his *Scènes et doctrines du nationalisme* (Paris: F. Juven, 1902), pp. 432–40 at p. 433.

[39] *Ibid.*, pp. 432–3. There is more to come on the parasite metaphor.

[40] Edmond de Goncourt, 16 April 1889, *Journal: mémoires de la vie littéraire*, 9 vols. (Paris: Charpentier, 1887–96), vol. VIII, p. 43.

(Pagodas, minarets, moucharabiehs, an entire imitation Orient in cardboard. Not a single monument recalling our French architecture. One is aware that this exhibition is going to be an exhibition of flashy foreigners. Incidentally, in present-day Paris, Parisian men and women are becoming rare … At base, Paris is no longer the Paris of old but a sort of open city, in which all the world's thieves, those who have made their fortune in business, come to eat badly and rub up against flesh that calls itself Parisian.)

These quotations from Barrès and Goncourt betray the ideas and ethics upon which the men would insist: the latter, an idealized conception of Old Regime France, its social hierarchy, *politesse* and aristocratic art;[41] the former, a political campaign for 'Nationalisme, Protectionnisme, Socialisme'.[42] Barrès in fact was one of the first to popularize the term 'nationalisme' (in an 1892 article for *Le Figaro*) and to promote a specifically socialist mandate, one that viewed national cohesion as the inevitable outcome of social integration and consensus.[43] Yet it was a constellation of nationalist anxieties that characterized French politics – as well as the broader cultural and intellectual climate – in the late nineteenth and early twentieth centuries. As historians have explained, it was only during this quarter-century before the First World War that nationalist ideology – distinct from a long-standing sentiment of nationhood – began to dominate French political thought and practice.[44] Turning on its head the revolutionary

---

[41] For more on Goncourt and his brother Jules, their distaste for their own period (its reigning ideologies of democracy and capitalism, and its burgeoning technological development) and their preferred identification with eighteenth-century aristocracy, see Pierre Sabatier, *L'Esthétique des Goncourts* (Geneva: Slatkine, 1970); Debora L. Silverman, *Art Nouveau in Fin-de-Siècle France: Politics, Psychology and Style* (Berkeley and Los Angeles: University of California Press, 1989), pp. 17–39; Elisabeth Launay, *Les Frères Goncourt, collectionneurs de dessins* (Paris: Arthena, 1991); and Jean-Louis Cabanès, *Les Frères Goncourt: art et écriture* (Presses Universitaires des Bordeaux, 1997).

[42] See Michael Curtis, *Three Against the Third Republic: Sorel, Barrès and Maurras* (Princeton University Press, 1959); Zeev Sternhell, *Maurice Barrès et le nationalisme français* (Paris: A. Colin, 1972); his 'National Socialism and Anti-Semitism: The Case of Maurice Barrès', *Journal of Contemporary History*, 8/4 (1973), pp. 47–66; and Eugen Weber, 'Inheritance, Dilettantism, and the Politics of Maurice Barrès', in his *My France: Politics, Culture, Myth* (Cambridge, MA: The Belknap Press, 1991), pp. 226–43. Barrès condemned the opening of French frontiers and campaigned for national protectionism, in particular for the protection of the French labour market from the competition of foreign workers; see his *Contre les étrangers: étude pour la protection des ouvriers français* (Paris: Grande Imprimerie Parisienne, 1893), as well as his numerous articles for *Le Drapeau*, *La Patrie* and the short-lived review *La Cocarde*, which he founded.

[43] See Barrès, 'Socialisme et Nationalisme', *La Patrie*, 27 February 1903; also see Pascal Ory, 'La Nouvelle Droite fin de siècle', in Ory (ed.), *Nouvelle histoire des idées politiques* (Paris: Hachette, 1987), pp. 457–65.

[44] See, in particular, Eugen Weber, *The Nationalist Revival in France, 1905–1914* (Berkeley and Los Angeles: University of California Press, 1959); Robert Tombs (ed.), *Nationhood and Nationalism in France: From Boulangism to the Great War, 1889–1918* (London: Harper Collins, 1991); and James F. MacMillan, 'The Right and Nationalism', *Twentieth-Century France: Politics and Society* (New York and London: Edward Arnold, 1992), pp. 31–8.

conception of nation (based on popular democracy and equal citizenship), the 'new nationalism' promoted a cult of authority and order, and defined national identity in specifically chauvinistic and racial terms. Indeed, the issue of race came to define contemporary politics (and was often blurred with profession, class, social provenance, psychology and physical characteristics).[45] Standard-bearers of self-styled nationalistic movements railed against the tide of invasive foreigners (including invasive southerners), convinced that the French nation might soon be subject to subversion – and that all sense of *le pays réel* would be lost for ever.

Clearly, this 'new nationalism' – founded on the fear of foreign infiltration, corruption and the declining prestige of French tradition – did not emerge out of nowhere. Rather, it related to a compound of ideas, values, facts and phenomena specific to the period. Of particular significance was the perceived lack of discipline within the Third Republic (which had itself emerged out of the context of war and invasion): the stagnation of French money markets; the neglect of the army, navy and police force; weaknesses in diplomatic planning; and the vagaries of colonial policy. According to Charles Maurras – the leader of the anti-Republican and proto-fascist *L'Action française* – France did not have enough ships to defend (and even to visit) its overseas territories.[46] Moreover, having seized these territories and thrown open its frontiers, the nation was struggling to control its colonial subjects; borders proved permeable, and thus anxieties about invasion increased. Invasion by neighbouring Germany was a particular fear. Following their humiliating defeat by the Prussians in 1870, the French became increasingly concerned over the expansion of the German Empire – its escalating scientific and technological progress, population growth, commercial clout and influence on intellectual circles. By 1907, the real possibility of war was in the air, at least according to this anonymous critic for the democratic paper *La Dépêche*:

De sombres jours se préparent pour nous ... L'Europe connaîtra encore quelques années de paix. Mais vers 1911 ou, au plus tard, 1912, le Kaiser deviendra belliqueux. C'est la France qui sera l'holocauste de ce bouleversement. Nous connaîtrons la guerre civile et les puissances voisines se disputeront nos débris.[47]

---

[45] As Gaston Méry wrote in the epigraph to his 1892 novel *Jean Révolte*, a war of race, not of class, would define the period; quoted in Weber, *My France*, p. 35.

[46] See Charles Maurras, *Kiel et Tanger* (Paris: Nouvelle Librairie Nationale, 1910) and his digest, *Mes Idées politiques* (Paris: Fayard, 1937). Of the secondary literature on Maurras, Michael Sutton's *Nationalism, Positivism, Catholicism: The Politics of Charles Maurras and French Catholics, 1890–1914* (Cambridge University Press, 2002) is especially useful.

[47] Un Badaud, 'Menus Propos', *La Dépêche*, 4 May 1907, p. 1. Important primary sources that document French perceptions of Germany include: Léon Daudet, *Hors du joug allemand* (Paris: Nouvelle Librairie Nationale, 1915) and *L'Entre-deux-guerres* (Paris: Nouvelle Librairie

(Sombre days are brewing for us . . . Europe will continue to know only a few years of peace. But towards 1911 or, at the latest, 1912, the Kaiser will become belligerent. France will be the sacrifice of this upheaval. We will experience civil war and the bordering powers will fight over our remains.)

How did this historical context inflect the French reception of Diaghilev and his Ballets Russes?[48] It is easy to assume that the Russians were exempt from contemporary debate – unaffected by the questions of national identity that so preoccupied French culture and politics.[49] Since the 1890s a mutual friendliness and respect had developed between France and Russia; their political and military alliance, signed in 1894, served to strengthen the bond, and to safeguard both countries from invasion (by Germany, Austria-Hungary and Italy).[50] A series of state ceremonials, military visits and dedicated art exhibitions gave the alliance (secret, though widely rumoured) a public face, as did the erection of monuments designed to leave lasting marks on the nations' capitals – the Pont Alexandre III in Paris, and the Trinity Bridge in St Petersburg.[51] Perhaps the Ballets Russes were a

---

Nationale, 1915); Joséphin Péladan, *La Guerre des idées* (Paris: Flammarion, 1916); Édouard Driault, *Plus rien d'allemand* (Paris: Tenin, 1918); and Gustave Téry, *Les Allemands chez nous* (Paris: L'Œuvre, 1918), a collection of articles (from as early as 1910) entitled 'L'Invasion allemande', 'Chauvinisme et patriotisme', 'Qu'y a-t-il encore de français en France?' and 'Fermons nos portes!' (amongst others). According to historian Charles Rearick, so intense was the fear and anticipation of war with Germany that the French 'lived it up with a gnawing intuition that tomorrow they would die'; see his *Pleasures of the Belle Époque: Entertainment and Festivity in Turn-of-the-Century France* (New Haven, CT, and London: Yale University Press, 1985), p. 202. Rearick describes a number of popular entertainments and daredevil activities that seemed to both ignite and absolve the collective dread: 'the street-fair *jeu de massacre* in which customers threw balls at dolls representing the jaundiced Jesuit, the officious gendarme and the red-whiskered Englishman' (p. 199); 'loop-the-loop bicycle tracks sensationally billed as "the circle of death"' (p. 204).

48 As is well known, nationalist feelings and fears defined not only political movements but a broader social and cultural reality: even when the most aggressively nationalist politics died down, France witnessed the 'cultural explosion' of nationalism, an explosion that, according to Robert Tombs, 'retained an enormous subversive potential despite the failures of political enterprises directly inspired by it'. See Tombs, *Nationhood and Nationalism in France*, p. xiv.

49 Certainly, this is assumed by the bulk of the secondary literature, from Lynn Garafola's *Diaghilev's Ballets Russes* (1989; repr. New York: Da Capo, 1998) to more recent cultural studies of Russia's influence on the West, such as Steven G. Marks, *How Russia Shaped the Modern World: From Art to Anti-Semitism, Ballet to Bolshevism* (Princeton University Press, 2003).

50 Seminal studies include George F. Kennan, *The Decline of Bismarck's European Order: Franco-Russian Relations 1875–1890* (Princeton University Press, 1979); his *The Fateful Alliance: France, Russia, and the Coming of the First World War* (New York: Pantheon, 1984); and Patricia Weitsman, *Dangerous Alliances: Proponents of Peace, Weapons of War* (Stanford University Press, 2004).

51 On the interaction of Franco-Russian politics, art and culture, see Debora L. Silverman, 'Rococco Revival and the Franco-Russian Alliance', in her *Art Nouveau in Fin-de-Siècle France*, pp. 159–71.

monument of a similar kind. Although Diaghilev and his company faced criticism back home in Russian court circles, in Paris their compatriots turned out in support, turning evening performances into gala assemblies of French and Russian officials – in the words of one observer, 'une manifestation politico-artistique de la plus haute importance'.[52] Certainly, the troupe endorsed a sense of mutual support and service, an artistic solidarity and collaboration between France and Russia. Moreover, French critics acknowledged a shared choreographic heritage: French ballet had migrated to Russia in the nineteenth century, only to return, decades later, under the guise of the Ballets Russes.[53] The company, then, moored in a history that intertwined both nations, not only contributed to a cultural programme of exchange. The Ballets Russes were a testament to Franco-Russian cooperation, goodwill and support; they represented 'un nouveau resserrement de l'alliance' (a further strengthening of the alliance).[54]

However, according to some reports, the much-vaunted principles of concord and collaboration were rarely observed in practice: 'Nous sommes loin de l'internationalisme ou du simple "libre-échangisme" desiré, en art!' (We are, in art, far from the desired internationalism or simple 'free trade'), wrote an anonymous French critic.[55] Others thought that the alliance itself had gone stale, with the Russians no longer interested in supporting French culture and colonial politics, though happy to continue to borrow from the French money market. The impressions of duplicity and pretence also emerged from the discourse surrounding the Ballets Russes: in particular, from articles written by designer Alexandre Benois, published in both the French-language *Journal de Saint-Pétersbourg* and the Russian newspaper *Rech'*. Benois reported on the Ballets Russes fairly regularly for the Russian press, describing the Parisians' fascination with Russian culture – its

---

[52] Un Monsieur de l'Orchestre, 'La Soirée: La Saison russe au Châtelet', *Le Figaro*, 20 May 1909, pp. 5–6 at p. 6.

[53] See, for example, Robert Brussel, 'La Saison russe', *Le Figaro*, 20 May 1909, p. 5: 'Ce qui frappe dès l'abord dans le ballet russe, c'est le mélange qui s'est précisément opéré du sentiment naturel de la danse et de la tradition chorégraphique française. Ces traditions sont très vivaces en Russie, M. Petipa les représentait encore il y a quelques années. M. Fokine, tout en les développant, ne les a pas oubliées et les représente très nettement aujourd'hui.'

[54] Un Monsieur de l'Orchestre, 'La Soirée', p. 5: 'C'était presque, cette répétition générale, une cérémonie officielle, quelque chose comme une seconde visite des Russes à Paris, un nouveau resserrement de l'alliance. Seulement, cette fois-ci, les Russes ne viennent pas conquérir notre sympathie avec des navires et des marins, ils viennent conquérir notre admiration avec des artistes chanteurs, danseurs et décorateurs.'

[55] Anonymous, 'Protectionnisme russe', *Le Courrier musical*, 15 March 1912, p. 186. Also see Jacques Daugny, 'La Puissance russe', *La Nouvelle Revue*, 15 September 1911, pp. 274–81.

'spontaneity', 'primitive wildness' and 'simplicity'.[56] According to Benois, the Russians 'had shown that they could outvie the French on their own ground', resurrecting the French Romantic ballet (in *Les Sylphides*) and the French rococo (in *Le Pavillon d'Armide*).[57] Yet Benois pushed further. In an article of July 1909, the designer made explicit the very same metaphors of invasion used by the French critics in their assessment of the company:

Oui, les Barbares ont encore une fois conquis Rome – et c'est curieux – les Romains contemporains saluent leur captivité, car ils sentent que c'est pour leur bien, que les nouveaux venus, avec leur art précis et jeune vont infiltrer un sang vigoureux dans leur corps rachitique![58]

(Yes, the Barbarians have once again conquered Rome – and, funnily enough – the contemporary Romans celebrate their captivity, because they feel that it is for their own good, that the newcomers, with their youthful and distinctive art, are going to inject new blood into their rickety bodies!)

The Russians as conquerors, the French their captives: Benois was jubilant – and so too, he jeered, were the French. With no less pride and prejudice, the artist went on to compare Russian and French music theatre:

Après notre mise en scène, les mises en scène du grand Opéra et de l'Opéra-Comique ne peuvent paraître que des absurdités de baraques. Après nos artistes, surtout après l'ensemble de notre ballet, les artistes français (ces connaisseurs de leur métier), produiront l'effet de *marionnettes montées sur des échasses!!*[59]

(After our stagings, the stagings of the mighty Opéra and the Opéra-Comique will only appear as absurdities from a fairground stall. After our artists, especially after our ballet dancers, French artists (these connoisseurs of their craft) will look like *long-in-the-leg puppets!!*)

Responding to Benois in an article sarcastically titled 'Nos bons amis les Russes!', French critic Louis Schneider was appalled.[60] Why such belittling of

---

[56] See, for example, Alexandre Benois, 'Russkiye spektakli v Parizhe', *Rech'*, 25 July 1909; trans. Richard Taruskin, *Stravinsky and the Russian Traditions*, vol. I, pp. 449–550. As Roland John Wiley acknowledges in his series of short studies on Benois's Russian commentaries, the designer sought to promote Diaghilev's company to Russian readers (with the hope of securing for the company a permanent home in Moscow); see Wiley, 'Alexandre Benois' Commentaries on the First *Saisons Russes*', *The Dancing Times*, 71/841 (1980), pp. 28–30.

[57] Benois, 'Russkiye spektakli v Parizhe'.

[58] Benois, 'Lettres artistiques: les représentations russes à Paris'; archival sources suggest that this article appeared in the *Journal de Saint-Pétersbourg*, 2 July 1909.

[59] *Ibid.*

[60] Louis Schneider, 'Nos bons amis les Russes!'; clipping, F-Pn, Ro 12518. The reference scribbled on this clipping – *Le Gaulois*, 30 July 1910 – is incorrect. Unfortunately, and despite extensive searches, I have been unable to identify the actual date and source.

the Paris Opéra, especially when the Ballets Russes hoped to perform there the following year? And why such ingratitude? Recalling the Ballets Russes' initial reception ('la mémoire de l'accueil chaleureux que les Parisiens ont fait à la troupe de ballet et d'opéra russe'), Schneider bawled:

On aurait pu croire, on croyait jusqu'ici que la généreuse hospitalité de Paris, qui ne fait jamais défaut à tous les représentants de l'Art, demeurerait gravée à jamais dans le cœur reconnaissant de nos amis. Il n'en est rien; et, si étonnant que cela puisse paraître, le *Journal de Saint-Pétersbourg* vient de publier, sous la signature autorisée de M. Alexandre Benois, un article fort désobligeant pour la France en général et pour Paris en particulier.

(We would have thought, we had thought until now, that Paris's generous hospitality, which extends to all representatives of art, would remain forever engraved on the hearts of our grateful friends. Far from it; and, so surprising it appears, the *Journal de Saint-Pétersbourg* has just published, under the authorized signature of M. Alexandre Benois, an article truly offensive to France in general and to Paris in particular.)

To Schneider, the article represented more than Benois's personal arrogance: it was tantamount to an official document, one that came from the pen of Diaghilev's right-hand man ('l'alter ego de M. de Diaghilew') and spoke on behalf of the entire company. Thus the points made were all the more 'odieux'.

This couple of articles gives more than a hint of the frictions under-pinning the reception of the Russians in France. Clearly, the Ballets Russes were caught up with questions of national identity, power and prestige, caught up in their immediate cultural and political context. On his showing here, Benois took particular pleasure in situating the troupe within this context, loudly proclaiming the triumph of the Ballets Russes and the capitulation of the French. That his comments so aggravated and enraged Louis Schneider is hardly surprising. Taking every opportunity to belittle French performers and institutions, and even the enthusiastic French fans of the company, Benois could not have written words more inflammatory.

Of course, such anti-French rhetoric was not new. Thirty-seven years previously, and in the thick of the Franco-Prussian war, Richard Wagner penned and published *Eine Kapitulation*, a political farce cum musical comedy.[61] Much like Benois's 1910 essay, *Eine Kapitulation* set out to rub salt in Gallic wounds, to jeer, mock and openly insult French tradition (including the figureheads Victor Hugo, Jules Ferry and Léon Gambetta); the

---

[61] Written in 1870 and first published in the ninth volume of Wagner's collected works (first edition, 1873), *Eine Kapitulation* is reprinted in *Richard Wagner's Prose Works*, trans. William Ashton Ellis (London: Kegan Paul, 1896), vol. V, pp. 3–33.

text also angered Frenchmen, prompting condemnation for its viciousness and chauvinistic tones.[62] Indeed, the general critical response to Wagner was cast in terms not dissimilar from those used to describe the Ballets Russes: 'pénétration', 'conquête', 'infiltration', 'envahissement'.[63] The two were conflated in a sixteen-page special edition of the satirical journal *La Baïonnette*, a comic-strip about the life of 'Marianne' during the Third Republic.[64] Formerly the epitome of grace and beauty, Marianne had succumbed to both the Russian ballet ('des barbares ballets') and Wagnerian music. These dangerous infatuations had left her delirious, and with the look of a madwoman: 'Marianne jolie! prends garde! – ton bonnet à cocarde prend des façons de bonnet de folie!' (Pretty Marianne! Be careful! – your bonnet with its cockade looks like a dunce's cap!).[65]

The comic-strip presented Marianne, the symbolic incarnation of the French nation, as the victim of *cosmopolitisme* – a *cosmopolitisme* itself represented by the Ballets Russes and by Wagner. Both were configured as dangerous, demoralizing influences, and both subsumed under the banner 'enemies of the state'. The anxieties provoked by Wagner are of course well known, as are the various ways in which *Wagnérophobie* related to broader cultural concerns (the emergence of the avant-garde, the dissolution of opera, the development and decline of Symbolism), not to mention the far-reaching French campaign to restore national art and tradition.[66] Lesser known are the

---

[62] For a detailed account of Wagner's text, see Thomas S. Grey, '*Eine Kapitulation*: Aristophanic Operetta as Cultural Warfare in 1870', in Grey (ed.), *Richard Wagner and his World* (Princeton University Press, 2009), pp. 87–122. As Grey notes (p. 105), the published text of 1873 included a 'shame-faced apologia' in which the author-composer revealed that the play actually depicted the 'capitulation' of his own countrymen to the frivolities of the Parisian way of life.

[63] See, for example, the articles written by Camille Saint-Saëns and published in *L'Écho de Paris*, 19 September, 6, 16 and 23 October, and 21 November 1914.

[64] Lucien Métivet, 'Marianne et Germania: l'histoire d'un bonnet et d'un casque', *La Baïonnette*, 18 April 1918, pp. 242–57.

[65] *Ibid.* The page featured illustrations of a stern-looking cubist painter (depicted as a cube), a couple dancing, ballet characters and a host of Wagnerian figures (Valkyries, Rhinemaidens, Siegfried and the dragon).

[66] Useful secondary sources include Gerald D. Turbow, 'Art and Politics: Wagnerism in France', in David C. Large and William Weber (eds.), *Wagnerism in European Culture and Politics* (Ithaca, NY: Cornell University Press, 1984), pp. 134–66; Marion Schmid, 'À bas Wagner!: The French Press Campaign against Wagner during World War I', in Barbara L. Kelly (ed.), *French Music, Culture, and National Identity, 1870–1939* (University of Rochester Press, 2008), pp. 77–91; and Grey (ed.), *Richard Wagner and his World*. The broader subject under discussion here – music, culture and French national identity – has become a significant growth area in musicological scholarship. See, for example, Jane Fulcher, *French Cultural Politics and Music: From the Dreyfus Affair to the First World War* (Oxford University Press, 1999); and her *The Composer as Intellectual: Music and Ideology in France* (Oxford University Press, 2005); Steven Huebner, *French Opera at the Fin-de-Siècle: Wagnerism, Nationalism, and Style* (Oxford University Press, 1999); Carlo Caballero, *Fauré and French Musical Aesthetics* (Cambridge University Press, 2001);

anxieties aroused by the Russian ballet: how and why they emerged, and what they might tell us about contemporary intellectual and cultural currents. Certainly, the French response to the Ballets Russes did not reach the level of intensity and outrage that characterized the reception of Wagner. Yet it was comparable in scope and significance, and similarly embroiled in a wider polemic about national identity. As Kenneth E. Silver puts it in his seminal account of the Parisian avant-garde, the Russian ballet was part of 'the deranged and un-French recent history of Parisian aesthetics'.[67] As such, the company contributed not only to a culture of Parisian cosmopolitanism, attracting an audience keen to sample and engage with the latest in worldly art and theatre.[68] Indeed, *cosmopolitisme* itself signified more than a stance of openness towards other cultures and peoples. The term gestured to an amalgam of threatening foreign elements in circulation within French society, elements – themselves considered *cosmopolite* – set out to influence and destroy traditional French values.[69]

La Saison russe: les ballets juifs

Certainly, the Russian ballet did not lack ambition. Diaghilev in particular was keen to capitalize on Western tastes, and, in doing so, to secure his company's popularity with audiences across Europe.[70] And the French were well aware of this: in the words of critic Henry Gauthier-Villars, better known as Willy (and the husband of Colette), the entire Ballets-Russes venture could be described as '[un] essai d'internationalisme saltatoire' (an attempt at choreographic

Jann Pasler, *Composing the Citizen: Music as Public Utility in Third Republic France* (Berkeley and Los Angeles: University of California Press, 2009); and Annegret Fauser and Mark Everist (eds.), *Music, Theatre, and Cultural Transfer: Paris, 1830–1914* (University of Chicago Press, 2009).

[67] Kenneth E. Silver, *Esprit de Corps: The Art of the Parisian Avant-Garde and the First World War, 1914–1925* (London: Thames and Hudson, 1989), p. 22.

[68] As Garafola has described, this audience comprised an amalgam of white-collar workers, diplomats, fashion designers, musicians, painters and personalities from across the creative arts – and across the globe; see her *Diaghilev's Ballets Russes*, pp. 273–99.

[69] The changing cultural currency of the term across the nineteenth and twentieth centuries is relatively little known. Once a proclamation of universal solidarity, exchange and (in art) stylistic synthesis, the term acquired a significant pejorative aspect in the French press, popular literature and politics: see Genrich, *Authentic Fictions*, pp. 13–42 and Philippe Hamon and Alexandrine Viboud, 'Cosmopolitisme', in *Dictionnaire thématique du roman de mœurs, 1850–1914* (Paris: Presses de la Sorbonne Nouvelle, 2003), pp. 180–1. The specialist cosmopolitan journals mentioned earlier provide useful accounts of the meaning of the term at isolated historical moments.

[70] According to Garafola, Diaghilev was a 'thorough-going cosmopolitan'; see her 'Diaghilev's Musical Legacy', *Legacies of Twentieth-Century Dance* (Middletown, CT: Wesleyan University Press, 2005), pp. 45–53 at p. 48.

internationalism).[71] According to Gauthier-Villars, the troupe sought to show-case different choreographic styles, dancing to music by composers from different countries in an attempt to convince spectators of their international reach: 'Ces artistes ... ont désiré nous prouver que leur art n'est pas étroitement local, qu'ils savent danser en plusieurs langues' (These artists ... wanted to show us that their art wasn't strictly local, but that they knew how to dance in several styles).[72]

This ability to appropriate different choreographic styles was not unrelated to a specifically racial aspect of the company's perceived cosmopolitanism. Since their arrival in Paris, the Ballets Russes had faced criticism for their association with the Parisian impresario Gabriel Astruc. Astruc had a reputa-tion as a xenophile; his passion for foreign theatre had led him to engage a steady stream of international artists, several of whom took to the stage of his purpose-built Théâtre des Champs-Élysées.[73] Yet he was also the son of an important rabbi, and thus attracted attention from militant anti-Semites. In a 1912 headline article, Léon Daudet, co-founder of *L'Action française*, affirmed Astruc's pernicious influence. The impresario, according to Daudet, was about to heap ruin on the European theatrical scene:

Le Juif de Grande Saison de Paris est en train de raser la saison parisienne, comme son congénère rase la forêt française, à blanc étoc. Il en résultera, ici comme là, l'appauvrissement puis la ruine. Ici comme là, le nomade campé est un fléau pour le sédentaire. Quand Astruc aura fait et refait Paris, il ira faire et refaire Vienne ou Berlin. Ce sont les procédés de la banque juive appliqués au banquisme théâtral.[74]

(The Jew behind the Grande Saison de Paris is demolishing the Parisian season, as his species demolishes the French forest, completely. As a result, here as in the forest, there will be impoverishment then ruin. Here as there, the itinerant camper is a curse on the sedentary population. When Astruc is finished with Paris, he will do the same with Vienna or Berlin. This is the behaviour of the Jewish bank applied to the theatre.)

Daudet's words illustrate the professional anti-Semitism sanctioned within some quarters of the press – here a decade beyond the Dreyfus Affair and its overtly racialist politics. This was an anti-Semitism that regarded Jews as a powerful and dangerous group within society, a group that, lacking any

---

[71] Henry Gauthier-Villars, 'Deux ballets russes de musiciens français', *Comœdia illustré*, 15 June 1912, no page numbers.

[72] *Ibid.*

[73] The theatre itself, designed by the Belgian-born Auguste Perret, was thought to betray foreign influence. Its ferroconcrete construction, clean lines, sharp edges and overall austerity of form were compared to the new architectural aesthetic of the German avant-garde.

[74] Léon Daudet, 'Les Engouements de Paris', *L'Action française*, 31 May 1912, p. 1.

national tradition or citizenship of its own, had infiltrated the French army, the magistrature, the ministries, the newspapers, the universities, the financial sector – and even the Russian ballet.[75] Charles Batson, one of few recent commentators to consider the effect of this racialist invective on the company's reception, describes a transparent line of influence: 'The Ballets Russes were read by their critics as not only a foreign enterprise; they were also seen as manifestations of a despised, and despisedly powerful, minority group.'[76]

As Batson reminds us, Astruc was not the only associate of Diaghilev subjected to anti-Semitic scorn.[77] Bakst, who seems to have made no secret of his religion (acquiring stationery adorned with the Star of David on his arrival in Paris), was also held to account, his erotic costumes and 'intense feeling for sex' (the words of one English commentator) adding grist to the anti-Semitists' mill.[78] Then there was the Ballets-Russes audience. Reflecting on the company from the vantage point of 1925, novelist Paul Morand underlined the significance of the 'great Israelite audience' – which included some of Europe's most prosperous Jewish families.[79] No doubt this audience contributed to the company's success, not to mention its Jewish credentials. Indeed, in a journal entry from 1910, critic Maurice Denis scribbled 'Saison russe: les ballets juifs'.[80] Marcel Proust even compared the brouhaha sparked by the Russian troupe to that aroused by the Dreyfus Affair: 'une fièvre de curiosité moins âpre, plus purement esthétique, mais peut-être aussi vive que l'affaire Dreyfus' (a fever of curiosity less combative, more purely aesthetic, but perhaps just as intense as the Dreyfus Affair).[81]

L'invasion des barbares

This 'fièvre de curiosité' was sparked by the company's perceived national character. Press reports and reviews of the Ballets Russes made repeated reference to *l'âme slave*, endorsing a set of specifically Russian characteristics:

[75] It may be important to note that the politics of Barrès, mentioned earlier, were strongly influenced by his anti-Semitic tendencies; Curtis offers a summary account in his *Three Against the Third Republic*, pp. 210–20.

[76] Charles Batson, *Dance, Desire, and Anxiety in Early Twentieth-Century French Theater* (Aldershot: Ashgate, 2005), p. 132.

[77] *Ibid.*

[78] Huntley Carter, 1912; quoted in *ibid.*, p. 130. Bakst also came under anti-Semitic attack from fellow designer Benois, following a series of spats about the sets for *Schéhérazade* and *Petrouchka*.

[79] Paul Morand, 'Paris Letter', *Dial* (June 1925), p. 499. Garafola describes the Jewish composition of the audience in her *Diaghilev's Ballets Russes*, pp. 273–99.

[80] Maurice Denis, 1910 entry from his *Journal*, 3 vols. (Paris: Éditions Vieux Colombier, 1957), vol. II, p. 133.

[81] Marcel Proust, *À la recherche du temps perdu* (1913–27; repr. Paris: Gallimard, 1954), vol. III, pp. 236–7.

instinct, vitality, vigour, sincerity, energy, spontaneity, naivety, innocence, youthfulness, simplicity, intuition, tribal communalism, originary unity, passion, primitivism and a spiritual at-one-ness with the world.[82] To the French, these characteristics were entirely the opposite of those that defined Western civilization. The latter was looked upon with increasing dissatisfaction: power, prestige, secularism, industrialization and an obsession with material well-being had left Westerners in search of a soul – an Arcadian fantasy that was both primitive and timeless. The Russians, it seemed, could make that fantasy a reality. In the words of Jean-Louis Vaudoyer:

Restés barbares dans une Europe qui est, si l'on peut dire, civilisée jusqu'à la corde, les Russes sont au moment le plus fécond, le plus beau, de leur développement intérieur. Très neufs, avides et sincères comme des enfants, ils se donnent tout entiers et se cherchent avec fièvre. Ils ne sont pas entravés comme nous par les formules, et l'incrédulité ne les a pas énervés; ils ignorent la satiété occidentale. Ils n'ont encore rien usé.[83]

(Having remained barbarians in a Europe whose every fibre is civilized, the Russians now have the most richly creative, beautifully developed inner selves. As fresh, avid and sincere as children, they give themselves over entirely and search their souls feverishly. They are not hindered like we are by conventions, and are not enervated by a lack of belief; they have no experience of Occidental satiation. They are yet to wear things out.)

'Usé', 'âgé', 'fatigué', 'plus guère curieux': Europe was spiritually bankrupt, the victim of its own mad rush towards modernization. Primitive cultures could offer a means of salvation: to quote Adhéaume de Chevigné, 'une saveur que notre vieille routine et notre soi-disant expérience aurait tort de mépriser' (an essence that our old routine and our so-called experience would be wrong to disregard).[84] Benois recalled this aspect of the troupe's reception in his

---

[82] On the history and genesis of the phrase *l'âme slave* (or *russe*), its associated characteristics, and its significance within the discourse of Russian nationalism, see Robert C. Williams, 'The Russian Soul: Western Thought and Non-Western Nationalism', in his *Russia Imagined: Art, Culture and National Identity, 1840–1995* (New York: Peter Lang, 1997), pp. 3–18. As Williams notes, the Russians – not their European enthusiasts – were the first to conceive of their 'soul' along specifically national lines. Borrowing from German Romantic philosophy (its ideology of organic growth from the soil of ancient culture, itself a response to Enlightenment rationality and universality), they determined to think of themselves as an individual nation, distinct from the West, with historical purpose and future potential.

[83] Jean-Louis Vaudoyer, 'Variations sur les Ballets Russes', *La Revue de Paris*, 15 July 1910, pp. 333–52 at p. 351.

[84] Adhéaume de Chevigné, 'À Propos de la *Flûte enchantée* et de la *Saison russe*', *Le Courrier musical*, 1 July 1909, pp. 442–3 at p. 443. For a similar comment, see Fernand Gregh, 'Ce que disent les danses du *Prince Igor*', *Revue musicale*, 9/7–8 (July–August 1913), pp. 8–11.

1941 memoir: 'Our French friends did nothing but repeat to us: "You have come at the most suitable moment, you are refreshing us, you are leading us to new themes and feelings."'[85]

These quotations hint at a related attribute. Hand in hand with their essential primitivism, the Ballets Russes offered sumptuosity, elegance and charm, sensuousness, refinement and luxury, and on a scale that had rarely between witnessed on the balletic stage.[86] Partly this had to do with the company's Eastern emphasis: that is, those Oriental ballets dreamt up by Diaghilev and his team to capitalize on prevailing European tastes for the exotic.[87] Then there were the ballets based on specifically Russian themes: in the pre-war period, *Le Festin* (1909), *L'Oiseau de feu* (1910), *Petrouchka* (1911), *Le Sacre du printemps* (1913) and *Le Coq d'or* (1914). These ballets betrayed shifting conceptions of Russia and Russianness, and were influenced to varying degrees by Russian folklore and peasant tradition, pagan pre-history and life in urban St Petersburg.[88] Yet each was injected with Eastern Orientalism: with eroticized choreography and lasciviousness,

[85] Benois, *Reminiscences of the Russian Ballet*, trans. Mary Britnieva (London: Putnam, 1941), p. 285. In a 1909 article for *Rech'*, Benois had proudly declared: 'It was Russian culture that triumphed in Paris, the whole essence of Russian art, its conviction, its freshness, its spontaneity . . . Our primitive wildness, our simplicity revealed itself in Paris as something more refined, developed, and subtle than the French themselves could do . . . This secret has been lost on the Western stage, where everything is technique, everything is consciousness, everything is artificiality, whence have gradually disappeared the mysterious charm of self-oblivion, the great Dionysiac intoxication, the driving force of art.' See Benois, 'Russkiye spektakli v Parizhe', p. 550. Incidentally, and according to Modris Eksteins in a seminal study, Diaghilev himself conceived of art in terms of redemption and regeneration. Advocating vitality, intuition and spontaneity, the impresario sought to break free from the stultifying conventions, moral conformity and materialist priorities of the time-conscious, work-orientated Western world. Art, to Diaghilev, was a means of invigorating the soul, enlivening one's emotional life and liberating society from the constraints of time and place. Eksteins offers a useful contextualization of this point of view, linking Diaghilev to a broader cultural and intellectual revolt against rationalism; see his *Rites of Spring*, pp. 9–54. Also see Taruskin, 'The Antiliterary Man: Diaghilev and Music', *On Russian Music* (Berkeley and Los Angeles: University of California Press, 2009), pp. 202–13.

[86] Vaudoyer described this combination of primitivism and refinement in his 'Variations sur les Ballets Russes', p. 351. After having described the Russians' essential sincerity and spontaneity, he added: 'Qu'une même troupe puisse offrir l'*Oiseau de Feu* et le *Pavillon d'Armide*, *Giselle* et *Schéhérazade*, est un exemple probant de cette savoureuse union de culture et de barbarie.'

[87] *Schéhérazade*, in particular, was known for its refinement and barbarism. Critic G. Jean-Aubrey described 'ce spectacle de volupté barbare et raffinée, cette page sensuelle et délicate à la fois'; 'Soliloque sur les Ballets Russes', *La Tribune musicale*, 16 June 1914, no page number.

[88] According to Garafola, this multifaceted view of Russia and Russianness reflected the company's own identity: 'For Diaghilev and his fellow Petersburgers, there was no single way of being Russian or experiencing their own Russianness'; see her 'At Home and Abroad: Paris/Petersburg 1913', *Legacies of Twentieth-Century Dance*, pp. 54–65 at p. 56.

unbridled pleasure and ritual, and lavish visual display. Bakst's costume design for Tamara Karsavina's Firebird (one of the mythical Russian characters in *Le Festin*) illustrates this Russian–Eastern synthesis (see Figure 4.2). The outfit has a real-world, Russian model and is based on traditional peasant fancy-dress: a vivid and richly printed overskirt (*poneva*) and chemise (*rubakha*), a decorative headdress (*kokochnik*) and spangly, feathered accessories. Yet Bakst adapted this model for the Orientalist imagination, with elaborate embellishments (beads, jewels, bracelets, brooches), excessive plumage and fabrics embroidered with gold.[89] Equally exotic in their depiction of Slavic tradition may be the costumes designed by Nikolay Roerich for *Le Sacre du printemps* (Figure 4.3). As well as their austere and 'earthy' primitivism, the tribal tunics suggest something of the Orient, its vivid colours, brilliant juxtapositions and textured tapestry.

Much was made in the press of this intense yet mystical Russianness, as critics attempted to situate the troupe – its dancing, decor and music – in the context of Russian history and aesthetics.[90] Yet all were quick to recognize, including the Russians themselves, that the mix of savagery and sophistication was a sure selling point, a key to the troupe's popularity with audiences: never before, according to one observer, had something so beautiful – 'so barbaric, so luxurious' – been seen on stage.[91] And not only on stage. Welcoming the 'invasion' of dancers from Russia ('a country regarded until a few years ago as semi-barbaric, [and] given to tyranny . . . and violent revolt'), Gordon Selfridge declared that his London department store would soon have 'a Russian season of its own'.[92] In Paris, too, department stores and fashion houses began to cultivate the foreign look, turning mannequins into 'les oiseaux de rêve', as beautiful and opulent as those seen on stage.[93]

[89] Davis compares this outfit to that worn by Karsavina in the title role of *L'Oiseau de feu*; see her *Ballets Russes Style*, pp. 79–84.

[90] As for music, French concepts of Russianness owed much to César Cui's *La Musique en Russie* (Paris: Fischbacher, 1880) and Alfred Bruneau's *Musiques de Russie et musiciens de France* (Paris: Charpentier, 1903): both endorsed the nationalistic 'New Russian School' (the 'kuchka', 'five' or 'mighty handful') and opposed the Europeanized outlook and style of Tchaikovsky. For more on this split conceptualization of Russian music, see Richard Taruskin, *Defining Russia Musically: Historical and Hermeneutical Essays* (Princeton University Press, 1997) and, more specifically, the dialogue between Calvocoressi and Will Junker fran Fredricksamn published in *Le Courrier musical*, August to December 1912.

[91] Arnold Bennet, 1910; quoted in L. Honigwachs, 'The Edwardian Discovery of Russia, 1900–1917', PhD thesis, Columbia University (1977), p. 268.

[92] Gordon Selfridge, 'Selfridge Editorial', 12 May 1911; quoted in Mica Nava, 'The Allure of Difference: Selfridges, the Russian Ballet and the Tango', in her *Visceral Cosmopolitanism: Gender, Culture and the Normalization of Difference* (New York: Berg, 2007), pp. 19–40 at pp. 26–7.

[93] For an illustrated account of the influence of the Ballets Russes on Paris fashion, see Davis, *Ballets Russes Style*.

Figure 4.2 Bakst, *Le Festin*, costume design for 'l'Oiseau d'or' (1909).

'Primitivisme! Primitivisme!', cried Jean Perros in *La Critique indépendante*: 'les Russes étaient venus et nous voyions enfin la lumière' (the Russians had come and, finally, we were seeing the light).[94] Perros went on to describe the instant popularity of the Ballets Russes, noting how their essential Russianness had influenced the French:

[94] Jean Perros, 'Après les Ballets Russes', *La Critique indépendante*, 15 June 1913, p. 1.

Figure 4.3 Roerich, *Le Sacre du printemps*, costumes (1913).

Nous étions un peuple de vieillards et d'aveugles . . . Ils nous enseignaient la jeunesse, la candeur et la vérité. Ils nous offraient leur âme innocente, leur sensibilité jeune, leurs sentiments ingénus. Leur simplicité, leur ardeur, leur dévotion en face de la nature, voilà ce qui expliquait leur art et le rendait admirable.[95]

(We were a nation of old fogies and blind men . . . They taught us youth, candour and truth. They offered us their innocent soul, their youthful sensibility, their ingenuous

[95] *Ibid.*

feelings. Their simplicity, their ardour, their devotion in the presence of nature, this is what explained their art and made it admirable.)

Yet Perros had grown tired of Russian teaching.[96] The initial enthusiasm for the company having died down, the critic could see the Russians for what they were – rather, for what they were doing. Making fun of their audience, parading their ingenuity over Western rationalism and restraint, laughing at the delirium they caused: the Ballets Russes were not the innocent Slavs of naive and wishful thinking; they were cold and calculating, deliberately subversive. According to Victor Debay, the troupe not only humiliated but manipulated their Parisian audience: 'Les étrangers considèrent Paris comme un patient docile sur qui toutes opérations peuvent être tentées' (Foreigners consider Paris as a docile patient on whom all operations can be attempted).[97]

This couple of quotations deserves our attention, for they hint at the significant negative discourse surrounding the Russians' Russianness, that which contributed in no small measure to the company's perceived dissidence and threat. Debay's description of Paris as a patient, operated upon by Russian hands, is particularly evocative. It recalls the idea, mentioned earlier, of the Ballets Russes as a redemptive force – a miracle medicine that could cure Western civilization of its excessive rationality and particularism. Yet it turns this idea on its head: the Ballets Russes, to Debay, are surgeon-hacks, experimenting on their unassuming patient in the most outlandish of operations.[98]

Hardly surprising, perhaps, these words from Debay – and those from Perros – are couched within a review of *Le Sacre du printemps*, the Ballets Russes' 1913 *succès de scandale*. The ballet of course is infamous, as much for its music (Stravinsky), dancing (Nijinsky) and visuals (Roerich) as for the rows it provoked inside both the theatre and the press. Critics variously debated the historical authenticity of the work, the sincerity of the authors and their intentions, the collaborative work ethic, the communalism of the dancers on stage, the originality of the choreography and that of the score, the appropriateness of the drama for stage production and the expectations of the audience. The idea of humiliation cropped up recurrently. The Parisian

---

[96] So too had Vuillermoz: 'Une fois de plus, les Barbares du Nord viennent démontrer aux Latins la supériorité de leur instinct sur notre culture et humilier l'Occident de tout ce subtil éclat de la sagesse orientale. Nous allons prendre docilement notre leçon annuelle de peinture, d'art décoratif, de chorégraphie, de mise en scène et d'orchestration.' See his essay, 'Igor Strawinsky [*sic*]', *Revue musicale S.I.M.*, 15 May 1912, pp. 15–21 at p. 15.

[97] Victor Debay, 'Les Ballets Russes', *Le Courrier musical*, 15 June 1913, pp. 340–2 at p. 341.

[98] Jacques-Émile Blanche offers something similar, asking whether the 'vaccine' offered by the Russian troupe, injected into the French, would turn out to be salutary or noxious; 'Un Bilan artistique de 1913', *La Revue de Paris*, 1 December 1913, pp. 517–34.

audience at the premiere had laughed, loudly and out loud; but why? Were they bored, irritated, dumbfounded or derisive, or were they simply unable to understand the stage goings-on? And what if the Russians, as some critics had suggested, were in fact having the last laugh, mocking the infatuations of an unassuming public?[99]

Casting a shadow over these questions and debates was the theme of primitivism. Once thought refreshing and redemptive, the Russians' Russianness was now the subject of regret. Some critics declared a sense of *déjà-vu*: they had seen enough of the Russian ballet and deemed the company incapable of renewing itself. Yet most thought the Russians had simply gone too far. To Debay, the scene of *Le Sacre* was reminiscent of Paris's Jardin d'Acclimatation, a human zoo that exhibited foreign peoples from colonized territories.[100] Gaston Carraud described a cat fight, Paul Souday a gymnastic meet in carnival costume.[101] Adolphe Boschot recalled the intended scenario:

On veut nous montrer les danses de la Russie préhistorique: on nous présente donc, pour *faire primitif*, des danses de sauvages, de Caraïbes et de Canaques . . . Imaginez des gens affublés des couleurs les plus hurlantes, de bonnets pointus et de peignoirs de bains, de peaux de bêtes ou de tuniques pourpres, gesticulant comme des possédés, qui répètent cent fois de suite le même geste: ils piétinent sur place, ils piétinent, ils piétinent, ils piétinent et ils piétinent . . . Couic: ils se cassent en deux et se saluent. Et ils piétinent, ils piétinent, ils piétinent . . . Couic: une petite vieille tombe la tête par terre et nous montre son troisième dessous . . . Et ils piétinent, ils piétinent . . . Au seconde acte, voici une délicieuse danseuse, Mlle Piltz. Le chorégraphe l'abime à plaisir: il lui déforme les jambes en la faisant rester immobile, la pointe des pieds aussi rentrée que possible. C'est hideux.[102]

[99] All the Paris reviews of the premiere have been collected and translated by Truman C. Bullard, 'The First Performance of Igor Stravinsky's *Sacre du printemps*', PhD thesis, University of Rochester (1971). As Bullard notes, *Comœdia* critic Gaston de Pawlowski (31 May 1913, p. 1) responded vehemently to the claim that the Russians had set out to ridicule their French fans: 'Se moquer du public? C'est la phrase que l'on entend en pareille circonstance et je n'en connais guère qui soit plus péniblement stupide. Quel est, je vous le demande, l'artiste digne de ce nom et même quel est le plus vil commerçant d'un art qui songerait jamais à se moquer du public? Quelle contradiction, quel défi au bons sens!' However, according to Pawlowski's *Comœdia* colleague Louis Vuillemin, rumours of Russian contempt circulated prior to the premiere: '"Prenons garde", prévenaient les sceptiques. On se prépare tout simplement à se payer nos oreilles! On nous prend pour des crétins. Défendons-nous!"' See Vuillemin, 'Le Sacre du printemps', *Comœdia*, 31 May 1913, p. 2.

[100] Debay, 'Les Ballets Russes', p. 141. For more on the Jardin and its ethnographic exhibits, see William H. Schneider, *An Empire for the Masses: The French Popular Image of Africa* (Westport, CT: Greenwood, 1982).

[101] Gaston Carraud, 'Au Théâtre des Champs-Élysées', *La Liberté*, 31 May 1913, p. 3; Paul Souday, 'Le Sacre du printemps', *L'Éclair*, 31 May 1913, p. 2.

[102] Adolphe Boschot, 'La Musique, *Le Sacre du printemps*', *L'Écho de Paris*, 30 May 1913, p. 6.

(They want to show us the dances of prehistoric Russia: so, in order to conjure the primitive, they present to us dances of savages, of the Caribees and the Kanaks ... Imagine people decked out in the most garish colours, pointed bonnets and bathrobes, animal skins or purple tunics, gesturing like the possessed, who repeat the same gesture a hundred times: they stamp the ground, they stamp, they stamp, they stamp and they stamp ... Suddenly: they break in two and salute. And they stamp, they stamp, they stamp ... Suddenly: a little old woman falls down headfirst and bares her underskirts ... And they stamp, they stamp ... In the second act, here is a delicious dancer, Mademoiselle Piltz. The choreographer destroys her at will: he deforms her legs by making her stand still with her toes turned in as far a possible. It is hideous.)

To the Parisian audience, decked in their material finery, seated in the amaranth- and gold-coloured auditorium, this ritual presentation of pre-civilized man – 'ces balbutiements d'une humanité demi-sauvage' (these stammerings of a semi-savage humanity)[103] – was almost inhumane.[104] The ballet lacked any identifiable ethical or moral purpose; even the sacrifice of the 'Chosen One', purportedly a celebration of life through death, was de-sentimentalized, devoid of thought and feeling.[105] It was not only the scenario that conveyed this darker side of primitivism.[106] Boschot underlined the feral force of the dancing, its manic repetitiousness, unnatural contortions and back-to-basics gestural vocabulary. He went on to invoke a similar brutishness about Stravinsky's score, describing 'une musique sauvage', 'déconcertante et désagréable', 'éminemment *amusical*'.[107]

The cohering idea – of aesthetic decomposition – echoed loudly within the press. The majority of critics agreed: whilst the ballet scenario reduced the (com)passion of life to its essential and defining elements (birth, death), both Nijinsky and Stravinsky had stripped their respective contributions of psychology and subjectivism, as well as conventional style and syntax. The choreographer 'decomposed' physical movement, deforming the dancing body in the process: choreography was limited to heavy stomping, quasi-automatic flinching, swaggers, swoons and jumps; classical poses were contradicted by knock-kneed angularity and asymmetry. As for Stravinsky, his music exhibited matching deconstructive features, from its non-conventional form and

---

[103] These words are from a press release published in *Le Figaro*, 29 May 1913, p. 6.

[104] To quote Perros, 'Après les Ballets Russes': 'Trop d'impulsion, pas de vérité, pas de mesure, pas de goût, en un mot pas de civilisation.' Perros concluded his article by hailing the 'véritable supériorité' of French art and culture, its 'intelligence' and 'exquise sensibilité'. The Russians, he argued, had these qualities yet to learn.

[105] On this point, see Jacques Rivière, 'Le Sacre du printemps', *La Nouvelle Revue française*, 1 November 1913, pp. 706–30.

[106] For a sophisticated account of primitivism in relation to art-historical aesthetics, see Hal Foster, 'The "Primitive" Unconscious of Modern Art', *October*, 34 (1985), pp. 45–70.

[107] Boschot, 'La Musique', p. 6.

tonality, through its lack of thematic recall and preparation, to its raw, pulsating rhythms synchronized to stage movement. Boschot spoke of music like noise; Pawlowski described primitive onomatopoeia.[108] According to Carl Van Vechten, the audience heard in Stravinsky's score no less than the destruction of music as art.[109]

This was a serious allegation, and one that was made against the ballet as a whole. *Le Sacre du printemps* challenged the conception and realization of art, throwing into question all matters of representation and mimesis, expression and communication, craftsmanship, intentionality and beauty. Jacques Rivière, in one of the most detailed and thoughtful reviews, spoke positively of this challenge. Describing both the sociological and biological significance of the ballet, Rivière applauded 'le renoncement à la sauce' (the renunciation of sauce) – the stripping away of the superfluous, the atmospheric, the incidental and impressionistic.[110] Yet this 'renoncement' had exposed the raw materials of ballet, had turned music and dance against the signifying functions they had formerly fulfilled. To the angry audience inside the theatre, ballet had become 'blasphemous', synonymous with the 'abuse of art'.[111] *Le Figaro*'s Alfred Capus envisaged the Théâtre des Champs-Élysées as a place of execution, a place where torture was inflicted with prehistoric cruelty.[112]

From *cosmopolitisme* through *primitivisme*

These accounts of *Le Sacre* furnish an idea about art – itself conspicuous within the mass of journalistic criticism – that follows directly from our discussion of belle-époque cultural politics. Capus, in the article quoted above, joins the dots: he begins by commenting on the tension provoked by the Ballets Russes during their 'seizure' of Paris; he describes this seizure in military terms, imagining border-incidents, frontiers and the company's armed camp; he goes on to report the impotence of the Parisian public in the face of Russian occupation; he recalls the Russians' cabalistic manner and

---

[108] *Ibid.*; and Gaston de Pawlowski, 'Au Théâtre de Champs-Élysées: *Le Sacre du printemps*', *Comœdia*, 31 May 1913, p. 1.

[109] Carl Van Vechten, *Music after the Great War* (New York: Schirmer, 1915), pp. 87–8 at p. 87.

[110] See Rivière, '*Le Sacre du printemps*', p. 706. Rivière was not alone in his positive response to the ballet. Léon Vallas, Cyril Beaumont and Florent Schmitt praised Stravinsky's music for its genius, originality and futuristic appeal; and almost all critics applauded the high standard of dance performance (although some rejected the 'dance' descriptor, preferring the terms 'movement' and 'manoeuvre').

[111] See Van Vechten, *Music after the Great War*, p. 87.

[112] Alfred Capus, 'Courrier de Paris', *Le Figaro*, 2 June 1913, p. 1.

their annihilation of art; and he concludes by recommending that a peace treaty is signed in order to ensure the rights and privileges of both parties.

To put this in other words: from Parisian *cosmopolitisme* through Russian *primitivisme*, the Ballets Russes were invested with cultural, social and aesthetic significance: Romain Rolland, French novelist and critic, described 'le miroir magnifique de nos puissances et de nos faiblesses, de nos espoirs et de nos terreurs' (the magnificent mirror of our strengths and weaknesses, our hopes and fears).[113] More than this, the company was a metaphor for invasion, and not only the literal invasion of Parisian society by seemingly dangerous and destructive foreigners. The Russians invaded the sanctified space of art itself, initiating an aesthetic revolution of which they were both the heroes and the villains. Their alleged intuition, irrationalism and higher spiritual 'truth' had first brought fame and full crowds; but then there was the dark side, the spectre of man's primeval origins, the possibility of degeneration. When darkness eclipsed the meaning and function of art – when only the raw materials, the faintest outlines, remained – critics cried 'sacrilège!'. These critics did not need to spell out the association, for the general perception amongst the European intelligentsia was that Russia, part of the mysterious East, was destined to break, in both aesthetic and moral terms, from a patriarchal authority that issued from the West. Russian *primitivisme*, then, was inevitably unstable, reactionary; it was bound to stir up contemporary debates about the status and supremacy of Western art.

In the following pages I should like to continue to envisage the Russian company as an invasive force – no longer in the literal terms (the armies, borders and frontiers) of Capus, but in the metaphorical terms of the creative or compositional process. This process resulted in the production of a number of ballets all of which, like *Le Sacre*, brought new insights to bear on the relation between music and dance, and on the conceptualization of works of art.

Tripatouillage

According to Vuillermoz, writing about *L'Après-midi d'un faune*: 'l'idée qu'un des chers barbares moscovites allait toucher au précieux prélude

---

[113] Romain Rolland, *La Vie de Léon Tolstoï* (Paris: Hachette, 1911), p. 4. Rolland's description is actually of the novels of Tolstoy, rather than the ballets of Diaghilev's company. But both share a similar history: first, 'invading' France and achieving critical and popular success; second, facing French 'counter-attack' and criticism of their influence. For these terms and more, see F. J. Hemmings, *The Russian Novel in France, 1884–1914* (Oxford University Press, 1950). Incidentally, it is not only the Russian novel and the Russian ballet that can be historicized in this way. Russian painting was also welcomed then worried over: see, for example, *Apollinaire on Art*, ed. LeRoy C. Breunig, trans. Susan Suleiman (New York: Viking Press, 1972), p. 394.

debussyste était secrètement désagréable' (the idea that one of those dear Moscovite barbarians was going to meddle with Debussy's precious prelude was secretly disturbing).[114] Here in a 1912 article for *Revue musicale S.I.M.*, Vuillermoz acknowledged a general anxiety about the ballet, one that arose prior to the production and betrayed ingrained critical concerns. Two of these will be familiar: concern for the identity and integrity of specifically French art; and concern for the nature and extent of Russian ('barbarian') influence. According to Camille Mauclair in a contemporary piece for *Le Courrier musical*, Nijinsky's choreography for *Faune* was bound to run into problems: the Russian dancer, by dint of birth and biology, was incapable of realizing the fundamentally French aesthetics of Debussy and Mallarmé.[115]

There was a third concern. As discussed in the previous chapter of this book, *Faune* provoked a torrent of press criticism for its seemingly dissociated and dissonant choreography. Nijinsky, critics complained, had deliberately ignored Debussy's music, preferring to work against the score, to counteract its *legato* lyricism with angular and asymmetrical gestures. Yet lurking beneath this complaint was a broader and more basic issue. As Vuillermoz made clear, the very thought of Nijinsky's contribution – whatever the reality of its physical form – was enough to induce anxiety, and this was not only because of the choreographer's Russianness (and any attendant 'primitivist' associations) or the composer's status as the pre-eminent French composer. It had to do with the more mundane matter of fiddling.

Meddling, manipulating, jiggery-pokery: the French called this *tripatouillage*, a term that cropped up repeatedly in press reviews of the Ballets Russes and gestured primarily to their handling of music. The company often fiddled with their musical accompaniments, orchestrating piano compositions, cutting and fragmenting large-scale dramatic works, linking extracts into a patchwork backcloth. At base, though, their fiddling matched music to dance – music that was not always intended for dance performance. *Faune*, as mentioned above, was set to Debussy's 1894 symphonic prelude; but there were plenty of prior examples. *Le Festin* (1909) featured pre-existing music by Glazunov, Glinka, Musorgsky, Rimsky-Korsakov and Tchaikovsky; *Les Sylphides* (1909) borrowed from Chopin; *Cléopâtre* (1909) comprised extracts from Glazunov, Glinka, Musorgsky, Rimsky-Korsakov, Sergey Taneyev and Nikolay Tcherepnin (along with new music by Anton Arensky); *Carnaval* (1910) showcased the music of Schumann;

[114] Émile Vuillermoz, 'La Grande Saison de Paris', *Revue musicale S.I.M.*, 8/6 (1912), pp. 62–8 at p. 66.

[115] Camille Mauclair, 'Nouvelles et familières réflexions à propos des Ballets Russes', *Le Courrier musical*, 15 June 1912, pp. 358–62.

Schéhérazade (1910) was set to Rimsky-Korsakov's symphonic suite; and *Le Spectre de la rose* (1911) presented a Weber waltz (orchestrated by Berlioz).

Tripatouillage, one might argue, constituted an essential component of the Ballets Russes' creative practice, as well as their historical legacy.[116] This legacy has tended to be regarded in terms of new composition: Richard Taruskin describes the Russians' 'crucial upgrading of the role of the ballet composer';[117] Lynn Garafola writes of their 'need for new music', a need that seemingly arose from their overthrowing of choreographic conventions.[118] But the spate of ballets set to pre-composed music deserves attention. Indeed, their ubiquity and significance may be unsurprising in view of the well-known words spoken by principal choreographer Michel Fokine:

> The new ballet . . . in contradistinction to the older ballet . . . does not demand 'ballet music' of the composer as an accompaniment to dancing; it accepts music of every kind, provided only that it is good and expressive.[119]

Equally unsurprising may be critics' reactions – 'la polémique générale et passionnée'.[120] Reconceiving *musique pure* as choreographic accompaniment, promoting new expressive parameters, interpreting the intangible on stage: the Ballets Russes, according to the critical consensus, spoiled their musical selections, staining formerly abstract art with all-too-tangible visual signifiers. The impact of these signifiers – in particular, of the body – should not be underestimated. As historian Tim Armstrong has shown in his seminal study of early twentieth-century modernism, the body was a primary site of social and scientific crisis, obscurity and experiment, identified with 'lack' and thus necessitating compensatory action.[121] Sexual and erotic bodies were

---

[116] It is important to note that the Ballets Russes were not the first to attempt the practice. Before the Russians' arrival in Paris, Isadora Duncan had famously danced to *musique pure* (famously influencing Fokine in the process); see Garafola, *Diaghilev's Ballets Russes*, pp. 39–42. Diaghilev's troupe, one might argue, established the theatrical significance of the practice, influencing a long line of twentieth-century dancers and dance companies.

[117] Taruskin, 'The Antiliterary Man', p. 209.

[118] Garafola, 'Diaghilev's Musical Legacy', p. 47. Garafola adds (p. 49): 'Diaghilev's fame does not rest on the old music he recycled for choreographic use, however much this expanded the literature for ballet. Rather, it rests on the new music he brought into being.'

[119] Michel Fokine, letter to *The Times*, 6 July 1914; reprinted in Roger Copeland and Marshall Cohen (eds.), *What is Dance? Readings in Theory and Criticism* (Oxford University Press, 1983), p. 260.

[120] See Svétlow, *Le Ballet contemporain*, pp. 115–18.

[121] Tim Armstrong, *Modernism, Technology and the Body: A Cultural Study* (Cambridge University Press, 1998). Armstrong writes of a 'revolution in perceptions of the body in the nineteenth century', noting not only developments in medical technology, but the emergence of Darwinian science, degeneration theory, psychophysics and psychoanalysis, and the capitalist fantasy of the 'complete' body (pp. 2–3). 'Modernism', he goes on, 'is characterized by the desire to *intervene* in the body; to render it part of modernity by techniques which may be biological, mechanical, or behavioural' (p. 6).

particularly threatening, iconic not only of raw physicality and bare flesh, but of marketable merchandise. The body was absorbed into the dominant culture of commodity fetishism, conceptualized as goods for sale; the prostituted body became an allegory of modernity, a pure commodity.[122] Considered in this context, the bodies of the Ballets Russes may have assumed Dionysian symbolism, smeared pre-existing music with associations of irrationality, carnal passion and excess. More than this, these bodies were doing the penetrating themselves – penetrating the surface of the musical 'body', mining the aesthetic interior for nuggets of expressive possibility. Perhaps they were even 'prostituting' the musical works, exalting not only the loss of musical autonomy, independence and purpose, but the transformation of music into material commodity.

Whatever the case, critics were enraged, as Vuillermoz reported: 'Nos critiques puristes se scandalisèrent bruyamment du sans-gêne de ces enfants terribles qui, dans leurs jeux barbares, ne respectaient pas les conventions musicales les plus sacrées' (Our purist critics were extremely shocked at the lack of consideration shown by these 'enfants terribles' who, in their barbaric games, had not respected the most sacred musical conventions).[123] Vuillermoz himself looked quite favourably on the Russian adaptations, praising the company for overturning the usual balletic hierarchy – which placed composers and their music on the bottom rung of the ladder. In a 1912 article for *Musica*, he explained:

Par un illogisme absurde, n'avons-nous pas trop souvent jusqu'ici subordonné la pensée du compositeur à l'étroite gymnastique du danseur? Humble servante des conventions chorégraphiques les plus saugrenues, la musique de danse, n'était-elle pas descendue chez nous à un degré un peu trop humiliant? Nous aurions mauvaise grâce à leur [les Ballets Russes] reprocher trop amèrement d'avoir brisé quelques barreaux de la prison où nous languissons.[124]

(By means of an absurd illogic, have we not too often until now subordinated the thoughts of the composer to the stringent demands of the dancer? Humble servant of the most ludicrous choreographic conventions, had our dance music not fallen to a level a little too humiliating? We would have bad manners to reproach them [the Ballets Russes] too bitterly for having broken a few of the bars of the prison in which we languish.)

---

[122] See Christine Buci-Glucksmann, 'Catastrophic Utopia: The Feminine as Allegory of the Modern', *Representations*, 14 (1986), pp. 220–9.

[123] Émile Vuillermoz, 'Les Ballets Russes', *Musica-Noël* (1912), p. 257.

[124] *Ibid*. Svétlow, though less enthusiastic than Vuillermoz, tried to make excuses for the Russians. If only there were more contemporary composers able and willing to write for ballet, he argued, then the Ballets Russes would no longer have to resort to music not composed with dancing in mind. See his *Le Ballet contemporain*, p. 118.

Yet reproach, in the main, they did – and in the most aggressive and excessive of terms: 'trahison' (treachery), 'injure', 'abus', 'mutilations sur mutilations'.[125] The Russian ballet had not only taken excessive liberties: they had falsified the sense and expression of music; they had betrayed the composer. This last point was particularly difficult to digest. Adapting *musique pure* for dance perform-ance was tantamount to blasphemy; *tripatouillage* signalled a refusal to honour and respect the composer, a selfish disdain for his authorial intentions. Even Vuillermoz, who had praised the practice in 1912, came round to this way of thinking. In a 1913 review of the *saison russe*, Vuillermoz deplored the seem-ingly criminal calculations of the troupe, especially those of Nijinsky: 'Nijinsky a péché contre Debussy . . . avec la même insouciance des droits les plus sacrés du compositeur' (Nijinsky sinned against Debussy . . . and with the same lack of concern for the most sacred rights of the composer).[126] Dancing to non-dance music represented a new kind of artistic warfare, and one from which music – especially the music of French composers – needed protection.

Metaphors of invasion

Here we confront the metaphor of invasion identified earlier: the invasion of art itself, of its integrity, autonomy, its aesthetic condition and purpose. For it was not only *Le Sacre du printemps* that appeared to defy the established doctrine of the arts; the Ballets-Russes productions set to pre-existing non-dance music posed a similar threat, penetrating the membrane of musical works, contesting the supremacy of authorial intentions. Indeed, it is irresis-tible to link the practice of *tripatouillage* to the literal invasion already outlined: Russian forces creep into French territory, infiltrating society, culture and art; French critics fear foreign influence, issuing calls for order, discipline and national protection. The affinity between scenarios is instructive. It alerts us to the interdependence of cultural-political and aesthetic-intellectual thinking: the shared anxieties about penetration and identity. And it leads us towards a diagnosis of the modernist 'self'. The nation, the society, the individual; the bodies on stage and the musical works to which they danced: all were open to outside forces, their surfaces and boundaries vulnerable to aggressive inter-vention. This conceptualization of identity even extended to the human

---

[125] See, for example, René Chalupt, 'Les Ballets Russes', *L'Occident*, 115 (June 1912), pp. 229–33.
[126] Émile Vuillermoz, 'La Saison russe au Théâtre des Champs-Élysées', *Revue musicale S.I.M.*, 15 June 1913, pp. 49–56. In a recent article, Hanna Järvinen suggests that Nijinsky's choreography for *Faune* may have emphasized the choreographer's authorial signature, thus turning the ballet into a new kind of choreographic 'work'; see her 'Dancing without Space: On Nijinsky's *L'Après-midi d'un faune* (1912)', *Dance Research*, 27/1 (2009), pp. 28–64.

sciences, coinciding with the development of germ theory and the discovery of bacteria – external agents, small but prolific, penetrating the body. In fact, the medical discourse on bacteria bore a remarkable semantic similarity to contemporary press commentary on Paris's foreign artists. Here, for example, is the German physician Robert Koch:

[Bacteria] creep around and live off the marrow of the army even in times of peace; but once the torch of war blazes, and then they creep out from their crevices, raise their heads to a colossal height, and destroy everything that is in the way. Proud armies have often been decimated, even destroyed, by epidemics; wars and thus the fate of peoples have been decided by them.[127]

And here is French critic Louis Laloy:

L'invasion des barbares est toujours à craindre. Les plus redoutables ne sont pas ceux qui contiennent les frontières. Les barbares de l'art sont parmi nous. Ni leur costume ne les distingue, ni leur langage, à part quelques incorrections. Ils nous observent depuis longtemps et d'abord ont ri de nos folles équipées avec la masse ignorante dont ils étaient les sentinelles avancées. Puis ils se sont approchés, enhardis, ont vu un butin de renommée qu'on oubliait dans l'ardeur de la bataille; leur convoitise s'est éveillée, et voilà qu'ils se sont glissés dans l'arène et se proclament artistes à leur tour.[128]

(The invasion of the barbarians is always to be feared. The most fearsome are not those who control the borders. The barbarians of art are amongst us. Neither their dress nor their speech, bar a few mistakes, distinguishes them. They have been observing us for a long time and at first they laughed at our silly antics along with the masses, who were unaware that they were our front-line guards. Then they drew closer, gained in courage, saw the opportunity for fame that we had forgotten in the heat of the battle; their covetousness was aroused, and *voilà*, they crept into the arena and now declare their turn to be artists.)

Bad press

The Ballets Russes and bacteria? The comparison may be a useful hyperbole: useful because it points to a relatively unknown aspect of the Ballets Russes

---

[127] Quoted in Christoph Gradmann, 'Invisible Enemies: Bacteriology and the Language of Politics in Imperial Germany', *Science in Context*, 13 (2000), pp. 9–30 at p. 25. For more on the discourse of bacteriology, including its broader historical resonance, see Laura Otis, *Membranes: Metaphors of Invasion in Nineteenth-Century Literature, Science and Politics* (Baltimore, MD: The Johns Hopkins University Press, 1999).

[128] Louis Laloy, 'Article critique concernant *L'Histoire de la Musique* de Camille Mauclair', *Comœdia* (1914); clipping, F-Pn, Ro 6019. Readers may also recall the 'parasite' references in earlier quotations from Barrès and Lefèvre.

and their French reception. As discussed more than once in this book, we have long luxuriated over the Russian troupe; its dancers and ballets are objects of our adoration. And we adore them still, happily paying a small fortune for a spin-off scarf, replica jewellery or a calendar of portrait prints. (I think particularly of the products on offer at the 2010–11 Diaghilev exhibition at the V&A Museum, London, including an Erdem Moralioglu limited-edition silk scarf, based on Ballets-Russes sketches by Bakst. Priced at £185, the scarf featured in *Harper's Bazaar*, the magazine thus continuing the long association between the company and the fashion press.) Our adoration has a long history, one that betrays the full force of Western ideology – at least, of some of its most salient cultural constructs. Cosmopolitanism, primitivism and (let's not forget) exoticism: each helped shape the reception of the Russian company, contributing to that company's 'fetish' status in the cultural consciousness.

Of course, the usual history – the story of infatuation and craze, of Parisian audiences enamoured by Russian art and culture – has been well documented by scholars. But there may be another story to tell, a story of anxiety, fear and hostile take-over – or, to quote Vuillermoz, of a decapitated statue, a broken mirror, a tear in the rug:

Enfin seuls! Nos hôtes turbulents sont partis après affolé, émerveillé et exaspéré Paris. Comme des maîtres de maison qui ont donné à danser et qui, après avoir reconduit les derniers couples, rentrent dans leurs salons bouleversés, nous nous regardons avec un peu d'effarement et de lassitude. Les invités furent exquis mais ils ont commis quelques dégâts: voici une statuette décapitée, une glace brisée, une soierie tachée et voici un accroc au tapis. Les Russes ont passé là, tout est ruine et deuil dans les salons de l'esthétique française.[129]

(Alone at last! Our wild guests, after maddening, overwhelming and exasperating Paris, have now departed. Like those hosts who, having given a dance and sent the last couples to the door come back to view their disarrayed rooms, we gaze at one another in bewilderment and weariness. The guests were delightful but they did some damage: here is a decapitated statue, a broken mirror, a stain in the silk, and here is a tear in the rug. The Russians have come our way, and now everything is in ruin and regret in the salons of the French aesthetic.)

Vuillermoz makes plain the anxiety felt by the French, as well as the destruction left by the Russians. Yet he also tells two stories at once. He acknowledges the allure of the Russian troupe, hinting at their popularity and influence, but he admits the duality of impression. 'The guests were delightful but they did some damage': read, the guests were fascinating but also feared.

---

[129] Vuillermoz, 'La Saison russe au Théâtre des Champs-Élysées', p. 49.

To follow Vuillermoz's lead may be to rediscover the complexities of the Russians' reception. For the press discourse surrounding the Ballets Russes was a contestatory discourse: critics engaged in praise and flattery, extolling the virtues of the Russian soul; but they also passed negative judgement, worrying over the scope and significance of Russian influence. Further study of these seemingly contradictory yet coexisting attitudes may help restore perspective, help us on our way towards a more comprehensive understanding of the historical scene. At the very least, it should be apparent that those ideological constructs mentioned above were themselves marked by oppositional tendencies. Cosmopolitanism, primitivism, exoticism: these were not unproblematic attitudes of xenophilia or straightforward expressions of desire. They generated similarly contestatory discourses, riven by ideas that pushed towards the polar opposites of belle-époque psychology: fascination for foreign art, culture and the promise of salvation; and fear of attack, degeneration and the collapse of national tradition.[130]

Vers l'erreur (conclusion)

Readers may sense something else, something larger, at stake here. For these pages on the Ballets Russes and their musical adaptations are provocative: they teeter on the edge of some of the most notorious – and notoriously loaded – issues of art and its ontology.

Abusing originals, sinning against authors, ignoring intentions in favour of bold, new interpretations: these were the charges brought against the Ballets Russes for their danced reworkings of *musique pure*. But not only the Ballets Russes came under fire. The *tripatouillage* phenomenon embraced a variety of musical activities, from restaging opera and reseating the orchestra, to editing, orchestrating, transcribing, recording and even relocating the music of J. S. Bach to the concert hall. According to critics of the period, these activities were increasing in number, and dangerously so. To quote Victor Debay in a 1912 article suggestively titled 'Vers l'erreur':

---

[130]   Two studies that focus specifically on the dualities embedded in the historical mindset are: Susan J. Navarette, *The Shape of Fear: Horror and the Fin de Siècle* (Lexington: University Press of Kentucky, 1998); and David Evans and Kate Griffiths (eds.), *Pleasure and Pain in Nineteenth-Century French Literature and Culture* (New York: Rodopi, 2008). Readers may also wish to consult Gundula Kreuzer's *Verdi and the Germans: From Unification to Third Reich* (Cambridge University Press, 2010), a book that tackles head-on the role of foreign cultures in creating and preserving national identities.

Nous vivons en des temps singuliers où il semble qu'en toutes choses on ait perdu la notion des convenances, des proportions et de la mesure ... Il y a, en ce moment, complot contre la sûreté de l'Art. Dans tous les genres règne la confusion.[131]

(We are living in remarkable times in which it seems that in everything we have lost the notion of propriety, proportion and moderation ... There is, at the moment, conspiracy against the security of Art. In all genres there is confusion.)

Debay began his article – a survey of 'le sabotage français' – by discussing the trend for dancing to non-dance music, as exemplified by the Ballets Russes (and by the solo Russian dancer Natalia Trouhanova). Where, he asked, would this end?

Quelque jour les fugues de Bach ou les chorals d'orgue de César Franck nous seront chorégraphiquement représentés.[132]

(One day the fugues of Bach or the organ chorales of César Franck will be represented choreographically.)

Next he turned to reorchestrations of Beethoven – acts of vandalism, he thought. And what was the point?

En tous cas, le sentiment exprimé par l'auteur n'y est plus. Si habile que soit la correction, il y aura toujours lieu de lui préférer la version originale dont un siècle a consacré la valeur et la signification.[133]

(In all cases, the feeling expressed by the author is no longer present. However skilful the correction, we will always prefer the original version, that which has acquired a century's worth of value and significance.)

According to Albert Bertelin, preferring the original was hardly the issue. Composers simply did not have the right to fiddle with other composers' works:

[Un] compositeur contemporain, même génial, a-t-il le droit de porter la main sur des œuvres consacrées? Peut-il y faire les modifications qu'il juge nécessaire pour les rajeunir, pour leur donner en quelque sorte une vie nouvelle? Sans hésiter, je réponds non; il n'est pas plus admissible de réorchestrer, même très discrètement, une symphonie classique que de repeindre une toile de Van Dyck ou de Rembrandt sous le fallacieux prétexte que les couleurs en sont ternies.[134]

---

[131] Victor Debay, 'Vers l'erreur', *Le Courrier musical*, 15 May 1912, pp. 290–3.
[132] *Ibid.*, p. 291.   [133] *Ibid.*
[134] Albert Bertelin, 'Restauration et réorchestration', *Le Courrier musical*, 15 February 1910, pp. 138–9 at p. 138. Bertelin concluded by recommending a hands-off approach: 'De tout ceci il résulte que le plus sage est de ne point toucher, même avec des mains pieuses, aux chefs-d'œuvre que nous ont légués les siècles précédents.'

(A contemporary composer, even a great one, has he the right to raise his hand to hallowed works? Can he make the changes that he considers necessary to bring the works up to date, to give them a kind of new life? Without hesitation, I say no; it is no more acceptable to reorchestrate, even very discreetly, a classical symphony than it is to repaint a canvas by Van Dyck or Rembrandt under the fallacious pretext that the colours have faded.)

Debay worried especially about opera. Discussing Reynaldo Hahn's recent production of Mozart's *Don Juan* at the Opéra-Comique, he grumbled about the singers:

[Ils] ont, par leur inexpérience, par leur ignorance et par leur insuffisance, trahi un chef-d'œuvre.[135]

([They] have, because of their inexperience, their ignorance and their insufficiency, betrayed a masterwork.)

Hahn, it seems, had wanted to restore 'le vrai Mozart', directing the orchestra with a precision and delicacy appropriate to the classical style. But his singers were incapable of sustaining Mozart's phrases, let alone portraying the complexities of dramatic character. Moreover, and according to critic Jean d'Udine, opera singers were taking liberties with the score, shamelessly showing off with seemingly spontaneous dramatic effects rather than adhering to the music's notated form.[136] Gaston Carraud looked upon this same tendency as an unfortunate consequence of the divided agency of operatic production:

Autour de la représentation d'un opéra s'agitent deux cent personnes; et chacune d'elles s'arroge le droit d'en tirer à soi quelque lambeau. Car chacune ne voit dans l'opéra qu'un prétexte à produire avantageusement son individu, et tient l'auteur, fût-il un maître, pour un niais, incapable de lui ménager ses avantages. Le dernier des musiciens de l'orchestre lui démontrera qu'il ne connaît rien à l'orchestre; le dernier des chanteurs, rien aux voix . . . L'auteur, pour tous ces gens-là, c'est l'ennemi.[137]

(Around the production of an opera there are two hundred people; and everyone claims the right to a piece of it. Because everyone regards opera as only a pretext for their individual performance, and they regard the author, even a great one, as a simpleton, incapable of showcasing their talents. The last of the orchestral players will show him that he knows nothing about the orchestra; the last of the singers, nothing about voices . . . The author, for these people, is the enemy.)

---

[135] Debay, 'Vers l'erreur', p. 292.

[136] Jean d'Udine, 'Artistes et interprètes', *Le Courrier musical*, 15 July 1911, pp. 494–6. According to d'Udine, opera singers were not 'artistes': they were mere 'interprètes', and not particularly sensitive ones at that.

[137] Gaston Carraud, 'Tripatouillages', *Le Courrier musical*, 15 March 1913, pp. 153–61 at pp. 154–5.

What are we to make of these reports? The critical backlash against *tripatouillage* was not, of course, new to the period; neither was critics' advocacy of a selfless and submissive obedience to the score, whether in performance or any other mode of musical realization. (Recall the words of Francesco Geminiani, 1749: 'Playing in good taste doth not consist of frequent Passages, but in expressing with strength and delicacy the Intention of the Composer.'[138] Or this anonymous critic, over one hundred years later: 'If you want to arrange, then leave things be. Your only goal is to capture – without unnecessary colouration – the impression of the original, whilst ensuring that you are forgotten as much as possible.'[139]) *Tripatouillage* itself was not new, the act of transcription being perhaps the oldest form of fiddling.[140] Moreover, and as recent scholars have shown, musicians throughout the nineteenth century variously reworked the musical work, at the very time that 'work' assumed definitive, text-bound form.[141] For example, and according to Jonathan Kregor, Franz Liszt was renowned not only for his virtuoso performance (based on extemporization rather than adherence to a pre-composed score); he also raised the status of the transcriber to that of a fully fledged artist on a par with the composer.[142] James Q. Davies has described how dancers in London and Paris created 'Dramatic Concerts', dancing to Beethoven's *Pastoral* Symphony in an attempt to 'secure the abstractions of the concert hall in a visual or gestural way'.[143] Clearly, this last example is of particular significance in the present context. Although Davies suggests that the trend for dancing to non-dance music soon disappeared, the history – and legacy – of the Ballets Russes suggests quite the contrary.

Indeed, the Ballets-Russes productions set to pre-existing music may be fully expressive of their context; for what was new in the early twentieth century was a sense of *tripatouillage* run amok. Debay, above, suggests as

[138] Francesco Geminiani, *Treatise of Good Taste in the Art of Music* (London: n.p., 1749; facsimile Wyton: King's Music, 1988), p. 2.

[139] 'Arrangements und Transcriptionen, *Leipziger Allgemeine musikalische Zeitung*, 26 January 1876, p. 52.

[140] A comprehensive history of transcription, from the fifteenth to the late twentieth centuries, can be found in Silke Leopold (ed.), *Musikalische Metamorphosen: Formen und Geschichte der Bearbeitung* (Kassel: Bärenreiter, 1992).

[141] On the emergence of a work concept, see Lydia Goehr, *The Imaginary Museum of Musical Works: An Essay in the Philosophy of Music* (1992; rev. edn Oxford University Press, 2007); for a summary account, see Jim Samson, 'The Musical Work and Nineteenth-Century History', in Samson (ed.), *The Cambridge History of Nineteenth-Century Music* (Cambridge University Press, 2002), pp. 3–28.

[142] Jonathan Kregor, *Liszt as Transcriber* (Cambridge University Press, 2010).

[143] James Q. Davies, 'Dancing the Symphonic: Beethoven-Bochsa's *Symphonie Pastorale*, 1829', *19th-Century Music*, 27/1 (2003), pp. 25–47 at p. 26.

much, singling out the historical moment for its conspiracy against 'Art'. Louis Vierne, in an article aptly titled, 'La Transcriptomanie', speaks similarly, describing the contemporary tendency towards disfigurement and excess.[144] Then there is Carraud. His article, quoted above, maintains the standard critical ideology of merely obedient performance, advocating fidelity to authorial intentions. Yet the critic imagines the exact opposite, a practical reality of interpretation in which selfless subservience to the composer – or any kind of spiritual communion – is overlooked. Carraud's final words – 'the author is enemy' – are particularly evocative, not least for their resonance with the single most seminal account of authorship in the modern period. Roland Barthes's 1967 essay 'The Death of the Author', a theoretical outline for literary criticism, famously locates the origin of the anti-authorial impulse in precisely the period in question here.[145] More specifically, Barthes speaks of Mallarmé and his famous remarks on compositional aesthetics, remarks that extolled the disappearance of the poet-speaker and the power of language, the anonymous unravelling words, to explain itself.[146] With this literary context in mind, Carraud's comments, and those others quoted here, acquire special salience: they point, quite unambiguously, to the literal underpinnings of this anti-authorialism – the casting aside of the author and his intentions, and the promotion of interpretive intervention.

One might argue that the aesthetic will-to-impersonality endorsed by Mallarmé, and of defining significance to Barthesian philosophy, is lacking in this analogy: the critics quoted above describe the exact opposite, a will-to-personality shared by opera singers, musicians, dancers, transcribers and others engaged in the business of adaptation. Yet the disappearance of the author, in all cases, looms large, and suggests something of the separability of art from its original and conceiving force. More specifically, one might describe a newly elastic conception of art itself, one that serves to question the nineteenth-century 'work' concept, as well as the economics of representation, the rules of aesthetic appropriateness, the ownership of art, the policing of adaptation, the influence of modernity and the relation of art to its audience. Examples of this conceptual 'elasticity' – across a range of contemporary art – abound. One need only recall the Futurist mandate for the 'Variety Theatre' ('Systematically prostitute all of classic art on the

---

[144] Louis Vierne, 'La Transcriptomanie', *Le Courrier musical*, 15 November 1911, pp. 679–81.

[145] Roland Barthes, 'The Death of the Author', in *Image-Music-Text*, trans. and ed. Stephen Heath (London: Fontana, 1977), pp. 142–8.

[146] *Ibid.*, p. 143: 'In France, Mallarmé, no doubt the first, saw and foresaw in all its scope the necessity to substitute language itself for the subject hitherto supposed to be its owner; for Mallarmé, as for us, it is language which speaks, not the author.' See Stéphane Mallarmé, 'Crisis in Verse', in T. G. West (trans. and ed.), *Symbolism: An Anthology* (London: Methuen, 1980), pp. 1–12.

stage');[147] the 'readymade' *Roue de bicyclette* (Bicycle wheel) by Marcel Duchamp ('Can one make works which are not works of "art"?');[148] the 'incompréhensible' *Embryons desséchés* (Dried-out embryos), a collection of piano pieces by Erik Satie (designed to mock the tradition of musical titles);[149] and, no less, the stealing of the *Mona Lisa* by the Italian carpenter Vincenzo Perugia (ostensibly in order to forge and sell copies).[150] This last example has an interesting history: during the period in which the painting was missing from its home at the Louvre, crowds flocked to see not the painting, of course, but its absence – the space on the wall where it had hung, the negative space of art.[151]

Futurist theatre, Duchamp's wheel, Satie's embryos and the theft of the Mona Lisa: each may be 'read' as a metaphor for the dissolution of the 'work' of art; or, for the emergence of a new creative nebula – a formless space, without clearly defined boundaries, drained of proprietary rights, essentially contestatory yet intensively transformative. The Ballets Russes' danced adaptations may be similar metaphors – and similarly embroiled in a contemporary debate about art, what it means, why it is created and how we respond to it. My next chapter will address a specific – and specifically generic – aspect of this debate. Focusing on the last of the Russians' pre-war adaptations, an example of *tripatouillage* writ large, I shall explore its reasons for being, its reception and the extent to which it resonates across the French theatrical scene.

[147] F. T. Marinetti, 'The Variety Theatre' (1913); repr. in Richard Drain (ed.), *Twentieth-Century Theatre: A Sourcebook* (London: Routledge, 1995), pp. 171–4 at p. 173.

[148] Marcel Duchamp, 1913; see *The Writings of Marcel Duchamp*, ed. Michel Sanouillet and Elmer Peterson (Oxford University Press, 1973), p. 74. Duchamp's *Roue* (1913) is lost; a replica, based on the original and constructed by Duchamp himself, is housed in the Museum of Modern Art, New York.

[149] See Mary E. Davis, *Erik Satie* (London: Reaktion Books, 2007), pp. 86–7.

[150] On the theft and the ensuing investigation, see the thriller-cum-social-history by Dorothy and Thomas Hoobler, *The Crimes of Paris: A True Story of Murder, Theft, and Detection* (Boston, MA: Little, Brown and Company, 2009). French crime fiction of the period also engaged with the conceptualization of art, undermining the distinction between the authentic and the forged art object, whilst maintaining the irrelevance of authorship; see Emma Bielecki, 'Faking It: Representations of Art Forgery from the Second Empire to the *Belle Époque*', in Louis Hardwick (ed.), *New Approaches to Crime in French Literature, Culture and Film* (New York: Peter Lang, 2009), pp. 35–50.

[151] Darian Leader explores the psychology behind this crowd phenomenon – and what it may reveal of our relationship to art – in his *Stealing the Mona Lisa: What Art Stops Us From Seeing* (New York: Counterpoint, 2002).

5 ❧ Beyond and behind *Le Coq d'or*

The 1914 production by the Ballets Russes of Rimsky-Korsakov's opera *The Golden Cockerel* (*Le Coq d'or* to the French) holds a special position in the work's history for the peculiarities of its staging.[1] The singers, dressed in identical reddish-brown caftans and fur-trimmed caps, sat on steep ramps along the sides of the stage; dancers in costume provided the action. As a consequence, there were two of each character: one centre stage, mute but mobile; the other 'un double momifié' (a mummified double), merely one of a mixed-sex mass.[2] (Figure 5.1, from the scrapbook album compiled by the Marchioness of Ripon and devoted to the Ballets Russes, illustrates the stage scene.)

The resulting 'opéra-ballet', complete with musical cuts, contrasted dramatically with the late composer's conceptualization of the opera; it even challenged his attitude towards theatrical performance. In a letter written only months before his death in June 1908, Rimsky-Korsakov expressed concern about the gestural realization of music: 'works not intended for it do not require any mimic interpretation, and, in truth, it is powerless to interpret them. All in all, miming is not an independent kind of art and can merely accompany words or singing, but when it foists itself unbidden upon music, it only harms the latter by diverting attention from it.'[3] This same

Portions of this chapter have been presented as papers at Columbia University, University of Melbourne, University of Auckland, Victoria University of Wellington, the 2008 meeting of the Francophone Music Criticism Network (University of London Institute, Paris) and the 2010 meeting of the American Musicological Society (Indianapolis).

[1] This history is quite convoluted. The opera, to a libretto by Vladimir Belsky (based on a poem by Alexander Pushkin), was not performed during Rimsky-Korsakov's lifetime, largely owing to the composer's refusal to sanction the significant cuts called for by the Tsarist censors. (The opera's plot, though cloaked in fairy-tale imagery, was thought to poke fun at Russia's recent history – namely, the disastrous Russo-Japanese War.) The premiere of the censored version was given by the private opera company of Sergey Ivanovich Zimin at the Solodovnikov Theatre in Moscow, 7 October 1909. Soon after, the opera was staged at the Bolshoi, Moscow, and went on to become a permanent fixture in the Russian operatic repertory. It is the only one of Rimsky-Korsakov's fifteen operas to attain international popularity and prominence.

[2] See Émile Vuillermoz, 'Les Ballets Russes à l'Opéra', *Comœdia*, 26 May 1914, p. 3.

[3] Letter to S. P. Byelanovsky, January 1908; see Nikolay Rimsky-Korsakov, *My Musical Life*, trans. Judah A. Joffe (1923; repr. London: Faber and Faber, 1989), pp. 446–7. In 1900, the composer described ballet itself as 'a degenerate art'; quoted in Richard Taruskin, 'The Antiliterary Man: Diaghilev and Music', in *On Russian Music* (Berkeley and Los Angeles: University of California Press, 2009), pp. 202–13 at p. 205.

Figure 5.1 Anonymous, *Le Coq d'or* (1914).

concern for gestural interference emerged from the composer's performance directions for *Le Coq d'or*, reprinted in the score. Forbidding cuts of any kind, and describing opera as 'first and foremost a musical work', Rimsky-Korsakov asked that characters avoid 'unnecessary by-play'; the diegetic dances to be performed by the two leading characters in Act Two were not to 'interfere' with the singing.[4]

Small wonder the family complained. Still angry about Diaghilev's *Schéhérazade* four years earlier, and no doubt with the composer's words in mind, the Rimsky-Korsakovs maintained the impropriety of this choreographic *Coq d'or* – that the staging 'distorted the fundamental features of the work as an operatic composition' – and moved to ban the production from the stage.[5] Issued through the French court and backed by the Société des Auteurs, the lawsuit they prosecuted was successful. Although the result came too late to affect Diaghilev's Paris premiere and two subsequent performances, all others were subject to the approval of the family. Moreover, the court decreed that if Diaghilev had designs on future

[4] 'Composer's Remarks' (1907); see, for example, the Peters edition of the piano–vocal score, p. 4.

[5] Andrey Rimsky-Korsakov (the composer's son) expressed the family's view in the Russian journal *Apollon*, 6–7 (1914), pp. 46–8; Richard Taruskin provides a useful summary in his *Stravinsky and the Russian Traditions: A Biography of the Works through 'Mavra'*, 2 vols. (Berkeley and Los Angeles: University of California Press, 1996), vol. II, pp. 1074–5.

productions, he would have to lay down a guarantee of 3,000 francs – a financial pledge that he would uphold the rights and wishes of the composer's heirs.[6]

There is much that is beguiling about this history – much, even, that might commend *Le Coq d'or* as a final port of call for this book. Throughout these pages I have discussed the manner in which music and gesture might achieve an ideal union or synthesis; I have also pondered moments of structural or stylistic disjunction, suggesting how such moments might betray specifically modernist choreographic aesthetics. In view of these topics, *Le Coq d'or* may offer a crowning case study, an example of music and dance (and words) that issue from separate sources, that are spatially detached yet dramatically entangled. The resulting paradox – an at once dislocated yet coherent theatrical text – could doubtless inspire a range of interpretive readings, from the recently modish metaphysics of musical disembodiment (brought to mind by those almost-acousmatic voices) to the doubling-up of characters – a case, maybe, of material and abstract bodies, of the vivisection of dramatic consciousness into worldly and unworldly forms. Then there is the production's historical significance, pinned to the date of its premiere: 24 May 1914, during the Ballets Russes' final pre-war season. It is tempting to sense an aura of finality about *Le Coq d'or*, to imagine that the Russian troupe were giving the two fingers to their conservative critics, their last gesture of irreverence signalling a temporary adieu.

This irreverence, of course, points to a further avenue of investigation, one that circles back to my previous chapter. Dancing to non-dance music – an example of the wide-ranging and widespread phenomenon of *tripatouillage* (fiddling) – was standard practice within the Ballets Russes. As discussed earlier, the troupe variously reworked pre-existing music – reworked the 'work' concept itself – to the incredulity of contemporary critics. Yet, with *Le Coq d'or*, the throwing-up of critical hands led to the involvement of legal

---

[6] Details of the lawsuit were reported in *L'Écho de Paris*, 29 May 1914, p. 2, and *Gil Blas*, 29 May 1914, p. 1. Incidentally, and despite the troubles of the Paris production, *Le Coq d'or* enjoyed a successful run at the Theatre Royal, Drury Lane, London (June and July 1914); a few years later, former Ballets-Russes dancer Adolph Bolm staged his version at the Metropolitan Opera House, New York, with sets and costumes designed by the Hungarian decorative artist Willy Pogany. Continuing the run of revisions, Colonel Wassili de Basil and his 'Ballet Russe de Monte Carlo' (comprising performers from the disbanded Russian company) presented a wholly balletic version at Covent Garden, London, in 1937. On this occasion, advice was sought from one Nikolay Tcherepnin, a former pupil of Rimsky-Korsakov who had previously guarded over foreign productions of Rimsky-Korsakov's works. Tcherepnin sanctioned de Basil's production, even helping to choose the musical instruments that were to substitute for the solo singers and chorus; the score for this production, with vocal lines crossed out, is housed at US-CAh, TMC, MS Thr 465 (200).

services, to the banning of the production and the issuing of financial control. Questions immediately arise about rules of aesthetic appropriateness, how they were established and by whom; about the identity and ownership of art, particularly after an author's death; and about the wider world of theatrical practice and the ways in which legal policing impacted the conception and realization of productions in a more general sense. These questions could certainly stimulate further study, even warrant essays in themselves. But here I should prefer to focus on a specific aspect of *Le Coq d'or*'s inherent revisionism, one that may carry a broader and more compelling significance in the context of this project.[7]

Put simply, what does it mean to turn an opera into a ballet, to sideline (literally) a singing component and foreground a newly designed dancing one? What does the resulting theatrical hybrid represent historically? How was it regarded in the press? And why did it come about in the first place? This chapter will begin with these last two questions, about the conception and reception of *Le Coq d'or*. Then I shall survey broader trends and trajectories in French music criticism and theatre, situating the production in its theatrical and aesthetic contexts. The sort of 'broad brush' enquiry I attempt will substitute for a close reading of *Le Coq d'or* – of its structural, musical and dramatic content, its enticing disembodied-ness. Yet the production – the facts of its staging, the conditions of its creation, the terms with which it was recognized – remains central to my discussion. *Le Coq d'or*, I suggest, illuminates an important if little-known historical debate: a debate about theatrical aesthetics and staging practices; about singing, dancing and standards of each; and, perhaps most important, about the status and reception of opera and ballet (not to mention the curious hybrids in between) in the early twentieth century.

The origins of *Le Coq d'or*

If their memoirs are to be believed, both Alexandre Benois and Michel Fokine were the brains behind the Ballets-Russes production – though neither one credits the other. Both maintain that the staging was 'my dream', 'my idea'; both describe that dream or idea as novel and peculiar;

---

[7] This chapter may also contribute to the emerging field of musicological research into the nature and significance of operatic revisionism. Exemplary texts include Roger Parker, *Remaking the Song: Operatic Visions and Revisions from Handel to Berio* (Berkeley and Los Angeles: University of California Press, 2006); and Richard Taruskin, 'Setting Limits', in *The Danger of Music and Other Anti-Utopian Essays* (Berkeley and Los Angeles: University of California Press, 2009), pp. 447–66.

and both recognize the suitability of Rimsky-Korsakov's opera for balletic treatment, acknowledging its air of fantasy and fairy tale, as well as a general ascendance of action over psychological development.[8] (The opera, set in a pseudo-Oriental kingdom, depicts the antics of bumbling Tsar Dodon and the war he embarks upon following a premonition from his magic cockerel.)

There is an additional point of convergence. Both Benois and Fokine express concern with the aesthetics of opera: specifically, with opera's visual aspect and stage acting. According to Benois, opera can be 'a very poor spectacle'; opera singers 'have no idea of acting' and 'stalk about like bears and gesticulate aimlessly'. Ballet, in contrast, is more dramatically 'present-able'. Dancers, 'if not always beautiful, have, nevertheless, an agreeable appearance'; moreover, trained in 'expressive mime', they render all charac-ters, even the 'grotesque or hideous', with control and elegance.[9] The same cannot be said of opera singers, as Benois quipped in a later essay: 'an Isolde whom Tristan can scarcely enfold in his arms; a pot-bellied, bandy-legged Faust paying court to a massive Marguerite. The ballet excludes such visual monstrosities.'[10] Fokine was of a similar mind, also complaining of singers' 'physical handicap'. His complaints, though, were fuelled less by size-ist insult than a concern for the physiological – and physiognomical – effects of singing: 'it is impossible to sing', Fokine writes, 'without opening the mouth wide and at times a bit askew'. The act of singing, he argues, compromised a visual effect: 'vocal perfection and theatrical excellence are very seldom found in the same person.'[11]

Le Coq d'or was to offer a solution to this problem. The plan for the production – whatever the truth of its conception – was to get the singers off the stage, to get them to blend with the wings and concentrate solely on singing; then the dancers could take centre stage in communicating the drama. There was, we are told, some concern that the singers, including famous names from the Russian Imperial Opera, would not agree to their repositioning – in the words of Benois, 'to limit themselves to the part of "orchestral instruments" . . . their only function . . . to "accompany" with their voices the real performance that was taking place on the stage'.[12] But Diaghilev managed to convince, a fact perhaps unsurprising in view of the

---

[8] See Alexandre Benois, *Reminiscences of the Russian Ballet*, trans. Mary Britnieva (London: Putnam, 1941), pp. 353–7 and pp. 362–3; and Michel Fokine, *Memoirs of a Ballet Master*, ed. Anatole Chujoy, trans. Vitale Fokine (London: Constable, 1961), pp. 225–33.

[9] Benois, *Reminiscences*, pp. 354–5.

[10] Alexandre Benois, 'The Origins of the Ballets Russes' (1944); published as the preface to Boris Kochno, *Diaghilev and the Ballets Russes*, trans. Adrienne Foulke (London: The Penguin Press, 1971), pp. 2–21; quotation at pp. 16–17.

[11] Fokine, *Memoirs*, p. 231.   [12] Benois, *Reminiscences*, p. 356.

impresario's well-documented powers of persuasion: as Fokine writes, 'What sacrifices wouldn't people endure under pressure from Diaghilev?'[13]

A simple fix, then, and a simple message: of the salience of opera's visuals. What Benois's and Fokine's comments make clear is that interest in the physical appearance of theatrical performers had taken on a new urgency, audiences and critics increasingly responsive to the visual spectacle before their eyes. And performers were aware of this. Here is Frances Alda (a New Zealand-born soprano who made her debut in Paris in 1904) with words that recall those of Benois, above:

Audiences today are more critical of a singer's appearance than they used to be. They demand not only that the singer shall sing well, but that she shall look lovely and be an actress, too. No more beefy Isoldes, pudgy Carmens and bovine Violettas. Who wouldn't rather look at a slim and virginal Elsa than one who bulges unromantically?[14]

This manner of thinking may well have been symptomatic of a contemporary theatrical tendency towards sexualized, exotic-erotic plots and a performing body framed in explicitly exhibitionist terms. It also suggests something of an emerging desire for a more dramatically motivated mode of physical expression, one that broke with the stylized theatrical conventions of the past. As opera historian Susan Rutherford has argued, singers of the early twentieth century were implored to offer 'truthful', almost psychologized performances, to immerse themselves in their dramatic roles (more on this later).[15] At base, singers had to look good and act appropriately – or else they would be cast aside, literally, as the case of *Le Coq d'or* confirms.

Le Coq d'or in the press

Examining some two dozen reviews of *Le Coq d'or* in French newspapers and specialist journals reveals an undertow of controversy, fuelled by the nature of the work and the underlying attitudes of those who commented on it.

---

[13] Fokine, *Memoirs*, p. 228.

[14] Frances Alda, *Men, Women and Tenors* (Boston, MA: Houghton Mifflin, 1937), p. 299. The American soprano Geraldine Farrar made a similar confession: '[I]t is hard to nurse poetic and fantastic illusions, no matter how fine a voice is trying to convey them, when the eye is oppressed by the sight of some three hundred pounds of human *avoirdupoids*, ill-fitting costumes, wigs, awkward stage deportment or ill-timed mannerisms.' Quoted in Lanfranco Rasponi, *The Last Prima Donnas* (London: Gollancz, 1984), p. 92.

[15] Susan Rutherford, *The Prima Donna and Opera, 1815–1930* (Cambridge University Press, 2006), pp. 266–74.

As we might expect, the controversy encapsulated a moral debate: whether the Russian troupe should have danced – again, and on this occasion without permission – to one of Rimsky-Korsakov's scores. There were those, the more conservative, who spoke of 'sacrilège', 'irrespect' and 'travestissement'; and there were those who admitted a fondness for the production, praising its originality and invention.[16] Of the latter, several maintained, as did Benois and Fokine, that the opera was more than suited to its new staging; one critic even suggested that Rimsky-Korsakov's music ('facile et heureuse', 'de bonne humeur') might have inspired the creative developments.[17] In the main, though, critics oscillated between impressions. According to composer Alfred Bruneau the production went beyond the boundary of 'libertés permises'; the dissociation of voice and body deprived the music of its life, its spirit, even its comprehensibility. But still, as Bruneau added, the dancing offered 'une joie rare', and the entire production was great entertainment for those 'grands enfants' in the audience.[18] Émile Vuillermoz also swung both ways, and also noted the production's comic effect: 'Voilà évidemment une blague excellente! Et, en effet, elle est bonne! Elle est même si bonne qu'on ne sait plus si l'on doit s'indigner ou rire de bon cœur' (This is evidently an excellent joke! And, in effect, it is good! It is even so good that one doesn't know whether to be outraged or to laugh in good humour). Reminding readers of Rimsky-Korsakov's performance directions, Vuillermoz described the production as morally unspeakable yet artistically impressive: 'Moralement, le "coup" du *Coq d'or* est inqualifiable. Mais, artistiquement, il est défendable' (Morally, the 'coup' of the *Coq d'or* is unspeakable. But, artistically, it is defensible).[19]

Besides this moral debate, critics commented on Diaghilev's enduring desire to shock the Parisian audience, as well as on Fokine's choreography and the production's folkloristic and toybox-like decor, designed by Natalia Goncharova, a leading artist within the Russian avant-garde.[20] (See Figure 5.2,

[16] Louis Schneider, 'Les Premières', *Le Gaulois*, 26 May 1914, p. 4, was especially positive: 'Ce *Coq d'or* est une féerie pour les yeux, une féerie pour l'oreille, c'est la mille et deuxième nuit bouffonne.'

[17] See Jacques Rivière, 'La Musique', *La Nouvelle Revue française*, 1 July 1914, pp. 150–62 at p. 161: 'Bien que la présentation qu'il en a faite pût être considérée à certains égards comme un travestissement de l'œuvre, j'avoue y avoir pris un plaisir extrême. Et d'ailleurs la musique de Rimsky-Korsakov ne donnait-elle pas toutes les permissions? Facile et heureuse (il est vraiment étonnant que ce soit une œuvre de vieillesse), à deux doigts de la banalité, mais préservée d'y tomber par je ne sais quelle ingénuité charmante, c'est une musique de bonne humeur et qui, moins sourcilleuse que les héritiers du maître, n'a fait que sourire aux libertés qu'on a prises avec elle.'

[18] Alfred Bruneau, 'À l'Opéra', *Le Matin*, 26 May 1914, p. 4.

[19] Émile Vuillermoz, 'Les Ballets Russes à l'Opéra', *Comœdia*, 26 May 1914, p. 3.

[20] Schneider is exemplary on all points; see his 'Les Premières', p. 4.

Figure 5.2 Goncharova, *Le Coq d'or*, scene design for Act One (1914).

Goncharova's design for Act One, with seated and stationary singers framing the stage. Described as 'neoprimitive', the sets and costumes captured the style of traditional Russian icon painting and *lubok* prints.) A handful of critics also noted parallels between *Le Coq d'or* and the 1896 play by Alfred Jarry, *Ubu Roi*.[21] Both works depicted a comic hero in a dehumanized, puppet-like manner: Ubu, Jarry's title character, wore a mask and hung a model horse from his neck for equestrian scenes; Tsar Dodon went to war on a similar toy horse, carrying an over-sized sword and a huge quiver.[22]

[21] See, for example, Paul Souday, 'Les Premières', *L'Éclair*, 26 May 1914, p. 2; and G. Linor, 'Les Ballets Russes à l'Opéra: l'interprétation', *Comœdia*, 26 May 1914, p. 3. Even the Russian dancer Tamara Karsavina observed a likeness between the opera-ballet and the play; see her short piece, 'Avant le rideau', *Le Figaro*, 24 May 1914, p. 5.

[22] An additional parallel concerns the 'absurdist' effect of both opera-ballet and play; see Martin Esslin, *Theatre of the Absurd* (Garden City, NY: Doubleday, 1961). According to musicologist Marina Frolova-Walker, Rimsky-Korsakov's *Golden Cockerel* spearheaded a specifically Russian brand of absurdist and anti-psychological 'anti-opera'; see her chapter 'Russian Opera: Between Modernism and Romanticism', in Mervyn Cooke (ed.), *The Cambridge Companion to Twentieth-Century Opera* (Cambridge University Press, 2005), pp. 181–96.

But the issue of genre, so important to the production's conception, weighed heavily. The more liberal-minded reviewers expressed a desire that *Le Coq d'or* might prove successful, might even signal a new direction for music theatre. In one of his weekly pieces for the theatrical daily *Comœdia*, critic Louis Laloy hailed the production as a redemptive force, a prototype of a new theatrical aesthetic based on the superposition of musical and gestural parameters:

Pourquoi ne pas superposer ce qui, jusqu'ici ne nous était donné qu'en succession, comme on superpose dans l'orchestre les mélodies? Il semble que ce soit un progrès. Le progrès dans l'art s'accomplit toujours par combinaison, non par élimination. C'est pourquoi le théâtre de l'avenir a toute chance de se rapprocher de ce genre nouveau du ballet chanté ou parlé.[23]

(Why not superpose that which, until now, was only presented to us in succession, as we superpose melodies in the orchestra? That would seem to be a progress. Progress in art is always accomplished by means of combination, not by elimination. That is why the theatre of the future has every chance of drawing near to this new genre of sung or spoken ballet.)

Daniel Chennevière, writing in the avant-garde journal *Montjoie!*, also complimented the production, though he wondered whether its strategy of split staging would be appropriate for other pre-existing works. Chennevière added a prediction about the future of ballet, sparing no opportunity to pass judgement on opera:

Enfin, étant donné que l'opéra est un genre monstrueux et difforme, la séparation du chanteur et du mime, imaginée par Fokine, et qui fut fort bien plastiquement réalisée, est une idée heureuse. Il serait peut-être curieux de l'appliquer aux drames lyriques déjà existants: pour ce qu'est de l'avenir, je pense bien que les musiciens se rendront compte que la forme du drame chanté sur la scène, est une forme stérile et maladroite, et que nous en viendrons bien vite au drame chorégraphique abstrait.[24]

(Finally, given that opera is a grotesque and distorted genre, the separation of singer and mime, imagined by Fokine, and realized extremely well by him from a gestural standpoint, is a fine idea. It might be strange to apply it to already existing lyric dramas: as for the future, I feel certain that musicians will realize that drama sung on a stage is a sterile and clumsy form, and that we will soon turn to an abstract choreographic drama.)

Grotesque, distorted, sterile, clumsy: similar descriptions of opera were offered by prominent Russian critics. In an article defending *Le Coq d'or*

---

[23] Louis Laloy, 'La Musique chez soi', *Comœdia*, 28 May 1914, p. 3. Also see Taruskin's account of the French press in his *Stravinsky and the Russian Traditions*, vol. II, p. 1076.

[24] Daniel Chennevière, '*Le Coq d'or*', *Montjoie!*, 2/4–6 (April–June 1914), p. 22.

against a largely negative Russian press, Diaghilev's cousin and former colleague Dmitry Filosofov argued that 'opera has entered its period of degeneracy'. He went on: 'We are all surfeited to the point of nausea with [opera's] stylized realism. The singer has killed the composer, has killed theatrical action as well.'[25] Ballet enthusiast Vilenkin Nikolay Maximovich (known as 'Minsky') spoke similarly of theatrical 'illusionism'. He added his own premonition: 'I have no doubt that this time the inspirers of the Russian Ballet have hit upon a new form of theatrical art, one that has a huge future.'[26]

The abundance of similar premonitions, and from a range of sources, is striking. There is Benois, for example, who describes in his memoirs how 'our *Coq d'or* might open a new era in opera'.[27] Even Rimsky-Korsakov's son Andrey could not help his words of protest turning into prophecy:

In all probability, given Diaghilev's luck, plenty of composers will turn up, eager to adopt that ballet-cantata form. It might be that the example of *Le Coq d'or* will inspire them to works of their own on this split-level format. Good luck to them! It is high time they got started.[28]

Sarcasm aside, it is clear that the Russian production was path-breaking, almost epochal, that it was thoroughly entangled with attitudes and assumptions about music theatre. But can we be more specific? The predictions quoted above suggest in capsule form how *Le Coq d'or* was regarded as a possible model for future theatre; but they also point towards specific lines of influence. To take the two French critics: Laloy speaks expressly of superposition, of parallel singing and dancing; Chennevière refers to the future of ballet, a future that seems predicated on the demise of sung lyric drama. Chennevière thus suggests a reason behind *Le Coq*'s assumed redemption, and one that chimes with the Russian response. But what was the general feeling amongst the French? Was opera really sterile and outmoded? And what of ballet? Was it widely regarded as the theatre of the future? Then there is the method of superposition, of simultaneous singing and dancing, of voices wrenched from bodies on stage. How pervasive was this theatrical strategy? And why was it considered so effective? This second set of questions – about superposition – will be tackled first, for here we are dealing with

---

[25] Dmitry Filosofov, *Russkoye slovo*, 29 May 1914; trans. Taruskin, *Stravinsky and the Russian Traditions*, vol. II, pp. 1073–4.

[26] Minsky, *Utro Rossii*, 24 May 1914; trans. Taruskin, *Stravinsky and the Russian Traditions*, vol. II, p. 1071.

[27] Benois, *Reminiscences*, p. 357.

[28] Andrey Rimsky-Korsakov, *Apollon* (1914), p. 54; trans. Taruskin, *Stravinsky and the Russian Traditions*, vol. II, p. 1076.

a seemingly open and shut historical case, one that has already been exhumed by scholars.

Superposition

The method of superposition – overlaying artistic parameters – was not unique to *Le Coq d'or*. From the late nineteenth century, and seemingly inspired by contemporary technological invention, artists of all kinds began to experiment with the temporal and spatial conceptualization of their work.[29] Take, for a random selection, painters Albert Gleizes and Jean Metzinger, poet-writer-critic Guillaume Apollinaire, and the Italian Futurists. Gleizes and Metzinger argued for the 'superposed' basis of Cubist painting: 'the fact of moving around an object to seize it from several successive appearances, which, fused into a single image, reconstitute it in time'.[30] Apollinaire wrote different kinds of superposed poems, some weaving remote times and places into continuous narratives, others offering both words and images – that is, images constituted from the typographical arrangement of words.[31] As for the Futurists, their interest in superposition was bound to a deep-seated desire to challenge aesthetic conventions: more specifically, they sought to create dynamic and seemingly spontaneous forms of art that would express the multiple and simultaneous realities of modern life.[32]

---

[29] Artistic interest in superposition can be related to *fin-de-siècle* developments in transport and communication (wireless telegraphy, aviation technology, the metro, early cinema), all of which appeared to shrink lived distances, allowing the public to experience a multidimensional perspective at a single moment in time. For many contemporary observers, the Eiffel Tower was the emblem and oracle of this new *simultanéisme*, at once an object of the gaze and a panoramic vantage point. The Tower also helped establish a global, synchronized time, owing to its wireless capabilities and electronic relaying system. At 10 a.m. on 1 July 1913 the Tower transmitted the first time signal around the world. The simultaneity of the present displaced localized time cultures; global affairs became superposed dramas enacted on a unified, multi-planar world stage. For more on this context, see Stephen Kern, *The Culture of Time and Space: 1880–1918* (Cambridge, MA: Harvard University Press, 1983).

[30] See Albert Gleizes and Jean Metzinger, *Du 'Cubisme'* (1912); trans. Robert L. Herbert, *Modern Artists on Art* (1964; rev. edn Mineola, NY: Dover, 2000), pp. 2–16 at p. 13. Of the secondary literature, David Cottington, *Cubism and its Histories* (Manchester University Press, 2004), provides a useful study of the Cubist significance of superposition and simultaneity.

[31] On Apollinaire and his poetic experimentation, see Willard Bohn, *The Aesthetics of Visual Poetry, 1914–1928* (Cambridge University Press, 1986), pp. 46–84, and Claude Debon, *'Calligrammes' de Guillaume Apollinaire* (Paris: Gallimard, 2004).

[32] On the Futurist movement in general, see Marjorie Perloff, *The Futurist Moment: Avant-Garde, Avant-Guerre, and the Language of Rupture* (1985; rev. edn University of Chicago Press, 2003) and Günther Berghaus, *Futurism and Politics: Between Anarchist Rebellion and Fascist Reaction, 1909–1944* (Oxford University Press, 1996).

The Futurists were also amongst the first to experiment with superposed theatre. Filippo Tommaso Marinetti, founder of the movement, wrote a number of short plays or 'sintesi' (literally, syntheses) that overlaid dramatic narratives, compressing actions, words and gestures into the briefest period of time. His first attempt was the aptly titled *Simultaneità* (1915), in which the stage was split into two sections, each depicting a different physical space: in one section, a bourgeois family spends a quiet evening around a living-room table; in the other, a courtesan prepares for an evening out.[33] The simultaneous unfolding of dramatic situations became a hallmark of Futurist theatrical practice, a means by which the group could challenge the structural and dramatic logic of traditional spoken theatre (its chronological development, motivated characterization and stylized theatricality) whilst evoking the multi-lateral modern-day experience. In one of the many theatrical manifestos issued by the group, Futurist author, journalist and playwright Emilio Settimelli argued this last point: 'from a purely artistic point of view the synthetic theatre attempted above all to offer a theatre matching our speed-mad, multi-faceted modern soul . . . He had to be given a total impression of life: its poetry, mystery, drama, smell, strangeness, oddities, witty agility, goodness, brutality, monotony, might, sun, calmness, storm.'[34]

If one is to pause here and think back to the matter at hand, to *Le Coq d'or* and its singing–dancing split, a parallel becomes clear. For both the Russian production and the Futurist 'sintesi' were designed to remedy perceived theatrical deficiencies; both challenged the spectator to attend to different and simultaneous sensory impressions; and both adopted the principle of superposition as compositional mode. Besides this, both emphasized the dramatic and structural salience of the vertical relation, of actions or effects occurring at the same time: the 'slicing' of time essential to Futurist theatre conveyed not only the brutality and dynamism of the modern world, but the meaning and impact of the unfolding drama; likewise, in *Le Coq d'or*, the simultaneous yet separated singing and dancing played an important dramatic role, adding to the effects of puppetry and pantomime central to the storyline. As for any specific line of influence, it is highly plausible that

---

[33] The playscript for *Simultaneità* is reprinted is Christiana J. Taylor, *Futurism: Politics, Painting and Performance* (Ann Arbor, MI: UMI Research Press, 1974), pp. 86–7. Some fifty additional playscripts, along with theatrical manifestos and a general survey of Futurist theatre, can be found in Michael Kirby, *Futurist Performance* (New York: E. P. Dutton, 1971). Also see Günther Berghaus, *Italian Futurist Theatre, 1909–1944* (Oxford University Press, 1998).

[34] See Emilio Settimelli, '"Balance Sheet" of the Synthetic Theatre' (1919); trans. Laura Richards in Claude Schumacher (ed.), *Naturalism and Symbolism in European Theatre, 1850–1918* (Cambridge University Press, 1996), pp. 473–5 at p. 474.

Benois and Fokine, known for their general receptivity to European theatrical practices, were aware of Futurist aesthetics; their multi-planar conception may even relate to the changes in spatio-temporal experience that the Futurists sought to transpose to the stage. And Louis Laloy, he who explicitly advocated the superposed principle in his review of *Le Coq d'or*, may also have had Futurist theatre in mind. Well versed in Futurist art and theory, Laloy made references to both in his press criticism; he also expressed views on contemporary theatre ('theatre is a victim of stylized realism', 'the rhythms of real life should be brought to the theatre') that were strikingly similar to those held by the Italian group.[35]

But the issue here – of *Le Coq d'or* and its dramaturgical significance – may be wrongly framed. In his seminal volume on twentieth-century music and culture, musicologist Glenn Watkins describes a series of works that employed the superposition strategy expressly à la *Coq d'or*: with parallel singing and dancing, rather than parallel-running storylines.[36] Watkins thus brings to light an important historical chronology, one that begins in 1914 and not only with *Le Coq d'or*: Igor Stravinsky's *Le Rossignol*, 'a lyric tale in three acts' produced by Diaghilev, also doubled up on performers, singers in the pit providing voices for mute characters on stage. As Watkins explains, Stravinsky and the Russian company experimented with similar staging in a number of later works: *Renard* (composed in 1916 but not premiered until 1922), originally conceived as puppet theatre with singers in the pit (unidentified with stage characters); *Pulcinella* (1920) and *Les Noces* (1923), both featuring pit singing with little direct relation to the drama on stage.[37] Watkins suggests a possible model for these works, describing theatrical traditions of the Far East, particularly Japanese Bunraku theatre. The latter, in which the voice of a narrator is separated from the body of a puppet, seems a likely antecedent: its principal ingredients – Orientalism, folklorism and puppetry – come clearly to the fore in the above works, their dramatic settings and scenarios.[38]

There is little to be added to Watkins's account, save mention of a second potential influence on the Russian *mise en scène*, one that emerges from a

---

[35] For these two quotations, see Laloy, 'La Musique chez soi: pour l'art du théâtre', *Comœdia*, 28 May 1914, p. 3: this is the same article in which Laloy reviewed *Le Coq d'or*.

[36] Glenn Watkins, *Pyramids at the Louvre: Music, Culture, and Collage from Stravinsky to the Postmodernists* (Cambridge, MA: The Belknap Press, 1994), pp. 42–9 and pp. 285–97.

[37] Singers also featured in the Ballets-Russes productions *Le Tricorne* (1919), *Les Biches* (1924) and *Ode* (1928).

[38] See Watkins, *Pyramids at the Louvre*, pp. 47–8. Daniel Albright also discusses *Le Rossignol* and *Les Noces* – specifically, their dramatization of nature, puppets and the machine – in his short book *Stravinsky: The Music Box and the Nightingale* (London: Gordon and Breach, 1989).

smattering of remarks by Diaghilev and Stravinsky.[39] In a 1910 interview, Diaghilev confessed an aversion to rational, concrete exegesis, and to words in particular; he preferred, he said, the 'elemental spontaneity' of physical gesture.[40] Stravinsky was more explicit, proclaiming his theatrical preference in an article of 1912: 'Opera does not attract me at all. What interests me is choreographic drama, the only form in which I see any movement forward, without trying to foretell its future direction'.[41] The previous year, the composer had offered something similar:

I love ballet and am more interested in it than in anything else. And this is not just an idle enthusiasm, but a serious and profound enjoyment of scenic spectacle – of the animated art form … I think that if you would attend the ballet regularly (artistic ballet, of course), you would see that this 'lower form' brings you incomparably more artistic joy than any operatic performance (even the operas with your favourite music), a joy that I have been experiencing now for over a year and which I would like to infect you all with and share with you. It is the joy of discovering a whole new continent. Its development will take lots of work – there's much in store![42]

The cohering point of view here – one that echoes Benois, Fokine, Filosofov and Minsky – leads back to the principal subject of this chapter. Clearly, the Russians shared an aversion to opera and an enthusiasm for ballet, tastes that played into their development of superposed theatre. As a potential

---

[39] There is also the curious case of Georges Migot, a French composer, painter and poet who, from the 1920s, began to combine elements of opera and ballet in a series of 'polylinéaire' or 'polyplanaire' stage works: *Hagoromo* (1920–1), *La Belle et la bête* (1938), *Mystère orphique* (1948) and *Le Zodiaque* (1958–60). To Migot, the concept of superposition, applicable to musical counterpoint as much as audio-visual relations, was of specifically French origin. In his theoretic writings, he argued that the French lyric tradition was founded on the principle of 'contrapunction' between words and music, and thus shared an aesthetic heritage with extra-Hellenic (Chinese, Hindu or Egyptian) theatre; see Migot, *Appogiatures résolues et non résolues* (Paris: Éditions de la Douce France, 1922) and his *Essais pour une esthétique générale* (Paris: Eugène Figuière et Cie, 1920).

[40] Diaghilev, *Utro Rossii*, 24 August 1910; trans. Taruskin, *Stravinsky and the Russian Traditions*, vol. II, pp. 1072–3. Taruskin describes the 'deep-seated antiliterary prejudice' of the Diaghilev circle (p. 1072), whilst Russian historian Harlow Robinson calls Diaghilev a 'snobbish opera hater' for whom opera was 'passé and clumsy, a dead art form'; see his 'The Case of Three Russians: Stravinsky, Prokofiev, and Shostakovich', *Opera Quarterly*, 6/3 (1989), pp. 59–75 at p. 59 and p. 62. It is important to note, however, that, according to Diaghilev's biographer Richard Buckle, the impresario was originally (and principally) interested in opera, and made plans for two seasons (although only one materialized); see Buckle, *Diaghilev* (London: Weidenfeld and Nicolson, 1979), especially p. 129, p. 158 and p. 178.

[41] Stravinsky, *Peterburgskaya gazeta*, 27 September 1912; trans. Taruskin, *Stravinsky and the Russian Traditions*, vol. II, pp. 973–4.

[42] Stravinsky, 21 July 1911, letter to Vladimir Rimsky-Korsakov; trans. Taruskin, *Stravinsky and the Russian Traditions*, vol. II, p. 982. For more from the composer, specifically on dance, see Stephanie Jordan, *Stravinsky Dances: Re-Visions Across a Century* (London: Dance Books, 2007), pp. 521–32.

influence, then, on the ripple of works by Stravinsky and Diaghilev, this critical consensus is persuasive. As evidence of a reception history – of both opera and ballet – it is equally so. Indeed, the Russians dangle a considerable carrot: they invite us to consider the ideological distance between their views and those of the French, the principal audience of their works. To do this we need to take a fairly detailed look at the French reception of opera; set against this, all other lines of enquiry will come more clearly into view.

The French response: opera (and singing)

Louis Laloy, once again, offers a useful lead:

Nous traversons une crise. Au lieu de sortir toutes du même moule, d'être taillées sur le même patron (malgré la différence des talents), comme ce fut le cas jusqu'en 1895, les œuvres importantes que l'on a mises à la scène en ces derniers temps diffèrent profondément entre elles; elles s'inspirent de principes distincts ou même opposés, relèvent d'esthétiques contradictoires. Il semble qu'il y ait incertitude, hésitation entre différents types; il semble, pour parler le langage de l'histoire naturelle, que nous soyons dans une de ces périodes de variation intense où, subitement, une espèce jusque-là uniforme se segmente en variétés dissemblables, dont les plus fortes feront souche d'espèces nouvelles.[43]

(We are going through a crisis. Instead of being moulded similarly and from the same design (despite differences of talent), as was the case until 1895, the important works that we have staged in recent years are extremely different from one another; they are inspired by different and even opposing principles, products of contradictory aesthetics. It seems that there is an uncertainty, a hesitation between different forms; it seems, to borrow the terminology of natural history, that we are experiencing one of these periods of intense variation, in which, all of a sudden, a species that was previously standardized begins to break down into different forms, the strongest of which will give rise to new species.)

One word sticks out: crisis. As Laloy explains, early twentieth-century opera was a heterogeneous beast: composers were unsure of their present and future direction; thus new and disparate forms had started to appear. What Laloy doesn't explain – perhaps doesn't need to – is the reason behind the predicament.[44] The impact of Richard Wagner on French operatic practice

---

[43] Louis Laloy, 'Le Drame musical moderne', *Le Mercure musical*, 15 May 1905, pp. 8–16 at p. 8. This was the first of four articles on the subject; all were transcriptions of conference papers presented at the École des Hautes Études Sociales, Paris, March and April 1905.

[44] The administration of the Paris Opéra was also held to account, as critics regretted its financial mis-management, poor production standards, the lack of employed understudies and even the putting of principal roles up for auction: see the suite of articles in *Comœdia*, April 1909.

was no doubt familiar to readers – and no doubt still is. A spate of scholarly studies has attempted to reconstruct the dialogue between French national identity and Wagner's legacy, charting the ways in which the composer's techniques and more general ideas influenced the creation of a Wagnerian *drame lyrique* in France.[45] In 1905, though, when Laloy wrote the above, critical interest in the composer-ideologue had begun to wane, even though public enthusiasm had helped entrench Wagner's works in the repertory of the Paris Opéra and elsewhere.[46] The previous year, Camille Mauclair had published an article in the newspaper *La Revue* entitled 'La Fin du wagnérisme'.[47] Before that, Alfred Bruneau had predicted a similar end, pondering how a Wagnerian eclipse might encourage French composers to unveil their true personalities, rediscover a genre and recapture an audience.[48]

That the future of French opera came under serious scrutiny in the press is evident from the December 1909 edition of the Marseilles-based monthly *Le Feu*. The journal had launched an enquiry into the French *drame lyrique*, its historical evolution, possible development and means of success; responses from composers and critics were published in December's special edition.[49] Although, as an editorial concedes, several composers abstained from comment (evidence, we are told, of their prudent reserve, as well as an inability to renounce the past), the replies received offer much of

---

[45] Of the secondary literature, Steven Huebner's monograph *French Opera at the Fin de Siècle: Wagnerism, Nationalism, and Style* (Oxford University Press, 1999) remains outstanding. Huebner offers an in-depth study of thirteen French operas, advancing an argument about the increasing interpenetration of Wagnerian ideas and French musical styles. Useful studies of Wagner's French reception include: Léon Guichard, *La Musique et les lettres en France au temps de wagnérisme* (Paris: Presses Universitaires de France, 1963); Danièle Pistone, 'Wagner à Paris (1839–1900)', *Revue internationale de musique française*, 1 (1980), pp. 7–84; the exhibition catalogue produced by Martine Kahane and Nicole Wild, *Wagner et la France* (Paris: Bibliothèque Nationale de France, 1983); Gerald D. Turbow, 'Art and Politics: Wagnerism in France', in David C. Large and William Weber (eds.), *Wagnerism in European Culture and Politics* (Ithaca, NY: Cornell University Press, 1984), pp. 134–66; and Marion Schmid, 'À bas Wagner! The French Press Campaign against Wagner during World War I', in Barbara L. Kelly (ed.), *French Music, Culture, and National Identity, 1870–1939* (University of Rochester Press, 2008), pp. 77–91.

[46] According to Schmid, this public enthusiasm contributed to the demise of Wagnerism as a critical and cultural movement; see her 'À bas Wagner!', p. 77.

[47] Camille Mauclair, 'La Fin du wagnérisme', *La Revue*, 15 February 1904, pp. 464–73.

[48] Alfred Bruneau, *Musiques d'hier et de demain* (Paris: Bibliothèque Charpentier, 1900), pp. 221–2. Of the 'religion wagnérienne', Bruneau writes: '[J]e pense, à mon tour, que son déclin est proche. On peut donc prévoir qu'elles seraient pour le drame lyrique français les conséquences de ce déclin qui permettrait à nos compositeurs de secouer un joug funeste, de dégager leur personnalité, de reprendre leur entière liberté, de retrouver un théâtre et un public.'

[49] 'L'Avenir du drame lyrique: enquête', *Le Feu*, 1 December 1909, pp. 193–209. I am grateful to Sabina Ratner for inadvertently leading me to this source.

interest – much, indeed, that may help us get a handle on paradigmatic French perspectives of the period.[50]

Critic Julien Torchet and professor Henri Lichtenberger confessed the disaffection with Wagner suggested by Bruneau and Mauclair; Lichtenberger offered some detail, acknowledging a general fatigue with Wagner's 'prétensions littéraires et philosophiques', as well as the mythic themes, grandiloquent diction and continuous thematic development favoured by the composer.[51] Antoine Mariotte, best known for his operatic *Salomé*, described the multiplicity of musical tendencies reported by Laloy (quoted above). In an account that leaned heavily on a contemporary theory of music history by Jean Marnold, Mariotte compared the evolution of opera to the unfolding of the harmonic series. The latter, he argued, could gauge the increasing rate of change within operatic composition: a shift from the 13th harmonic to the 17th then 19th signified a period in which change was increasingly frequent.[52] One such change, according to French composer Jean Gabriel-Marie, was the 'symphonisation' of opera, the result of the mounting presence of the orchestra in both the theatre and the concert hall, where operatic extracts were frequently performed without words, singers or dramatic action.[53] Another development was bound to the public prerogative. Lichtenberger described how the 'public d'opéra' was unfamiliar with the musical language of modern French composers and thus tended to overlook works such as Paul Dukas's *Ariane et Barbe bleue* or Albéric Magnard's *Le Guercœur* in favour of repertory staples from Meyerbeer, Verdi and *l'école vériste*. According to Lichtenberger, a split between two types of art – 'l'art industriel' and 'l'art artiste' – was imminent; Dukas, Magnard and their kind were likely to be appreciated only by the musical elite.[54]

Entangled with these ideas – particularly Gabriel-Marie's 'symphonisation' – was a concern for vocal expression. As Mauclair acknowledged: 'personne n'écrit pour la voix: on la méprise, on l'étouffe et on la casse, on ne s'occupe jamais de savoir les facultés et les impossibilités d'un larynx humain. La mélodie est tenue pour une hérésie' (no one writes for the voice: we despise it, stifle it, devalue it, we never get to know the capabilities and incapabilities of the human larynx. Melody is taken as heresy).[55] This view,

---

[50] *Ibid.*, p. 193.   [51] *Ibid.*, pp. 195–8 and pp. 208–9.   [52] *Ibid.*, pp. 199–201.

[53] *Ibid.*, pp. 198–9.   [54] *Ibid.*, pp. 195–8.

[55] *Ibid.*, pp. 201–4 at p. 203. Mauclair expands on the role of singers in opera in his *Histoire de la musique européenne, 1850–1914* (Paris: Fischbacher, 1914), especially pp. 126–33. For an interesting account of the perceived demise of melody, see Wanda Landowska, 'Pourquoi la musique moderne n'est pas mélodique?', *Revue musicale S.I.M.*, 9/3 (March 1913), pp. 1–6. In response to the question of her title, Landowska raises the matters of prior exposure and generic convention, arguing that any new musical style to which the ear is unaccustomed will inevitably sound unmelodic. She sums up (p. 3): 'La musique mélodieuse c'est la musique d'hier; celle d'aujourd'hui ne l'est pas encore, elle le sera plus tard.'

widespread amongst composers and critics, was not unrelated to the influence of Wagner.[56] In a letter of 1897, Camille Saint-Saëns implied that the suppression of singing was a direct consequence of the substitution of one form of operatic logic (that of the nineteenth-century 'number' opera) for another (the Wagnerian *drame lyrique*):

À l'obligation d'écrire des airs, des duos, des ensembles, a succédé l'interdiction; il n'est plus permis de chanter dans les opéras, et, à ce jeu, le bel art du Chant s'étiole et tend à disparaître ... N'est-ce pas excessif, et ne saurait-on sortir d'un esclavage que pour retomber dans un autre?[57]

(From being obliged to write airs, duos, ensembles, we are now forbidden to; singing is no longer allowed in operas, and, as a result, the beautiful art of singing withers and disappears ... Is it not ridiculous to escape one form of slavery only to fall into another?)

Saint-Saëns was still bemoaning the decline of singing some twelve years later. In an essay entitled 'Drame lyrique et drame musical', the composer described how singing had been overshadowed by dramatic declamation, as well as by an instrumental discourse that was shapeless, like porridge ('réduite en bouillie insaisissable et fluide').[58] Although the Wagner factor was mentioned only in passing, the composer's influence on the (im)balance of vocal and instrumental parts described by Saint-Saëns, and on a general tendency towards the complicated, mysterious and incomprehensible, was evident.

There were other contributing factors. In a 1914 lecture (subsequently published in his monograph *Du Chant*), composer Reynaldo Hahn regretted the decline of singing, acknowledging the impact of contemporary modernity.[59] Singers, Hahn observed, were driven by ambition, caught up in the pace and superficiality of the modern world; they were motivated by a desire not to further their knowledge or understanding of music but simply to advance their careers – which they did, Hahn notes, by copying the latest singing

---

[56] It is well known that Wagner sought to downgrade the singer's status, along with the musical structures and melodic formulae that had previously supported it; see Wagner, 'The Destiny of Opera' (1871) and 'On Actors and Singers' (1872); *Richard Wagner's Prose Works*, trans. William Ashton Ellis, 8 vols. (London: Kegan Paul, 1896) , vol. V, pp. 127–55 and 157–228. For a historical perspective on Wagner's influence and 'abuse' of the voice, see Jane Meyerheim, *L'Art du chant technique* (Paris: Costallat, 1905), especially pp. ix–xxiii.

[57] Camille Saint-Saëns, 'Lettre de Las Palmas' (30 March 1897, to Madame Juliette Adam), in *Portraits et souvenirs* (Paris: Société d'Édition Artistique, 1900), pp. 230–43 at p. 240. For more on Saint-Saëns's response to Wagner, see Georges Servières, 'Le "Wagnérisme" de C. Saint-Saëns', *Rivista musicale italiana*, 30 (1923), pp. 223–44.

[58] Saint-Saëns, 'Drame lyrique et drame musical', in *Portraits et souvenirs*, pp. 177–90 at p. 178.

[59] Reynaldo Hahn, *Du Chant* (1920), in *On Singers and Singing*, trans. Leopold Simoneau (London: Christopher Helm, 1990), pp. 135–48, especially pp. 143–4.

sensations.[60] Hahn also claimed that the public, too, had succumbed to the lures of the modern condition – not to success, fame and personal gain, but rather to new technologies and sports. There was little interest in going to the opera or in singing (though 'everyone used to love it'); the public could recognize cars and gadgets, but not singers good or bad.[61]

Education and teaching were also held to account. Hahn was quick to regret the disappearance of the church choir, an institution that had provided comprehensive training in vocal technique and ensemble singing. Sadly, as Hahn grumbled, specifically musical skills were becoming less and less important: 'A handsome appearance, a few striking notes and some two dozen friends in the hall are all one needs to launch a career today.'[62] Perhaps this had led to the abundance of 'unmusical teachers of singing' noted by soprano Emma Calvé in her memoirs:

[I]t is curious and sometimes absurd to note that among those who undertake to teach the difficult art of singing will be found pianists, theatre managers, professors of solfège, teachers of pantomime, ladies in reduced circumstances, even ex-chorus women. I know of one instance where the lady's maid of a famous opera star has become a teacher of singing, and, incidentally, has made a very good business of it![63]

As for the 'official' Conservatoire, music critic Sauveur Selon called for training in both 'la technique de la voix' and 'la psychologie et l'histoire de l'art lyrique'.[64] Selon admitted that singers' artistic education was almost

---

[60] In her autobiography, the American mezzo-soprano Kathleen Howard also noted French singers' ambitious streak, along with their reliance on money and influence, and their general lack of musical education. Recollecting – but not recommending – her experience as a student in Paris from 1905 to 1906, Howard described how some of her fellow students held 'the most disproportionate views of their own importance'; see her *Confessions of an Opera Singer* (London: Kegan Paul, 1920), pp. 57–8. Egotism and ambition, it seems, were entrenched characteristics. Writing her memoirs, renowned singing teacher Mathilde Marchesi (resident in Paris in the late nineteenth century) lamented students' unwillingness to dedicate themselves to long and patient study. 'Everybody is impatient to get money and fame', Marchesi complained: 'Oh, holy art of singing, how sad a fate hath befallen thee!' See *Marchesi and Music: Passages from the Life of a Famous Singing Teacher* (London and New York: Harper, 1897), pp. 141–2.

[61] Hahn, *On Singers and Singing*, pp. 144–6.   [62] *Ibid.*, p. 146.

[63] Emma Calvé, *My Life* (London: Appleton, 1922), pp. 228–9. Marchesi noted something similar, describing how the art of singing had 'fallen victim to empiricism': 'This art, which was formerly a subject of unceasing care and attention, and was only imparted to students by competent teachers, has now become common property. Every musician – amateur or instrumental professor – fancies himself capable of undertaking the production of the voice and competent to teach singing. Each one seeks to invent a new system, and each one thinks he has found the right thing.' See *Marchesi and Music*, p. 179.

[64] Sauveur Selon, 'De l'Éducation artistique des chanteurs lyriques', *Le Feu*, 1 October 1909, pp. 53–64. Also see Maria Gibello, 'La Musique criée et la musique chantée', *Revue musicale*, 15 February 1909, pp. 98–103; Louis Vierne, 'La Décadence de l'art du chant', *Le Courrier musical*, August 1912, pp. 449–53; and the anonymous article 'Les Bases de l'enseignement du chant', *Le Monde musical*, 30 January 1914, p. 23.

non-existent. With poor diction and articulation, a lack of interpretive awareness and (no less) big heads, singers tended to discredit the operas they performed. But what if they were to improve? Selon arrived at an interesting conclusion:

Et si par hasard, les chanteurs lyriques devenaient en majorité des véritables artistes, qu'arriverait-il? *Bone Deus*! ce serait probablement dans une pareille conjecture la mort lente de l'opéra. L'opéra est inesthétique, anti-musical, grossier, lourd, tissé de banalités et de faux-semblants. Un chanteur lyrique vraiment artiste aura hâte de s'évader hors de ce pandemonium de cartons peints.[65]

(And if by chance, most operatic singers were to become true artists, what would happen? Good God! it would probably lead to the slow death of opera. Opera is non-aesthetic, non-musical, vulgar, clumsy, full of banalities and false appearances. A truly artistic singer will be eager to escape from the stage pandemonium.)

Singers, it seems, would be the death of opera: either they would be too bad and disgrace the genre, or too good and want nothing to do with opera's inherent 'fakery'.

Ballet (and gesture)

Like the Russians, then, the French were uneasy about opera – about singers, singing and a particularly operatic brand of theatrical illusionism. But the similarity did not end there, for the French, too, began to gravitate towards ballet, enamoured by its silent bodily forms and suggestive gestural vocabulary. This gravitation is of course well known. Countless books, including this one, have described the ascendance of dance on Parisian stages both 'low' and 'high', have noted the number of danced entertainments in the French capital on any one evening, the 'stature' of composers who turned to ballet, the amount of journalistic ink expended on the genre, the almost-religious audience following, the institutional support, the available capital, the international audience and the emerging intrigue amongst intellectual types about how the moving body might function, might *mean*. According to French author and playwright René Peter, ballet became the primary locus of dramatic expression during the period. In his 1947 monograph on French theatre of the Third Republic, Peter reflects on the migration of 'la poésie dramatique' from one art to another:

---

[65] Selon, 'De l'Éducation artistique des chanteurs lyriques', p. 64.

La poésie dramatique semble d'ailleurs, à cette époque singulière, quitter son expression traditionnelle, le vers parlé, et ce n'est pas une des moindres curiosités de ce temps-là que de la voir se réfugier, sur la scène, derrière les grâces et les mouvements d'un art muet dont tout à coup grandit la vogue: le ballet.[66]

(In this remarkable period, dramatic poetry, moreover, seems to forsake its traditional mode of expression, spoken verse, and it is no small quirk of the time that it takes refuge, on stage, behind the graceful movements of a silent art that is all of a sudden in vogue: ballet.)

Peter goes on to suggest a possible reason for this shift, describing how ballet may have symbolized and satisfied the collective 'état d'esprit', may even have offered spectators the opportunity to experience something other-worldly, far from the mundane realities of daily life. Peter seems to have had in mind both a pre- and post-war discontent, one that ballet – with its fleeting, fantastical impressions – could soothe:

Le public, dans la contemplation de cette danse ailée et comme baignée d'irréel, peuple de rêves apaisés ces fresques vivantes; il prête tout un monde d'intentions aux grâces d'un entrechat ou d'un jeté-battu … il oublie les soucis de l'heure! Rare fortune, miraculeuse évasion dans un temps où l'on n'a plus le droit de croire à rien, où l'on n'espère plus rien.[67]

(The public, contemplating this winged dance bathed in illusion, fills these living frescoes with calm dreams; it attributes a world of meanings to the grace of an *entrechat* or of a *jeté-battu* … it forgets the worries of the day! This is a rare stroke of luck, a miraculous escape during a time when one no longer has the right to believe in anything, when one no longer hopes for anything.)

There are of course other possible reasons behind the drift towards dance, including the development of organized sport and recreational activities, and the burgeoning scientific interest in the body, its physical comportment and capabilities.[68] Since the 1870s, independent researchers – amongst them, the

---

[66] René Peter, *Le Théâtre et la vie sous la Troisième République*, 2 vols. (Paris: Marchot, 1947), vol. II, p. 298. British author Arthur Symons made a similar point in his aptly titled essay 'The World as Ballet' (1898): 'How fitly then, in its very essence, does the art of dancing symbolise life; with so faithful a rendering of its actual instincts! … And something in the particular elegance of the dance, the scenery; the avoidance of emphasis, the evasive, winding turn of things; and, above all, the intellectual as well as sensuous appeal of a living symbol, which can but reach the brain through the eyes, in the visual, concrete, imaginative way; has seemed to make the ballet concentrate in itself a good deal of the modern ideal in matters of artistic expression.' See Symons, *Studies in Seven Arts* (London: Constable, 1906), pp. 387–91 at pp. 389–91.

[67] Peter, *Le Théâtre et la vie*, vol. II, p. 300.

[68] On the growth of a mass sporting culture in France (and the official promotion of sport by Republican leaders), see Eugen Weber, 'Gymnastics and Sports in *Fin-de-Siècle* France: Opium of the Classes?', *American Historical Review*, 76 (1971), pp. 70–98; and H. L. Wesseling, 'Pierre de

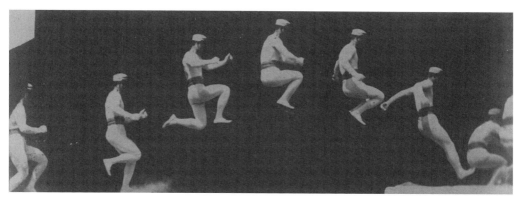

Figure 5.3 Marey, chronophotograph of a man jumping (1882–3).

famous physiologist Étienne-Jules Marey and his assistant Georges Demenÿ – had been studying human and animal locomotion, primarily by photographic means. The development of 'chronophotography' enabled scientists to capture consecutive phases of movement on a single photographic surface; published photographs and analytical studies were instrumental in contemporary physiology and athletic training, as well as the development of film and Futurist art.[69] (Figure 5.3, an example of chronophotography, overlaps a sequence of images of a man jumping.) As historian Lynda Nead has argued, the concept of motion gained special currency during the period, particularly across visual media. Not only painting, photography and early cinema, but poster advertisements, astronomy and magic-lantern shows: all sought to mobilize the visual image, to challenge conventional means of visual representation and, in doing so, to inspire new modes of sensory perception.[70]

In the present context, readers may anticipate an additional determining factor: the critical consensus about opera and singing. Looking back at the belle époque from the vantage point of the present day, it is difficult to imagine a more opportune historical moment at which dance might have

Coubertin: Sport and Ideology in the Third Republic, 1870–1914', *European Review*, 8/2 (2000), pp. 167–71. Wesseling notes how organized sport, which came late to France, was considered as preparation for military action (p. 171): 'Sport had fostered patriotism and self-confidence, team spirit and a sense of sacrifice, cool-headedness and endurance, solidarity and discipline – in short, a complete litany of virtues and qualities that could also be of importance in times of war.' For primary sources, see the exhibition catalogue *La Mise en scène du corps sportif, de la Belle Époque à l'âge des extrêmes* (Lausanne: Musée Olympique, 2002).

[69] See François Dagonet, *Étienne-Jules Marey: A Passion for the Trace*, trans. Robert Galeta (Cambridge, MA: The MIT Press, 1992) and Marta Braun, *Picturing Time: The Work of Étienne-Jules Marey (1830–1904)* (University of Chicago Press, 1994).

[70] See Lynda Nead, *The Haunted Gallery: Painting, Photography and Film c.1900* (New Haven, CT, and London: Yale University Press, 2007).

flourished; it is difficult to imagine, in other words, how the crisis facing sung theatre could not have encouraged the balletic. On this point, French ballet-enthusiast Maurice Brillant is clear. In a 1953 monograph, Brillant recalled how the ascendance of ballet was intensified by 'l'essoufflement du théâtre musical, du "drame lyrique" qui a succédé à l'opéra et qui agonise lentement' (the drying-up of music theatre, of the *drame lyrique* which had succeeded opera and was slowly dying).[71] Brillant made this same point in an article of 1924, reflecting on ballet's theatrical status:

Dans la décadence, ou mieux dans la crise de croissance du théâtre 'parlé', dans l'épuisement du drame lyrique, qui a remplacé l'opéra . . . le ballet est notre véritable spectacle d'art. Ce n'est pas sans motif que les artistes et les lettrés les plus fins lui marquent une tendre prédilection et qu'ils courent vers ses enchantements multiples et bariolés.[72]

(In the decadence, or better in the troubled development of spoken theatre, in the exhaustion of the *drame lyrique*, which replaced opera . . . ballet is our true artistic spectacle. It is not without reason that the finest artists and men-of-letters profess a fondness for ballet and that they tend towards its multiple and colourful enchantments.)

Paul Lombard, also writing in the 1920s, was of similar mind. Lombard, though, flipped the issue, intimating that the success of ballet (the Russian ballet in particular) had contributed to the demise of opera – the genre that had held sway over the theatre and even over culture at large.

Depuis quelques années, depuis l'aurore des ballets russes . . . l'opéra voit son rôle dans la hiérarchie des genres se déplacer peu à peu. Autrefois il était le gardien de la tradition musicale, il en a été même le mainteneur aux époques confuses, le voici désormais posé en arbitre au milieu de l'effervescence générale que manifestent un peu partout les équipes, les clans, les écoles.[73]

(Since several years ago, since the dawn of the Ballets Russes . . . opera's status in the hierarchy of genres has been dislodged little by little. Once upon a time, opera was the guardian of musical tradition, it even upheld that tradition in troubled times and,

---

[71] Maurice Brillant, *Problèmes de la danse* (1953; repr. Paris: Librairie Théâtrale, 1979), p. 6.

[72] Maurice Brillant, 'Danse classique et danse rythmique', *Le Correspondant*, 28 August 1924, pp. 682–95 at p. 682; see F-Pn, Ro 9981. Also see Émile Vuillermoz, *L'Art cinématographique* (Paris: Félix Alcan, 1927), p. 53: 'Ce n'est un secret pour personne que les musiciens de la génération actuelle se détachent de plus en plus de la technique de l'opéra. Pour beaucoup de jeunes gens d'aujourd'hui, le drame chanté représente une formule d'art d'une insupportable lourdeur . . . C'est pourquoi beaucoup d'entre eux se tournent vers le ballet expressif.' Incidentally, Vuillermoz goes on to discuss *Le Coq d'or*, suggesting that the production might have inspired early cinema.

[73] Paul Lombard, 10 June 1923; clipping, F-Po, Dossier d'œuvre, *Padmâvatî* (more on this work later).

henceforth, has acted as arbiter in the midst of the general agitation that flairs amongst groups, clans and schools.)

Clearly, times had changed, along with compositional and creative priorities: ballet was toppling opera from its erstwhile pedestal; the dancer was ousting the singer. This historical trajectory is important, and not only because it has been left largely unexplored in the scholarly literature.[74] During the period in question, opera gave way to ballet both in the critical-intellectual popularity-stakes and in the theatre, where operatic performance deferred increasingly to the physical, the gestural and even the balletic. In other words, the essential and defining component of ballet – movement – began to assert itself on the operatic stage, just as ballet itself asserted its status as the pre-eminent form of music theatre. A 1910 article for *Comœdia illustré* sets this idea in context, describing how contemporary theatre was becoming 'plus *mouvementé*'.[75] Artists, we are told, had taken up sports, including dance, in order to learn how to fully exploit the expressive potential of their bodies.[76] To wrench this discussion back to its ostensible subject, then, may be to suggest that *Le Coq d'or* was not as peculiar in its *mise en scène* as it first appears. A plausible case can be made for the production as representative of a widespread theatrical tendency, one that mobilized the concept of gesture as a mode of communication and expression. The 'gesticulation' of opera is the subject of the remainder of this chapter.

The 'gesticulation' of opera: operatic performance

A first and obvious example of this trend concerns some of the most famous singers of the day: Victor Maurel, Fyodor Chaliapin, Emma Calvé and Mary Garden. Each sought to cultivate a style of operatic performance that relied as much on bodily movement as on vocal technique, thus contributing to the development of operatic dramaticism initiated by nineteenth-century singers Giuditta Pasta, Wilhelmine Schröder-Devrient and Maria Malibran – a development described in detail by Susan Rutherford.[77] Chaliapin, for instance, described gesture as 'the very soul of dramatic creation', 'the first

---

[74] Maribeth Clark is one of few to consider the relation between vocal and gestural modes of theatrical performance. In a fascinating article on the performance history of Daniel Auber's opera *La Muette de Portici*, Clark notes a nineteenth-century trajectory that runs contrary to the one I describe here. Between 1828 and 1879, Clark argues, critics privileged the act of singing over that of gesticulating, praising performers who de-emphasized bodily histrionics. See Clark, 'The Body and the Voice in *La Muette de Portici*', *19th-Century Music*, 27/2 (2003), pp. 116–31.
[75] Georges Rozet, 'Les Artistes sportifs', *Comœdia illustré*, 1 August 1910, pp. 636–7 at p. 636.
[76] *Ibid.*, p. 637.   [77] Rutherford, *The Prima Donna and Opera*, especially pp. 231–74.

principle of dramatic art';[78] he wanted to avoid melodramatic movements and static oratory ('lifeless and mechanical', part of the reason for 'the whole condemnation of operatic art') and, instead, to offer an external image of a character's psychological interior.[79] Garden, too, maintained the dramatic significance of gesture. In an article of January 1909, the soprano advised budding singers in her native USA to learn how to act, to use 'brains' and 'personality', to 'get a drama as well as an aria over to your audience';[80] she went on, the following month, to claim that 'were it not for the actor's art, modern opera could not endure'.[81] Students took heed. As Rutherford notes, Garden and Calvé inspired a generation of actor-singers, some of whom went on to cultivate their gestural talents in silent film and dance.[82] Kathleen Howard, a Canadian mezzo-soprano and student in Paris from 1905 to 1906, described how she had wanted to learn to act à la Garden, 'to make voice, face, and … body an articulate expression of all that the role had to say'.[83] The American Geraldine Farrar, who also studied in Paris, had similar priorities. In a 1910 interview with writer and critic Carl Van Vechten, Farrar described her vocation: 'I am an actress who happens to be appearing in opera. I sacrifice tonal beauty to dramatic fitness every time I think it is necessary for an effect, and I shall continue to do it. I leave mere singing for the warblers. I am more interested in acting myself.'[84]

---

[78] Fyodor Chaliapin, *Man and Mask: Forty Years in the Life of a Singer*, trans. Phyllis Mégroz (London: Victor Gollancz, 1932), p. 130.

[79] *Ibid.*, p. 81 and p. 408. For an idea of the traditional histrionics and formulaic gestures that Chaliapin objected to, see Jules Audubert, *L'Art du chant, suivi d'un traité de maintien théâtral* (Paris: Brandus et Cie, 1876). Despite acknowledging the importance of natural and intuitive bodily comportment, Audubert describes and categorizes the exact poses and movements that singers should use in a variety of dramatic situations (falling to the ground, exiting the stage, engaged in conversation with other characters) and when experiencing different emotions. Mary Ann Smart discusses a number of similar treatises in her *Mimomania: Music and Gesture in Nineteenth-Century Opera* (Berkeley and Los Angeles: University of California Press, 2004), pp. 11–20. Smart notes how nineteenth-century taxonomies of gesture relied heavily on established eighteenth-century authorities such as François Riccoboni and Johann Jakob Engel.

[80] Mary Garden, 'Opera Stars and "Roman Candle Roles"', *The New York Times*, 24 January 1909, page number unknown.

[81] 'The Debasement of Music in America', *Everybody's Magazine*, February 1909; clipping, US-NYpl, Robinson Locke Collection, Mary Garden Scrapbooks. Also see Garden, 'Acting in Lyric Drama', *Century Magazine*, February 1911, page number unknown.

[82] Rutherford, *The Prima Donna and Opera*, p. 272. There was even a rumour that Chaliapin would make his debut in ballet during the 1914 Russian season at Drury Lane, London; see *Revue française de musique*, 25 February 1914, p. 376.

[83] Howard, *Confessions of an Opera Singer*, p. 50 and p. 54.

[84] Geraldine Farrar, 1910; quoted in Carl Van Vechten, 'Geraldine Farrar' (1916), in *Interpreters and Interpretations* (New York: Knopf, 1927), pp. 54–5. I am grateful to Kerry Murphy for alerting me to the continuation of a contrasting and specifically Italianate manner of operatic performance, closely associated with the teaching of Marchesi. Known nowadays for her development of the *bel canto* style, Marchesi strove for purity and evenness of tone, and forbade

This cultivation of 'moyens physiques' was not to everyone's tastes. Reflecting on his interview with Farrar in an essay of 1916, Van Vechten regretted 'that Mme Farrar carries her theories out literally'; he wished that she would withdraw from the stage for a while and devote herself to the study of singing.[85] Van Vechten also spoke unfavourably of Garden in the title role of Richard Strauss's *Salome* (at the Manhattan Opera House, New York, 1909): 'Nervous curiosity seemed to be the consistent note of this hectic interpretation. The singer was never still; her use of gesture was untiring.'[86] In Paris, Louis Handler offered something similar: 'Dieu! que c'est curieux! Elle n'a pas fait trois pas, Miss Garden, que déjà elle a fait cent trente-trois gestes avec la main droite, soixante-seize avec le bras gauche, et trois cent quatorze avec le reste' (God, it is odd! She has not taken three steps, Miss Garden, but has made 133 gestures with her right hand, 76 with her left arm and 314 with the rest of her body!).[87] Not even Chaliapin, 'le grand tragédien', was immune from criticism. The Russian's performance in Arrigo Boïto's *Mefistofele* was variously received for its vocal and visual tendencies. Here is W. J. Henderson, a reporter for the *New York Sun*:

He [Chaliapin] is constantly snarling and barking. He poses in writhing attitudes of agonized impotence. He strides and gestures, grimaces and roars . . . How long did he study the art of singing? Surely not many years. Such an uneven and uncertain emission of tone is seldom heard . . . The splendid song, 'Son lo Spirito Che Nega', was not sung at all in the strict interpretation of the word. It was delivered, to be sure, but in a rough and barbaric style. Some of the tones disappeared somewhere in the

gestures during singing, so as not to disturb sound production. Marchesi's pupil, the Australian Nellie Melba (who debuted in Paris in 1889), epitomized the Marchesi method. Melba was applauded for her pure and flexible voice, but criticized for her formulaic and pantomimic acting, as well as her perceived lack of emotional engagement with the operatic text. For more on Melba and Marchesi's teaching, see Kerry Murphy, 'Melba's Paris Debut: Another White Voice?', *Musicology Australia*, 33/1 (2011), pp. 1–11.

[85] Van Vechten, 'Geraldine Farrar' (1916), p. 55.

[86] Van Vechten, 'Mary Garden' (1916), in *Interpreters and Interpretations*, p. 81. Press commentary on Garden's New York Salome tended to focus on the infamous 'Dance of the Seven Veils'. According to the *Musical Leader*, the dance, performed by Garden herself, was 'one of the most astounding pieces of realism ever seen on the operatic stage'; clipping, US-NYpl, Robinson Locke Collection, Mary Garden Scrapbooks.

[87] Louis Handler, 'La Soirée', *Comœdia*, 7 March 1910, p. 2. Writing in the same paper, Henry Gauthiers-Villars offered an appraisal and an explanation of Garden's gestural performance: 'Ses poses étudiées, ses gestes échappés des toiles célèbres, sa robe, ruisselante de pierreries "qui semble un voile léger sur ses hanches", sa nervosité, sa sensualité sauvage ne sont point articles courants dans la maison qu'elle honore actuellement de sa présence. Elle a eu cette idée très littéraire de composer Salomé en danseuse, dès sa première scène, en danseuse irrésistible qui sait que les regards de taupe d'Antipas, et les yeux de flamme du Syrien et toutes les prunelles masculines, incendiées de désirs, ne quittent plus son corps dès qu'ils l'ont rencontré, et elle a joué l'œuvre entière avec ses bras purs, avec ses reins houleux et ses jambes voluptueuses.'

rear spaces of the basso's capacious throat, while others were projected into the auditorium like stones from a catapult.[88]

Too many gestures and unsung exclamations: according to Paul de Stoeklin in an article for *Le Courrier musical*, these were to blame for the general decline of operatic singing.[89] Stoeklin regretted that it was possible for singers with the roughest of voices – even with no voice at all – to find employment:

Ce qui ne peut se chanter se raconte. Il y a le geste rédempteur, il y a l'attitude, il y a le cri et la note bienfaisante, que tout être humain, si mal doué soit-il, a au fond du gosier.[90]

(Those who cannot sing tell the story. There are redeeming gestures, poses, the cry and that salutary note that everyone, even those lacking talent, has at the back of the throat.)

There is much to ponder here, not least the general gist of this criticism: that singers relied too heavily on gesture, as well as on declamatory effects. Readers may want to consider this perspective in more detail: clearly, the 'gesticulation' of operatic performance had detractors, as well as impassioned advocates. The topic may also benefit from a more specific scrutiny of the types and kinds of gestures cultivated by singers. Reviews of Calvé's performances, for example, tend to emphasize an extreme and alarming realism, describing the singer's movements in terms of 'le vrai' (the truth) of a drama.[91] Garden, too, was known for her powers of suggestion: an ability to fuse naturalistic and seemingly spontaneous gestures with poses more

---

[88] Quoted in Van Vechten, 'Feodor Chaliapine' (1916), in *Interpreters and Interpretations*, pp. 107–8. According to historian Kristi A. Groberg, Chaliapin's performance in Boïto's opera was part of his 'three-decade campaign to put a truly evil Mephistopheles on the stage'; see her chapter 'The Shade of Lucifer's Dark Wing: Satanism in Silver Age Russia', in Bernice Glatzer Rosenthal (ed.), *The Occult in Russian and Soviet Culture* (Ithaca, NY: Cornell University Press, 1997), pp. 99–133 at p. 114.

[89] Paul de Stoeklin, 'L'Art du Chant', *Le Courrier musical*, 1 February 1910, pp. 94–8.

[90] *Ibid.*, pp. 97–8. These same singers, Stoeklin explained, tended to struggle when performing non-theatrical works, those lacking the dramatic and gestural safety nets: 'Toute une partie de la musique vocale, la plus pure, la plus musicale, la plus riche, la plus belle est condamnée à l'oubli. Par un vague accès de snobisme, on s'évertue encore à chanter Bach avec une rare incompréhension. Mais le beau lied, celui de Gluck, de Beethoven, Schubert, Brahms, Duparc, Fauré et les autres, où est-il?'

[91] Several reviews are quoted by Rutherford, *The Prima Donna and Opera*, pp. 268–70. Also see the numerous press clippings compiled at F-Po, Dossier d'artiste, Emma Calvé. In her memoirs, Calvé admits her 'passion for realism' (and that she occasionally 'overstepped the mark'), describing an almost archaeological interest in the roles and dramas she performed; *My Life*, pp. 80–2.

symbolic, abstract and, at times, even 'classically' evocative.[92] As for Chaliapin, there are reports of gestural versatility and vividness, of a style of acting that negotiated a fine line between naturalism and stylization.[93] And Victor Maurel, according to opera scholar Karen Henson, cultivated an 'excessive' and 'modern' style of performance, characterized by impulsive gestural and declamatory effects (shudders, groans, sudden immobility).[94] Henson also makes a larger point: that singers' new approaches to operatic acting and declamation may undermine the period's well-known anti-performance rhetoric – issued by the likes of Stravinsky and Schoenberg – and thus reveal a practical reality in which 'singers continued to be important'.[95]

As for the impetus behind these new approaches, the spectre of Wagner looms large. It is well known that Wagner sought to transform gesture from a fairly neglected element of stage performance to an essential core – the core of his ideal music drama or 'total work of art'.[96] This concern for the renovation of operatic acting – Wagner invoked 'an ideal naturalism' as opposed to the 'unnatural affectation' of previous generations – no doubt contributed to the development of a specifically physical mode of operatic performance.[97] Equally influential, and itself influenced by Wagnerian

---

[92] Unlike Calvé, Garden maintained that she never 'studied' her roles – never read books or visited museums. She insisted nonetheless upon her total absorption in a role, going as far as to talk in the first person whilst in character ('I, Salome . . .'). For more on Garden and her manner of operatic performance, see Rutherford, *The Prima Donna and Opera*, pp. 270–2; Michael Turnbull's biography *Mary Garden* (Aldershot: Scolar Press, 1997); and, on Garden's most famous role, Gillian Opstad, *Debussy's Mélisande: The Lives of Georgette Leblanc, Mary Garden and Maggie Tayte* (Woodbridge: The Boydell Press, 2009), pp. 65–131.

[93] To some, the effect of Chaliapin's performances stemmed from the singer-actor's dramatic realism. Others, notably Vsevolod Meyerhold, described a non-naturalistic style that arose from a careful mapping of musical and gestural rhythms; see *Meyerhold on Theatre*, ed. Edward Braun (New York: Hill and Wang, 1969), pp. 82–3.

[94] Karen Henson, 'Verdi, Victor Maurel and *Fin-de-Siècle* Operatic Performance', *Cambridge Opera Journal*, 19/1 (2007), pp. 59–84.

[95] *Ibid.*, p. 59. Catherine Hindson makes a similar point in her *Female Performance Practice on the Fin-de-Siècle Popular Stages of London and Paris* (Manchester University Press, 2007), arguing that female celebrity performers were innovative and experimental practitioners, rather than merely passive sources of inspiration ('muses') for male artists.

[96] See, for example, Martin Puchner, *Stage Fright: Modernism, Anti-Theatricality and Drama* (Baltimore, MD, and London: The Johns Hopkins University Press, 2002), pp. 31–55.

[97] As is well known, Wagner heaped praise on the German soprano Wilhelmine Schröder-Devrient, celebrating her mimetic prowess and manner of 'self-divestment' whilst admitting, seemingly without concern, that 'she had no "voice" at all'; see Wagner, 'Actors and Singers', pp. 217–20; and, for more, Susan Rutherford, 'Wilhelmine Schröder-Devrient: Wagner's Theatrical Muse', in Maggie B. Gale and Viv Gardner (eds.), *Women, Theatre and Performance: New Histories, New Historiographies* (Manchester University Press, 2000), pp. 60–80. For a highly nuanced account of Wagner's practical and theoretical conceptualization of gesture, see Smart, *Mimomania*, pp. 163–204.

practice, was the standard set by silent film, a standard of expressive, intelligent acting by educated men and women. Press articles and reviews from the early twentieth century describe the development of film acting from the 'easy excesses' of vaudeville clowning to the psychologized art of pantomime. According to critic Jacques de Baroncelli, 'genuine cinema actors' acknowledged and investigated the expressive capacity of the body:

The new actors have put their whole selves into their roles. They have sat down in front of a mirror, like the spectator before the screen, observed their image as something strange and possessed (lacking a definite script of responses and tirades), as a kind of psychological map, as a series of 'moods' and 'moments'; they have spoken in turn to their reflected body, face, mouth, gaze: 'You are going to mean.' They have done mime. A feeling, the deepest of their being, has come to lodge in a fold of the lip, to realize itself in a contraction of the eyebrow, to take shape in a gesture, a pose . . . It is pantomime, but how much more deliberate and severe.[98]

This privileging of visual and gestural expression (essential to silent film) extended to spoken theatre: in particular, to the new styles of acting employed in private, avant-garde institutions as a means of challenging the perceived vapidity of the official stage. In France, self-proclaimed modernist directors André Antoine and Aurélien François Lugné-Poë (to name but two) were committed to trying to understand the origins and meaning of human behaviour and thus gave special attention to physical gesture and physical performance. Antoine, an advocate of a naturalistic *mise en scène*, developed an acting style that demanded total absorption in character. Nowadays associated with the Stanislavski method of psychologized performance, this acting style was designed to be 'true to life', to communicate character and emotion more effectively than the declamatory conventions, grand postures and gestural clichés of the traditional stage.[99] Antoine even suggested that, in the theatre, declamation was not necessarily of primary

---

[98] See Jacques de Baroncelli, 'Pantomime, Music, Cinema' (1915), trans. Richard Abel in Abel (ed.), *French Film Theory and Criticism, 1907–1939* (Princeton University Press, 1988), pp. 125–8 at p. 126. Abel's volume includes a number of contemporary reports on film acting and gesture.

[99] The definitive study of Antoine and his theatrical initiatives is Samuel Waxman, *Antoine and the Théâtre Libre* (Cambridge, MA: Harvard University Press, 1926); also see James B. Sanders, 'Antoine et la mise en scène', *Aux Sources de la vérité du théâtre moderne: actes du colloque de Londres* (Paris: Minard, 1974) and Bettina L. Knapp, *The Reign of the Theatrical Director: French Theatre, 1887–1924* (New York: Whitston, 1988), pp. 8–79. For comprehensive surveys of the Stanislavski method, see Jean Benedetti, *Stanislavski: An Introduction* (London: Methuen, 1982) and his *Stanislavski and the Actor* (London: Methuen, 1998); Colin Counsell, *Signs of Performance* (London: Routledge, 1996); Bella Merlin, *Konstantin Stanislavski* (London: Routledge, 2003); and, of course, Stanislavski's own writings, *An Actor Prepares* (1936), *Building a Character* (1949) and *Creating a Role* (1961), all translated by Elizabeth Reynolds Hapgood and published by Methuen.

importance; to him, lighting, decor, physical movement and even an actor's feet 'can be more expressive than any oral ranting'.[100] Lugné-Poë may well have agreed, though he differed from Antoine in his pursuit of specifically hieratic and dehumanized gestures, rather than ones than mimicked real-life bodily comportment. Moreover, whilst Antoine sought to capture the external, flesh-and-blood reality of a character, Lugné-Poë wanted to give the impression of mythic, mediumistic beings, of archetypal visions born from the depths of man's soul. In accordance with his Symbolist leanings, Lugné-Poë renounced the possibility of an objective portrayal of human character. To him, gestural formulae ceased to exist; bodily expressions were unique symbols of the corporeal unconscious.[101]

All these types and manners of movement – Antoine's naturalism, Lugné-Poë's symbolism, the 'real human activity' of cinema (and its disclosure, to quote Louis Delluc, of 'something beyond art, that is, life itself') – had an impact on operatic performance.[102] Calvé describes her enthusiasm for naturalistic theatre (in particular, for the 'simple, human, passionately sincere' acting of the Italian Eleonora Duse);[103] Garden expresses a similar debt to contemporary actresses (Duse, Sarah Bernhardt, *café-concert* performer Yvette Guilbert), betraying the Stanislavskian tendency towards total immersion in dramatic character;[104] Maurel was purportedly partial to the 'special effects' of Victorian spoken theatre; and Chaliapin was influenced by the 'plastic expressionism' of Russian actor Ivan Platonovitch Kiselevski, going on to inspire Stanislavski's performance theory and the stylized theatre of Vsevolod Meyerhold.[105]

---

[100] André Antoine, 'Causerie sur la mise en scène', *La Revue de Paris*, 1 April 1903, p. 610. Also see Antoine's 1890 brochure-cum-artistic-program, repr. and trans. Knapp, *The Reign of the Theatrical Director*, pp. 46–8.

[101] Frantisek Deak offers a useful account of Lugné-Poë's preferred acting style, as well as 'the semiotics of Symbolist *mise en scène*', in his *Symbolist Theatre: The Formation of an Avant-Garde* (Baltimore, MD, and London: The Johns Hopkins University Press, 1993), especially pp. 167–83. For a comprehensive overview, see Claude Schumacher (ed.), *Naturalism and Symbolism in European Theatre, 1850–1918* (Cambridge University Press, 1996). Incidentally, readers familiar with theatre history will note a line of influence from both Lugné-Poë and Antoine, through Jacques Copeau, Edward Gordon Craig, Jean-Louis Barrault, Antonin Artaud and Étienne Decroux, to Suzanne Bing and Jacques Lecoq. The last provides a useful outline of the development of gestural theatre in his 1987 volume *Le Théâtre du geste*; see the abridgement and translation by David Bradby, *Theatre of Movement and Gesture* (London: Routledge, 2006).

[102] Both quotations are from Louis Delluc, 'La Beauté au cinéma' (1917); trans. Abel, *French Film Theory and Criticism*, p. 137.

[103] Calvé, *My Life*, p. 60.

[104] See Mary Garden and Louis Biancolli, *Mary Garden's Story* (London: Michael Joseph, 1952), pp. 105, 145 and 268.

[105] See Chaliapin, *Man and Mask*, p. 153. For a discussion of Chaliapin, his interpretive manner, his roles and relation to the private opera company run by the Russian Savva Mamontov, see Olga Haldey, *Mamontov's Private Opera: The Search for Modernism in Russian Theater* (Bloomington: Indiana University Press, 2010). Haldey describes Chaliapin as Mamontov's ideal singer – 'a singing actor, capable of an interpretation blending drama with music' (p. 170).

The influence of music

In her memoirs, Calvé insinuates that the increasingly gestural mode of operatic performance was also symptomatic of 'a new type of music'.[106] Garden implies something similar, advising her students to 'learn that there are new works to be interpreted, new operatic tendencies to be fostered, new things clamouring at our doors to lead us forward'.[107] These 'works', 'tendencies' and 'things' comprised what the American critic James Huneker dubbed the 'New Opera', a genre that developed alongside 'new methods of interpretation'.[108] Stoeklin was more specific. In his article of 1910 (cited earlier), the critic grumbled about a number of nineteenth-century French composers, including Ambroise Thomas, Charles Gounod and Jules Massenet. These composers, Stoeklin argued, were responsible not only for musical atrocities, but for works that were explicitly theatrical, designed to underscore and inspire both bodily gestures and dramatic effects.[109] One wonders if Stoeklin had in mind music such as that shown in Example 5.1, from Massenet's *Esclarmonde*.[110]

It is now a scholarly commonplace that music can provide wordless stage directions, can give hint – in its rhythm, pulse, contour, theme or thematic structure – of physical movements taking place on stage. Mary Ann Smart has devoted several pages of her seminal study of nineteenth-century opera to this very issue, describing musical effects of mimicry, synchronization and cartoon-like pictorialism.[111] No such effects are apparent in Example 5.1, the orchestral interlude from Act Two of Massenet's 1889 opera. But this is not to deny the music's real sense of 'embodiment'. Here, played in front of a closed curtain, the orchestra illustrates the physical act of intercourse between characters silenced and hidden from view. The interjecting frissons from the distant spirits, the pulsating chordal accompaniment, the upward chromatic movement, the arching melodic lines and carefully graduated climax (based on tempo, dynamics, orchestral sonority and harmonic resolution): all

---

[106] Calvé, *My Life*, pp. 230–1.   [107] Garden, 'Opera Stars and "Roman Candle Roles"'.

[108] James Huneker, 'Mary Garden: Superwoman', *The New York Times*, 13 April 1919, page number unknown.

[109] Stoeklin, 'L'Art du Chant', p. 95. According to Cléricy du Collet, a combination of modern music, gesture, costume and decor had conspired and converged to promote the personality of the singer yet to overshadow the art of singing. See her 'La Méthode scientifique est-elle indispensable à l'art du chant?', 7 May 1909, pp. 3–7 at p. 5; unidentified source, F-Pn, 8-V 16675.

[110] A second example would be the music of Camille Erlanger (especially that of his 1906 opera *Aphrodite*), often criticized in the press for its gestural and physical tendencies, and even its 'violence'; see F-Po, Dossier d'œuvre, *Aphrodite*.

[111] Smart, *Mimomania*.

Example 5.1 Massenet, *Esclarmonde*, Act Two, interlude.

Example 5.1 (cont.)

Example 5.1 (cont.)

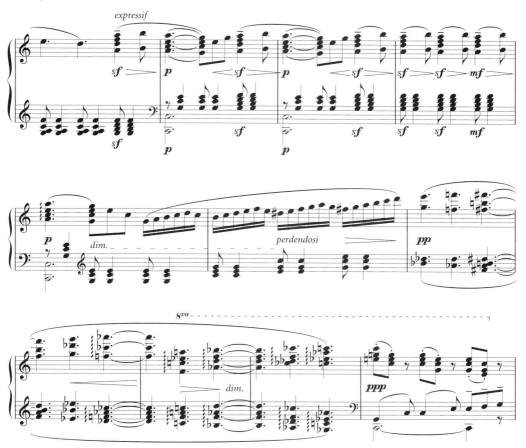

these musical components help construct an erotics of desire – to quote critic Camille Bellaigue, 'un éclat général et terriblement significatif' (a general burst that is terribly significant).[112] Bellaigue added:

Nous sommes témoins par les oreilles, ne pouvant l'être par les yeux. Jamais encore on n'avait, je crois, fait une description sonore aussi fidèle, aussi détaillée, de la manifestation physique des tendresses humaines.[113]

[112] Camille Bellaigue, 'Revue musicale', *Revue des deux mondes*, 1 June 1889, pp. 698–706 at p. 704.
[113] *Ibid*. Similar comments were made about the music's voluptuousness and transparency; see Annegret Fauser (ed.), *Dossier de presse parisienne: Jules Massenet, 'Esclarmonde' (1889)* (Heilbronn: Édition Lucie Galland, 2001).

(We witness with our ears what we cannot with our eyes. Never before, I believe, has such an accurate and detailed musical description of the physical manifestation of human love been made.)

The accuracy and detail that Bellaigue recalls is not the result of straight-forward musical mimesis. Massenet's score does not trace individual move-ments executed (or rather imagined) on stage: it offers none of the sharply etched, moment-by-moment graphic clarity that one might associate with, say, the overstated mode of discourse characteristic of the nineteenth-century *mélodrame*. Instead, the music short-circuits the representational mode: what we hear is a powerful homology for modern subjective expe-rience. As readers will be aware, the emergence of subjectivity as the critical object of artistic practice was a defining feature of modernist logic. The latter, dominating the logic of realism, sought to explore the individual consciousness, to construct subjective and physiological models of vision and audition with a view to capturing more accurately a new perceptual experience. With this modernist logic in mind, one might recall the direct-ness and sauciness of Olympia's stare in Édouard Manet's painting of 1863: how the nude unseats the authority of the viewer (and his viewing experi-ence) in the construction of her own subjectivity – if you like, her own 'erotics of desire' (see Figure 5.4).[114] Massenet's music might be doing something similar, confronting the listener with a basic and primal urge that is central to his or her consciousness. Indeed, the music offers a 'centre of consciousness' point of view: it 'stands in' not for the out-of-sight, objective narrator, but for the bodies themselves, their internal dynamics of tension and release.

We are teetering on the edge of some large issues here, from the materi-ality of music to the limits of theatrical representation. What does it mean that music might play a role in stoking libidinal desire, might function, not as a prop for a physical effect, but as a physical effect itself? And what of the music as body, entirely physical and manifest? This last question is especially interesting in light of the descriptive tendency of musical commentaries: Debussy compared Massenet's melodies to the napes of necks, his harmonies to arms;[115] Jules Lemaître spoke of the caresses of a woman.[116] According to critic Richard O'Monroy, Massenet's music even aroused like a body itself,

---

[114] The most influential and debated interpretation of the painting is offered by T. J. Clark, *The Painting of Modern Life: Paris in the Art of Manet and His Followers* (New York: Knopf, 1984).

[115] Debussy, 'D'*Ève à Grisélidis*', *La Revue blanche*, 1 December 1901, pp. 552–3 at p. 553.

[116] Jules Lemaître, *Billets du matin*, 14 May 1889; quoted in René Brancour, *Massenet* (Paris: Félix Alcan, 1922), p. 99.

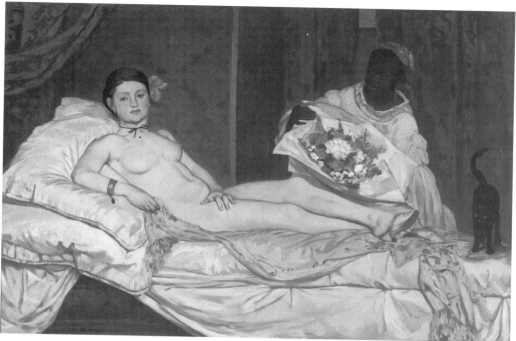

Figure 5.4 Manet, *Olympia* (1863).

male and female members of the audience succumbing to erotic frenzy during *Esclarmonde*'s sexual interlude.[117]

Further study will help us think critically about these ideas, as well as the business of intention: how and why a composer such as Massenet, to say nothing of his contemporaries, might have wished to underscore bodily movement, to develop a musical discourse with a view to the nature and function of its relation with an increasingly physical mode of operatic performance.[118] On this last point, the paragraphs above sketch the outlines of an analogy: on stage, a familiar lexicon of gestures was displaced by a more intuitive, dramatic and 'psychologized' manner of physical expression; in the orchestra pit, conventional mimetic approximations gave way to instances

[117] Richard O'Monroy, *Gil Blas*, 17 May 1889; quoted in Eugène de Solenière, *Massenet: étude critique et documentaire* (Paris: Bibliothèque d'Art de la Critique, 1897), p. 47.

[118] James Hepokoski comes close to addressing these questions in relation to the music of Verdi. In his handbook *Giuseppe Verdi: 'Otello'* (Cambridge University Press, 1987), pp. 186–7, Hepokoski writes: 'If in the libretto we sense a cool separation of the writer from the text, the high polish of an aesthetically manipulated poetry, in the music we are confronted with a direct series of body blows. Verdi's music is always direct, aggressive, tactile. We are continually struck by its sheer physicality and energy, by the way that Verdi can repeatedly take a polished, mannered line . . . and convert it into palpable presence.'

not of musical mystery or shadowy significance, but of flagrant sensuality, puissance and physical effect.

Dance within opera

For a third manifestation of opera's 'gesticulation' we can turn from stage acting and orchestral music to the status and function of dance within the operatic narrative. As even a cursory glance through libretti will reveal, dance has almost always featured in opera, French opera in particular, often contributing to the brilliance of a spectacle, the 'couleur locale' of a scene, or simply offering distraction from the development of plot: examples include the gypsy dances in Fromental Halévy's *La Juive* (1835), the ice-skating in Giacomo Meyerbeer's *Le Prophète* (1849), the orgiastic ballet in Charles Gounod's *Faust* (1859) and the *fête populaire* (including an 'idylle écossaise' and a 'pas des Highlanders') in Saint-Saëns's *Henry VIII* (1883). At the turn of the century, though, a new and different role for dance within opera's dramatic structure began to emerge. The iconic example is Strauss's *Salome* (1905) and the 'Dance of the Seven Veils'. Salome's dance is no mere diegetic appendage or exotic signifier: instead, it is integral to the plot, to the seduction game between Salome and her stepfather Herod, and to the latter's sexual arousal; it is symbolically loaded with powerful emotions buried deep within the characters' psyches and exposed through music and gesture. According to scholar Daniel Albright, Salome 'dances away from normal earthly behaviour'; she represents a 'plane of being' one step removed from the rational, realistic diegesis.[119] With little exaggeration, one could argue that Strauss's opera dances away from normal operatic behaviour: that, at least in the notorious striptease, it communicates primarily through gesture and bodily image rather than verbal exegesis.[120] Certainly, this could be said of the composer's later opera *Elektra* (1909), the plot of which culminates in a solo dance by the title character – a wild, Dionysian 'Totentanz' (dance of death) intended to gratify and transcend the opera's bloody sacrifices. The dance liberates Elektra from her terrible hatred and vengeance; but it also

---

[119] Daniel Albright, 'Golden Calves: The Role of Dance in Opera', *The Opera Quarterly*, 22/1 (2006), pp. 22–37 at p. 31.

[120] So popular was Salome's dance with audiences and solo performers that, as reported in *The New York Times* (16 August 1908), producer Oscar Hammerstein planned to introduce it into every opera staged at the Manhattan Opera House: 'Not only that, but he insists that all the plots of the operas in question must be altered in such a way that there shall be a logical reason for said dance. As soon as he got the idea, he at once called an expert play tinkerer and gave him, as a starter, the libretto of *Götterdämmerung* with strict instructions to insert the "Salome" dance in an artistic and convincing manner.'

signifies her self-fulfilment, thus necessitating her collapse. As Linda and Michael Hutcheon have noted, audio recordings of the opera obscure the significance of the dance: the listener may not register the fatality, that Elektra has danced herself to death.[121] Here, as in *Salome*, the climax is unsung and embodied. Opera is mute; words have no place; dance communicates to all.

(That both *Salome* and *Elektra* are adaptations of plays – by Oscar Wilde and Hugo von Hofmannsthal respectively – is of no small importance. In a 2007 monograph, theatre historian Mary Fleischer describes the function of dance within spoken theatre, arguing that the turn of the century witnessed an evolving non-verbal tradition in which dance held an important role.[122] Not only Wilde and Hofmannsthal, but Henrik Ibsen, August Strindberg, Gabriele d'Annunzio, Paul Claudel, Fyodor Sologub, William Butler Yeats and Gerhart Hauptmann all experimented with 'allegorical' dance, gesture functioning as a means of accessing individual psychology.)

French equivalents of Strauss's operas – in terms of their promotion of dance – are not uncommon, despite the relative decline of the 'number' format (with its set and often danced *divertissements*) and the evolution of a more continuous music drama. Balletic or gestural episodes, no longer purely 'spectacular' but dramatically expressive, can be found in several operatic works of the period, some of which present highly sexualized, exotic-erotic characters – thus respecting the conventional association of geographical 'otherness' with bodily freedom. An interesting example is *La Montagne noire* (1895), the last of four operas by Augusta Holmès. In her article on the opera, Henson describes the episodes of danced seduction, sensing their debt to contemporary exotic models in Bizet's *Carmen* and Delibes's *Lakmé*.[123] But she also notes the composer's sketch of an additional dance, one that signified 'a radical shift in genre'.[124] This 'allegorical' ballet offered none of the usual Oriental fare; instead, it depicted a battle between dancers dressed as clouds and shooting stars (with electrically lit head-pieces), and the entrance of Venus, 'shining and pure'.[125] To Henson, this episode illustrates

---

[121] Linda and Michael Hutcheon, *Bodily Charm, Living Opera* (Lincoln: University of Nebraska Press, 2000), pp. 16–22. The authors maintain the 'corporeal' orientation of the entire opera, noting the introduction of the dance motif in Elektra's opening monologue, as well as the many diegetic accounts of her physicality, physical abuse and physical relationships.

[122] Mary Fleischer, *Embodied Texts: Symbolist Playwright-Dancer Collaborations* (New York: Rodopi, 2007). In her *Legacies of Twentieth-Century Dance* (Middletown, CT: Wesleyan University Press, 2005), p. 87, Lynn Garafola also mentions a couple of French plays, staged by Jacques Rouché at his Théâtre des Arts, that gave prominence to dance.

[123] Karen Henson, 'In the House of Disillusion: Augusta Holmès and *La Montagne noire*', *Cambridge Opera Journal*, 9/3 (1997), pp. 233–62.

[124] *Ibid.*, 255.   [125] *Ibid.*, 256.

'feminine resistance to the conventions of exotic opera': Holmès's subversion of the exotic stereotype relates to her position as a female composer, her essential 'difference'.[126] Yet, equally, one might note the composer's enthusiasm for a different type of ballet – for an almost Symbolist, almost Mallarméan conceptualization of gesture, its dramatic and sensual potential.

Henson leads us to a second example: the 'Ballet de la Tentation' from the original version of Massenet's *Thaïs* (1894). As publicity materials made plain, this ballet was not only 'nouveau et original', with some 'très beaux effets de mise en scène'; it was dramatically essential.[127] Dancers dressed as gnomes, sphinxes and deadly spirits ('Esprits de la Tentation') attempt to seduce the monk Athanaël in his sleep; only a vision of the heroine Thaïs offers Athanaël an escape, helping to extinguish the spirits and their revelrous dance. The ballet thus underscores Athanaël's psychological torment and his devotion to Thaïs, making plain and making visual the erotic fantasies upon which the opera as whole appears to pivot.[128]

But there is more. The opera's significance, in the present context at least, extends beyond the integrity and prominence of this ballet to the general expressive function of gesture. In a 2005 article, Annegret Fauser outlines Massenet's interest in gesture: she notes the sheer number of 'nonvocal' episodes in the original *Thaïs* and describes a couple of archival documents that detail the gestural presentation of specific passages.[129] One such document is a letter from Massenet to Louis Gallet (his librettist) in which the composer refers to the seduction scene in Act Three:

Il ne s'agit pas d'une apparition calme, plastique – il s'agit de Thaïs paraissant près de la couche d'Athanaël et le tentant par des paroles et encore plus par *les gestes* qui accompagnent et soulignent cette scène jouée.[130]

(This is not a static appearance. This is Thaïs appearing close to Athanaël's bed and tempting him with words and even more with *the gestures* that accompany and underline the performed scene.)

---

[126] *Ibid.*, p. 257. Henson spies a possible historical model for Holmès's ballet, pointing to the operas of Lully and Rameau.

[127] *Le Ménestrel*, 23 July 1893; quoted in Patrick Gillis, '*Thaïs* à l'Opéra: du roman à la comédie lyrique, pertes et profits', in Marie-Claire Bancquart and Jean Dérens (eds.), *Anatole France: humanisme et actualité* (Paris: Bibliothèque Historique de la Ville de Paris, 1994), pp. 107–34 at p. 117.

[128] Huebner describes the 'innovative' ballet in his *French Opera at the Fin de Siècle*, pp. 109–11.

[129] Annegret Fauser, 'Visual Pleasures–Musical Signs: Dance at the Paris Opéra', *South Atlantic Quarterly*, 104/1 (2005), pp. 99–121.

[130] Massenet, letter of 28 July 1893; cited in *ibid.*, pp. 109–10. Also see Gillis, '*Thaïs* à l'Opéra', pp. 131–3.

Then there is the 1894 staging manual and a note as to how Athanaël should communicate during the 'Ballet de la Tentation':

Athanaël . . . s'agenouille au milieu de la scène et dit par gestes: 'C'est le réveil, c'est le salut!' Il comprend. . . il comprend!. . . Mais où donc était-il? Explosion de joie et de reconnaissance: Il est sauvé! sauvé![131]

(Athanaël . . . kneels in the middle of the stage and says through gestures: 'This is the awakening, this is salvation!' He understands. . . he understands!. . . But where was he? Explosion of joy and of recognition: He is saved! saved!)

According to Fauser, these comments attest to Massenet's appreciation of gesture as a dramatical tool, one with 'even more impact than text'. The composer, she suggests, understood that gesture could access and express individual psychology in ways 'not available to song and instrumental music'.[132]

The whiff of an argument here is enticing. Indeed, a closer look at the staging manual reveals a number of gestural indications: at the end of Act One, scene 1, Athanaël gesticulates to express his belief in God's will (p. 9); at the end of Act One, scene 2, Athanaël recoils from Thaïs's advances, making 'un geste d'horreur' as he exits the stage (p. 23); at the end of Act Two, scene 1, he gesticulates his farewell during Thaïs's attack of nerves (p. 29); at the end of the 'Ballet de la Tentation', he falls to his knees (p. 41); and he does so again at the end of the opera (p. 45).[133] These physical exclamations would seem to bolster Fauser's idea, providing further evidence of Massenet's 'gestural' impulse. They may also allude to the function of gesture as a structuring tool or end-of-scene punctuation, or even to the specifics of Athanaël's bodily comportment. It may also be significant that the gestural directions in the manual are to Athanaël, not Thaïs – and that the extant visual sources (at least those that I have seen) depict Athanaël, not Thaïs, in the act of 'gesticulation'.[134]

Again, one might wish to go further along this interrogatory path: to explore the textual, iconographic and musical evidence of Massenet's gestural agenda; and to ask, because it seems important, about the deletion of the 'Ballet de la Tentation' from the definitive version of *Thaïs* (premiered in 1898).[135]

---

[131] *Thaïs*, 'Mise en scène' (Paris: Au Ménestrel, 1894), p. 40; see F-Po, B 398 (10).
[132] Fauser, 'Visual Pleasures–Musical Signs', p. 109.
[133] *Thaïs*, 'Mise en scène', pp. 9, 23, 29, 41 and 45.   [134] See F-Pn, 4-ICO THE-2894.
[135] The 'Ballet de Tentation' was omitted from *Thaïs* following only nine performances at the Opéra; thereafter, and before the replacement was composed, a 'repertoire' ballet was inserted in its place (most often from Widor's *La Korrigane* or Paul Vidal's *La Maladetta*); see Patrick Gillis, 'Thaïs dans tous ses états: genèse et remaniements', *L'Avant-scène opéra: 'Thaïs'*, 109 (1988), pp. 66–74 at p. 71. In his memoirs, Massenet describes how opera director Pedro Gailhard requested an alternative ballet (along with a new scene). This new ballet was more conventionally conceived; it offered little dramatic continuity and less eroticism; see Jules Massenet, *Mes souvenirs* (Paris: Lafitte, 1912), p. 194.

For the present, it will be sufficient to register the opera's integration of gesture: the ways in which a distinctly physical mode of expression could contribute not only to a visual scene, but to an essential dramatic core. Fauser pushes further. Massenet, she writes, wanted to explore how dance and mime might function in a 'renewed French spectacle', helping to formulate a response to the 'challenge of Wagner'.[136] The 'gesticulation' of opera, thus conceived, was an ideologically motivated theatrical practice, one that contributed – as Fauser says, 'from the inside out' – to the renovation of French opera. This idea resonates with a set of examples across the contemporary operatic scene.

Opera-ballet

As is well known, the genre of opera-ballet dates from the late seventeenth century and the three- or four-act works composed for the Académie Royale de Musique. These works, popular until about 1770, tended to be light in tone, with colourful and dramatically discrete tableaux, fancy costumes, comic intrigue and, in terms of structure, alternating episodes of dance (often merely decorative) and song.[137] Lesser known is the revival of the hybrid genre in the second decade of the twentieth century and the enthusiasm of a handful of Frenchmen. One was theatre director Jacques Rouché. During his tenure at Paris's Théâtre des Arts (from 1910 to 1913), Rouché produced a number of opera-ballets and other hybrid forms (the court ballet and lyric tragedy): some were reconstructions of long-forgotten works; others were attempts at the recreation of past historical performances. (The historicist impulse was central to Rouché's theatrical aesthetic: his 'ambition', printed at the head of each programme for the 1912–13 season, was to 'trace the framework of theatre', to offer the public 'some of the beauties from different historical periods'.[138]) As well as Rouché, Debussy confessed an interest in the genre. In response to an enquiry into the future of opera

---

[136] Fauser, 'Visual Pleasures–Musical Signs', pp. 108–9.

[137] For more on opera-ballet, its genesis and characteristics, see James R. Anthony, 'The French *Opéra-Ballet* in the Early Eighteenth Century: Problems of Definition and Classification', *Journal of the American Musicological Society*, 18/2 (1965), pp. 197–20; and Jérôme de la Gorce, 'De l'opéra-ballet aux fragments', *XVIIe siècle*, 198 (1998), pp. 37–50.

[138] See the programmes housed at F-Pn, Ro 11128. It should be noted, however, that the works staged by Rouché at the Théâtre des Arts had a distinctly modern edge. Rouché sought to realize the scenic innovations of European directors (particularly Adolphe Appia and Edward Gordon Craig) and thus scorned historical verisimilitude in favour of experimental decor and minimal props. His 1910 book, *L'Art théâtral moderne*, summarized European theatrical practice whilst providing the foundations for his own experimentation; see the revised edition (Paris: Bloud et Gay, 1924).

launched in 1913 by the newspaper *L'Excelsior*, Debussy proposed a return to the hybrid form:

À mon avis, ils [les compositeurs d'aujourd'hui] pourraient adapter et rajeunir – en lui ôtant toutes ses rides – le vétuste opéra-ballet de nos ancêtres.[139]

(In my opinion, they [the composers of today] could adapt and rejuvenate – removing all its wrinkles – the venerable opera-ballet of our ancestors.)

Debussy never realized this idea: despite initial enthusiasm, his one opera-ballet, *Fêtes galantes* (begun in 1913), was abandoned in favour of other theatrical projects.[140] But he did make inroads into hybrid theatre, collaborating with both the Italian poet Gabriele d'Annunzio and the Russian dancer Ida Rubinstein in the mystery play *Le Martyre de Saint Sébastien* (1911), a work that combined dance and mime with solo and choral singing.[141]

To Debussy (and to Rouché as well), opera-ballet may have offered a means of resuscitating and replenishing French music theatre, of responding to the contemporary operatic malaise with a specifically national and cross-bred theatrical form. Certainly, this was the view of Albert Roussel, composer of the opera-ballet *Padmâvatî*, commissioned for the Paris Opéra in 1914 by Rouché (newly engaged as director). Roussel had expressed enthusiasm for opera-ballet as early as 1908. In a letter to the Belgian critic Octave Maus, he remarked: 'je crois que l'opéra-ballet ou plutôt le ballet avec soli et chœurs pourrait être une chose délicieuse … si les poètes voulaient s'y mettre!' (I think that opera-ballet or rather ballet with soli and chorus could be a delight … if only the poets would get on with it!).[142] Several years later, and in response to the same *L'Excelsior* enquiry mentioned above, Roussel

[139] 'L'Opéra de demain', *L'Excelsior*, 15 September 1913, p. 2. Debussy had spoken previously of combining singing, dance and pantomime. In an article of 1903, he described a possible remedy for the current operatic malaise: 'Retrouvons la Tragédie, en augmentant son décor musical primitif des ressources infinies de l'orchestre moderne et d'un chœur aux innombrables voix; sans oublier non plus ce qu'on pourra tirer d'effet total de la Pantomime et de la Danse, et en développant le jeu lumineux à l'extrême, c'est-à-dire à la mesure d'une foule. Pour cela, on trouverait de précieux renseignements dans les divertissements que donnent les princes javanais, où la séduction impérieuse du langage sans paroles qu'est la Pantomime atteint presque à l'absolu, parce qu'il procède par des actes et non par des formules. – C'est la misère de notre théâtre que nous ayons voulu le limiter aux seuls éléments intelligibles.' See his 'Pour le peuple', *Gil Blas*, 2 March 1903, p. 2.

[140] For an account of the genesis and abandonment of *Fêtes galantes*, see Robert Orledge, *Debussy and the Theatre* (Cambridge University Press, 1982), pp. 206–16.

[141] Orledge notes that Debussy's initial interest in *Le Martyre* was financially rather than artistically motivated; see *ibid.*, p. 219. For more on the play, and, in particular, on the presence and physicality of its performing bodies, see Fleischer, *Embodied Texts*, pp. 19–76.

[142] Roussel, letter of 31 March 1908; quoted in Albert Van der Linden, 'Albert Roussel et Octave Maus', *Revue belge de musicologie*, 4/4 (1950), pp. 198–206 at p. 203.

remarked that the hybrid genre might be particularly suited to the physical space of the Opéra:

> [J]e ne vois pas pourquoi on ne chercherait pas précisément à profiter de l'ampleur de cette scène, qui permet les grands mouvements de foules, les jeux de lumière, les décors somptueux, pour ressusciter l'opéra-ballet et retrouver ainsi une formule de spectacle parfaitement appropriée à son cadre.[143]

> (I do not understand why we would not look specifically to profit from the size of the stage, which allows for large-scale crowd movements, effects of lighting and sumptuous decor, in order to resuscitate the opera-ballet and thus rediscover a type of spectacle perfectly suited to the stage.)

This idea – of opera-ballet's practical advantage – cropped up again in a letter of 1923, written a few months before *Padmâvatî*'s long-delayed premiere.[144] But Roussel added something else: '[J]'ai voulu sortir complètement du drame lyrique wagnérien, et ne pas retomber pour cela dans l'opéra de Meyerbeer' (I wanted to break free entirely from the Wagnerian *drame lyrique*, but not to fall back into Meyerbeerian opera).[145] He expanded on this in an interview:

> Au nom de la vérité, le drame lyrique écarte le chant pour se rapprocher de la déclamation, de l'articulation et des inflexions du langage. En réalité, je pense . . . que tout est conventionnel au théâtre. Il est donc inutile de chercher à faire vrai. C'est pourquoi je crois opportun un retour à certaines formes délaissées ou peu exploitées: opéra-bouffe, ballet, opéra-ballet.[146]

> (In the name of verisimilitude, the *drame lyrique* discards singing in order to be closer to declamation, articulation and inflections of language. In reality, I think . . . that everything about the theatre is conventional. Thus it is useless to seek truth. That is why I think the time has come to return to long abandoned and little exploited forms: opera-bouffe, ballet, opera-ballet.)

Roussel, it seems, was motivated by a number of interrelated enthusiasms: to exploit the resources of a national institution and an ample stage, to flaunt music theatre's essential and spectacular unreality, and to escape

---

[143] 'L'Opéra de demain', *L'Excelsior*, 13 September 1913, p. 2. Roussel maintained, as did several of his contemporaries, that the physical space of the Opéra was unsuited to the modern-day *drame lyrique*: 'il sera toujours, sauf de rares exceptions, plus à sa place sur une scène moins vaste, où l'auditeur peut entrer en communion plus directe et plus intime avec les interprètes'.

[144] *Padmâvatî*'s premiere was planned for 1915; Roussel's score was three-quarters complete prior to the war, and was finished and orchestrated in 1918. For more on the genesis of the work, see *Cahiers Albert Roussel: 'Padmâvatî'*, 2 (1979), numéro spécial.

[145] Roussel, letter to G. Jean-Aubry, 31 March 1923; repr. in *Cahiers Albert Roussel: 'Padmâvatî'*, p. 90.

[146] Quoted in *Cahiers Albert Roussel: 'Padmâvatî'*, p. 6 (no source given).

nineteenth-century operatic convention by recourse to eighteenth-century forms. *Padmâvatî* was his theatrical testimony. The opera-ballet, based on Hindu legend and a libretto by Louis Laloy, required a large orchestra with triple woodwind and quadruple brass; it featured dancers, singers, chorus and soloists, and comprised scenes of festivity and ritual, murder and sacrifice, as well as a good deal of Oriental imagery. Several critics of the period perceived the scale and sumptuosity of the spectacle as a reaction against the 'austerity' of the *drame lyrique*; others described the work's succinct action and lack of character development in similar terms, lamenting the *drame lyrique*'s usual 'psychological' focus.[147] But, and despite these features, *Padmâvatî* offered no simple 'retour aux traditions'. As critics noted, Roussel and Laloy had refashioned the genre: 'voilà le premier essai d'un rajeunissement de l'opéra-ballet, forme d'art merveilleuse, abandonnée depuis le dix-huitième siècle' (here is the first attempt at the rejuvenation of opera-ballet, that marvellous form of art abandoned since the eighteenth century).[148]

The new and non-traditional aspects were variously identified: some critics thought that the overt exoticism and tragic storyline were far removed from the 'galant' heritage of the genre; others mentioned the collaboration between Laloy and Roussel, the dramatic significance of the music and the substitution of discrete *tableaux* for a continuous, unified narrative. But the principal difference between *Padmâvatî* and its historical antecedents was thought to be the role of dance. Whereas the traditional opera-ballet had tended towards dramatically extraneous danced *divertissements*, *Padmâvatî* featured danced episodes of, to quote one critic, '[une] puissance magnifique'.[149] Reviews and pre-premiere articles described a choreographic aesthetic that was not only unique but dramatically contingent. André Messager credited the librettist:

Nous voici en présence d'une œuvre considérable, œuvre fortement conçue, longuement méditée, l'une des plus intéressantes que la scène lyrique nous ait données

---

[147] See the press clippings compiled at F-Pn, Ro 10940, and F-Po, Dossier d'œuvre, *Padmâvatî*.

[148] Maurice Brillant, *Le Correspondant*, 29 June 1926; clipping, F-Pn, Ro 4245.

[149] Roland Manuel, n.d.; clipping, F-Po, Dossier d'œuvre, *Padmâvatî*. Roussel scholar Arthur Hoérée makes this same point: 'nous avons ici une action continue en opposition à l'opéra-ballet traditionnel où chaque entrée formait un divertissement distinct . . . Dans *Padmâvatî*, les défilés, les danses, les ensembles vocaux, les mouvements de foule, sont justifiés par l'action . . . On voit comment l'opéra-ballet avec Roussel a été rénové. Il en fait un spectacle où le divertissement n'est pas gratuit et comme ajouté artificiellement sur une trame préétablie.' See *Cahiers Albert Roussel: 'Padmâvatî'*, p. 8. It may be important to note that, whilst the danced *divertissement* was certainly characteristic of the eighteenth-century opera-ballet, works by Jean-Philippe Rameau in the genre tended to allocate greater dramatic significance to dance.

depuis plusieurs années. M. Louis Laloy a voulu faire revivre une forme depuis longtemps abandonnée, l'opéra-ballet, en imaginant un drame où la danse puisse être partie intégrante du sujet et non élément juxtaposé comme divertissement dans l'action.[150]

(Here we are witness to a work of considerable importance, a work solidly conceived, considered at length, one of the most interesting that the lyric stage has offered in several years. M. Louis Laloy wanted to revive a long-forgotten genre, opera-ballet, whilst imagining a scenario in which dance could be integral to the action, rather than a *divertissement*.)

The centrality of dance comes clearly to the fore in *Padmâvatî*'s second act, when a supernatural pantomime prepares and delivers the title character to her death. To recall: after having murdered her husband (to prevent his betrayal), Padmâvatî, the Queen of Tchitor, offers herself as a sacrifice. Priests enact a religious rite, lighting a funeral pyre for the king, whilst Padmâvatî's female attendants await her death. From the fire emerge the invoked deities, fantastical spirits that dance and encircle the queen. Ritualist chanting begins. Padmâvatî is consumed by flames.

In the words of Daniel Albright, 'it is the dance that leads us into the pyre: by the end of the opera, almost all singing is left behind in favor of the pure domain of wordless, world-less music and gesture'.[151] Indeed, the incantations of the priests and spirits are, for the most part, purely sonorous: magic syllables replace conventional spells – and even conventional singing. Casting an eye over the score, one might sense that the entire work sidelines singing. The chorus, for example, tends to function more as an instrumental ensemble than an operatic narrator. As Hugh Macdonald writes: 'they [the singers] do not express common thoughts in a traditional, sung manner: they murmur, they hum, they enunciate vowels like wind instruments; they form processions, oscillating and expressive movements, like dancers. Their role is more befitting of ballet than opera.'[152] To put this another way, *Padmâvatî* plays out on stage the eclipse of vocality and the ascendance of physical expression – the 'gesticulation' that characterized the contemporary

---

[150] André Messager, n.d.; clipping, F-Po, Dossier d'œuvre, *Padmâvatî*. Roussel, it appears, shared Laloy's reported intention: in a programme note, the composer maintained his desire to resuscitate the eighteenth-century opera-ballet by weaving dance into the drama; see Basil Deane, *Albert Roussel* (London: Barrie and Rockliff, 1961), p. 87. (I have been unable to trace the programme note described by Deane.)

[151] Albright, 'Golden Calves', p. 32.

[152] Hugh Macdonald, '*Padmâvatî*: œuvre lyrique ou chorégraphique', in Manfred Kelkel (ed.), *Albert Roussel: musique et esthétique* (Paris: Vrin, 1989), pp. 93–103 at p. 98. Macdonald also notes the expressive limitations of the solo lines; he describes a lack of melodic interest symptomatic of a Debussyste declamatory style – a style that, he writes, is ill befitting of *Padmâvatî*'s poetic libretto.

theatrical scene. A final couple of examples illustrates the pinnacle of this phenomenon.

Danced opera

Opera that was danced to, and/or sung, was greeted with a mixture of applause and scepticism. At bottom, the idea of unseating opera's essential and defining aspect was stupendous; it brought into question the nature and function of operatic expression (visual and musical, besides vocal), as well as the coherence of drama, character and point of view.

The first to essay this 'technique' was Isadora Duncan. From the outset of her career, in both France and her native USA, Duncan danced to operatic excerpts. These were mainly by Wagner and from the unsung episodes of his scores: the prelude to *Lohengrin*, the flower maidens' scene from *Parsifal*, Siegried's funeral march from *Götterdämmerung* and the 'Liebestod' from *Tristan und Isolde*.[153] Duncan had long professed an allegiance to the German composer, gushing at length about ideal unity, 'total theatre' and, no less, about the essential 'dance-ness' of Wagner's music:

He [Wagner] was the first to conceive of the dance as born of music. This is my conception of the dance also ... For in the depths of every musical theme of Wagner, dances will be found: monumental sculpture, movement which only demands release and life. It is of this music that critics are wont to say, 'It is not written for the dance'; but it is from this music that the dance, so long lifeless in the embryo, is being born again.[154]

As her words suggest, Duncan danced to Wagner's music because it was dance-like: not in the traditional sense of comprising rhythms and melodic motifs characteristic of 'set' dances (such as the minuet or waltz); but rather in the sense that it inspired physical movement, that it gave rise to 'the glorious child-birth of the Dance'.[155] What is more, in dancing to Wagner,

---

[153] Danced versions of *Carmen* – such as that performed by the Spanish mime artist Rosario Guerrero – were also popular during the period, as described by Elizabeth Kertesz in a conference paper ('*Carmen* "De-ranged": Melodrama, Ballet and Film in the Re-casting of Bizet's Opera, 1896–1915') presented at a one-day symposium on the Ballets Russes, University of Melbourne, 12 March 2010. Kertesz discusses this topic in more detail in her book on *Carmen*, co-authored with Michael Christoforidis (forthcoming, Oxford University Press).

[154] Isadora Duncan, 'Richard Wagner' (1921); repr. in Roger Copeland and Marshall Cohen (eds.), *What is Dance? Readings in Theory and Criticism* (Oxford University Press, 1983), p. 266.

[155] *Ibid.* Duncan did applaud the general rhythm of Wagner's music (as well as that of other 'great' composers), but only in terms of its correspondence with rhythm of a natural, bodily and 'earthy' kind. In 1909 she wrote: 'Ce sont les compositeurs comme Bach, Beethoven et Wagner

Duncan sought not only to 'wrench' from the music its innate gestural content; she wanted to promote the expressive significance of dance in music theatre. To Duncan, the contemporary *drame lyrique* was 'nonsense', 'all out of proportion': music had risen to prominence at the expense of visual and gestural display.[156] Duncan preached change: 'The theatre will live again in all its glory only when the dance once more takes its true place, as an integral and inevitable part of tragedy. It is because I believe this that I have dared to dance to the music of Wagner – yes, that I have raised my hands, vibrant with ecstasy, to the harmonious chords of *Parsifal*.'[157]

This same concern for the status of dance alongside music and drama led Duncan to the operas of Christoph Willibald Gluck, particularly his *Orphée* and *Iphigénie en Aulide*. To Duncan, Gluck's eighteenth-century works offered fertile terrain for the development of a new kind of *Gesamtkunstwerk*, one with dance at its centre. Duncan appreciated Gluck's own operatic renovation, particularly his integration of balletic, dramatic and musical forces. But she wanted to go further, towards dance as the visual incarnation of operatic expression. More specifically, she wanted to incarnate the ancient Greek chorus, that which, she proclaimed, Gluck appreciated like no other: 'Gluck, plus que les autres, a compris le chœur grec, le rythme, la beauté grave de ses mouvements et la grande impersonnalité de son âme émue, mais jamais désespérée' (Gluck, more than any other, understood the Greek chorus, the rhythm, the solemn beauty of its movements and the pronounced impersonality of it soul, emotional but never desperate).[158]

Duncan was not alone in her enthusiasm for Gluck. Concurrent with her various and varied operatic productions – extracts or full-length works, some with borrowings from other composers, with singing soloists in the pit, interspersed declamations or no words whatsoever[159] – were the choreographic stagings by Swiss music pedagogue Émile Jaques-Dalcroze. On 23 June 1913, Dalcroze created Gluck's *Orphée* at the *Festspielhaus* in Hellerau, a small garden city north of Dresden, Germany. Hellerau was carefully

---

qui, dans leurs œuvres, ont réuni, dans une perfection absolue, le rythme de la terre et le rythme humain. Et c'est pourquoi j'ai pris comme guide le rythme des grands maîtres. Non pas parce que je pense pouvoir exprimer la beauté de ces œuvres, mais parce que, en ployant sans résistance mon corps à leur rythme et cadence, je peux, peut-être, découvrir le rythme naturel des mouvements humains, perdu depuis des siècles.' See Isadora Duncan, *Écrits sur la danse* (Paris: Éditions du Grenier, 1927), pp. 25–6.

[156] Duncan, 1915; quoted in Ann Daly, *Done into Dance: Isadora Duncan in America* (Bloomington: Indiana University Press, 1995), pp. 144–5.

[157] Duncan, 'Richard Wagner', 1921; quoted in Copeland and Cohen (eds.), *What is Dance?*, p. 266.

[158] Duncan, *Écrits sur la danse*, p. 49.

[159] For more on Duncan's different stagings of Gluck's operas, see Daly, *Done into Dance*, pp. 145–50.

designed as a unified, organic community, one that offered its members (mainly workers at a local factory) an aesthetically pleasing living space with affordable housing and communal cultural activities. In 1910, Dalcroze founded his institute for 'rhythmic gymnastics' in the city's *Volksheime* (its central, community building): the institute offered free training for children in physical and musical study and was thought to help realize the city's social and moral ambition.[160] In the present context, the location should not deter: not for its distance from mainstream city life, and not, certainly, for its distance from Paris. The facts of Hellerau and *Orphée*, or *Orpheus* as it was known in German, tie in with those of Duncan's Gluck performances and, no less, with the broader 'gesticulatory' trend under discussion here.

Dalcroze, like Duncan, believed in the expressive potential of gesture – over and above that of the spoken or sung word.[161] And also like Duncan, Dalcroze was concerned about opera, the credibility of its singers and visuals, and the relation between gesture and music. To Dalcroze, opera singers lacked not only gestural intelligence (their movements were 'mechanical', 'false' and 'absurd'), but musical intelligence too. His 1910 article for *La Grande Revue* is worth quoting at length:

[R]egardons sur la scène de nos premiers théâtres lyriques, observons le jeu des acteurs tout en écoutant l'orchestre et nous nous apercevrons bien vite qu'il existe un mur entre l'orchestre et la scène, que la musique orchestrale semble un simple accompagnement au chant ou à l'attitude des acteurs et qu'elle ne pénètre pas en eux, qu'elle ne les marque pas à son empreinte. La musique s'élève, s'enfle, grossit, se déchaîne en grandioses sonorités: le geste ne suit pas le *crescendo* ou n'en donne pas l'illusion au spectateur. La musique s'apaise, s'endort, susurre et murmure comme dans un rêve: l'attitude sur la scène révèle une tension musculaire qui est un *fortissimo*! Et même les rythmes musicaux qui caractérisent non pas des mouvements de l'âme, mais de simples déplacements corporels, mouvements de marche, de course, arrêts brusques, soubre-sauts, etc., ne sont pas réalisés sur la scène ou le sont mal, ce qui est encore pire.[162]

---

[160] On the Hellerau project and its relation to the contemporary movement known as the 'Reform of Life', see Marco de Michelis, 'Modernity and Reform: Heinrich Tessenow and the Institute Dalcroze at Hellerau', *Perspecta*, 26 (1990), pp. 143–70.

[161] After attending a production of Strauss's *Salome* in Vienna, 1909, Dalcroze declared: 'À la dernière scène, Électre chante son triomphe en un crescendo magnifique, puis, ne pouvant plus chanter, elle *danse*! Et l'on se rend compte alors combien le corps est plus expressif que la parole, même chantée.' Quoted in Alfred Berchtold, 'Émile Jaques-Dalcroze et son temps', in Frank Martin (ed.), *Émile Jaques-Dalcroze: l'homme, le compositeur, le créateur de la rythmique* (Neuchâtel: Éditions de la Baconnière, 1965), pp. 27–158 at p. 81.

[162] Émile Jaques-Dalcroze, 'Le Rythme au théâtre', *La Grande Revue*, 10 June 1910, pp. 539–49 at p. 541; see F-Pn, Ro 9903.

(Let's watch the stage of our principal lyric theatres, let's observe the actors' play whilst listening to the orchestra, and we will soon notice that there is a wall between the orchestra and the stage, that the orchestral music seems to be a simple accompaniment to the actors' singing or postures, and that it never penetrates them, that it fails to make an impression on them. The music rises, swells, breaks out in grand sonorities: gesture does not follow the musical *crescendo* or, at least, it doesn't give this impression to the spectator. The music becomes calm and sleepy, whispers and murmurs like in a dream: stage posture betrays a muscular tension that implies a *fortissimo*! And even the musical rhythms that characterize, not the movements of the soul, but simple bodily movements such as footsteps, running steps, abrupt halts and sudden starts, etc., these are not realized on stage or are badly done so, which is even worse.)

Concerned about this perceived discordance between music and visuals, Dalcroze hoped for a renovation of opera – for singers not only to conduct themselves in time to a musical beat (something that, he added, was rarely in evidence), but to submit to the music, to visualize its essential 'soul' and, in doing so, recreate a synaesthetic ideal:

Il faut encore que les mouvements corporels et les mouvements sonores, l'élément musical et l'élément plastique soient étroitement unis . . . Chacun des mouvements rythmiques musicaux doit trouver dans le corps de l'interprète un mouvement musculaire adéquat, chacun des états d'âme exprimés par la sonorité doit déterminer sur la scène une attitude qui le caractérise. Chaque nuance orchestrale, chaque crescendo, diminuendo, stringendo, ou rallentando doit être ressenti par l'interprète et exprimé . . . la musique sera entrée en communication immédiate avec l'organisme, lorsque les vibrations sonores éveilleront dans les tissus et dans le système nerveux des vibrations analogues, et que le corps devenu récepteur des émotions musicales, saura instantanément les transformer en émotions plastiques.[163]

(Bodily movement and musical movement, the musical element and the plastic element, must be strictly bound to one another . . . Each musical rhythm must generate an adequate muscular movement in the body of the interpreter, each musical emotion expressed through sonority must inspire a stage posture that characterizes it. Each orchestral nuance, each crescendo, diminuendo, stringendo or rallentando must be experienced by the interpreter and expressed . . . the music will enter into immediate communication with the bodily organism when sonorous vibrations awaken analogous vibrations in the body's tissues and its nervous system, and the body becomes a receptor of musical emotions, instantly transforming them into plastic form.)

The production of *Orpheus* was something of an experiment in the expressive and dramatic possibilities of this musical-gestural ideology.

---

[163] *Ibid.*, p. 540 and p. 542.

Indeed, Dalcroze was keen to maintain a pedagogic agenda: that the production, preceded by gestural and rhythmic exercises, was an exercise in itself. (The *Festspielhaus* was regarded as more of a working studio than a concert hall or theatrical venue.) With singers standing behind the curtain and dancers engaged in constant movement (based on the Greek iconography so popular with Duncan), Dalcroze offered spectators the first, full-scale and specifically operatic realization of his 'rhythmic gymnastics'.[164] What is more, Dalcroze tweaked both Gluck's original score and the opera's scenario in order to further foreground the dancing bodies on stage, bodies engaged not in arbitrary diegetic spectacle but in dramatically motivated expression – the collective depiction of abstract emotions, memories and desires.[165]

What was made of the production? Swiss stage designer Adolphe Appia, who collaborated with Dalcroze on the opera and created some austere, geometric decor, spoke of a 'perfect fusion of expression'; he went on to recall that 'someone has written that *Orpheus* is miraculous!'.[166] This was the general consensus. George Bernard Shaw described the production as 'most remarkable', 'one of the best performances of Gluck's *Orfeo*';[167] French playwright Paul Claudel admitted: 'c'est la première fois que je vois au théâtre de la véritable beauté' (for the first time I see true beauty at the theatre).[168] Several critics – of several nationalities – also spoke of the potential significance of the production, how it inspired 'd'innombrables possibilités d'avenir' (countless possibilities for the future) and provided 'ample matière à discussion pour les praticiens de la scène et les esthètes' (ample talking points for stage practitioners and connoisseurs).[169] To an anonymous reviewer in *Le Monde musical*, the production superpassed its original pedagogic impulse, offering instruction not only to students but to

---

[164] The complete staging of Gluck's opera at Hellerau in June 1913 was preceded, in June 1912, by a danced version of the opening scene of Act Two.

[165] For more on the Dalcroze production and its choreography, see Tamara Levitz, 'In the Footsteps of Eurydice: Gluck's *Orpheus und Eurydice* in Hellerau, 1913', *Echo*, 3/2 (2001), no page numbers.

[166] For these quotations, see Richard C. Beacham, *Adolphe Appia: Artist and Visionary of the Modern Theatre* (London: Routledge, 1994), p. 98 and p. 100. Appia, of course, had long confessed a dissatisfaction with traditional stagings of opera: his well-known essay 'La Musique et la mise en scène' (1897) advocates a similar integration of music and body to the writings of Dalcroze. Also see his 'La Gymnastique rythmique et le théâtre', published in the Hellerau yearbook, 1911, which underscores not only his views on 'le mensonge inévitable de nos scènes lyriques' but on the necessity of singers' training in 'la gymnastique rythmique'.

[167] George Bernard Shaw, letter of 30 June 1913; repr. in *Bernard Shaw and Mrs Patrick Campbell: Their Correspondence*, ed. Alan Dent (New York: Knopf, 1952), p. 139.

[168] Paul Claudel, letter of 4 July 1913; quoted in Berchtold, 'Émile Jaques-Dalcroze et son temps', p. 99.

[169] Paul Bekker; quoted in Adolphe Appia, 'La Presse à Hellerau', in *Œuvres complètes*, ed. Marie L. Bablet-Hahn, 4 vols. (Lausanne: L'Âge d'Homme, 1988), vol. III, p. 207.

professional men of the theatre: 'On voit que les représentations d'Hellerau ne sont pas de simples essais, mais qu'elles marquent des résultats réels, qu'elles comportent des enseignements dont il faudra désormais tenir compte' (We realize that the performances at Hellerau are not simple experiments, but that they generate real results, that they offer guidance that we will need from this day on to take into account).[170]

These 'real results' and 'guidance' were bound in large part to Appia's decor – its simple, plain lines and lack of realistic detail. Auguste de Morsier, writing in the *Journal de Genève* quipped: 'Tout le bagage de l'opéra du type habituel est abandonné' (All the baggage of conventional opera is abandoned).[171] But Morsier may have had more in mind than Appia's 'abstraction architecturale'. The production's musical-gestural design was also exceptional – not to mention essential to the purported 'renovation' of music drama. According to one S. D. Gallwitz, Dalcroze's *Orpheus* signalled 'un nouvel style de drame', one in which stage movement was inspired by music:

[L]es nouvelles formes d'expression nées de l'esprit de la musique . . . ouvriront la voie à un nouvel art musico-plastique. Le réalisme presque insupportable de l'opéra moderne, qui offre sempiternellement un jeu superficiel accompagné de musique, connaîtra une re-naissance.[172]

(New forms of expression born out of the spirit of music . . . will open the way to a new musico-plastic art. The almost unbearable realism of modern opera, its superficial visual display accompanied by music, will be reborn.)

These words appear reminiscent of Duncan's musical-gestural thinking (she spoke similarly of gesture's musical 'birth'), as well as Dalcroze's predication for the future of operatic bodies on stage:

Et une fois que les chanteurs dramatiques auront appris à connaître le mécanisme admirable de leurs mouvements et l'alliance étroite de leur corps et de leur intelligence, de leur pensée, de leur volonté et leur instinct esthétique, ils triompheront complètement de tous les préjugés qui sont encore emmagasinés en eux, grâce à l'éducation et grâce à l'hérédité, ils considéreront leurs corps comme un moyen d'élévation physique – comme un instrument d'art pur et de beauté.[173]

(And once opera singers have learned about the admirable mechanism of their movements and the strict link between their body and their intelligence, their

---

[170]   *Le Monde musical*, 15 and 30 July 1913, p. 212.
[171]   Auguste de Morsier, *Journal de Genève*, 30 June 1913; repr. in Appia, *Œuvres complètes*, vol. III, p. 218.
[172]   S. D. Gallwitz; quoted in Appia, *Œuvres complètes*, vol. III, pp. 206–7.
[173]   Dalcroze, 'Le Rythme au théâtre', p. 549.

thought, their will and their aesthetic instinct, they will triumph completely over all the preconceptions that still accumulate in them, thanks to their training and inheritance, they will consider their body as a means of physical elevation – as a beautiful and pure artistic instrument.)

A trump card and a passport (conclusion)

Also reminiscent is *Le Coq d'or*: its similar reception and similar *mise en scène*, and the similar prophecies, anxieties and aspirations expressed by its producers. Both *Orpheus* and *Le Coq d'or* were extrinsically balletic; both pitted singing against dancing and staged only the latter, and both dissected an operatic narrative (and an operatic apparatus) into material and non-material forms. Moreover, the producers of both were uneasy about opera, about its fundamental illusions and inherent unreality, not to mention the perceived failings of its stage performers. They planned 'renovation'; they reshuffled their workforce: in Paris at the Opéra, and in Hellerau at the *Festspielhaus*, opera enacted a gross, physical transformation; opera became ballet.

To return to my beginning, then, and with all the examples of this chapter in mind, one might envisage *Le Coq d'or* as a barometer of critical-theatrical trends. The production encapsulates entrenched ideas and assumptions about ballet, opera, singing, dancing and the future of music theatre. More than this, it points to a widespread and widely endorsed 'gesticulatory' phenomenon, one that interconnects various individuals (Chaliapin, Massenet, Dalcroze) and productions (*Salome*, *Orphée*, *Padmâvatî*). My goal in these pages has been to reconstruct this phenomenon, to piece together the individuals and productions, and to re-establish their historical relationships. There is no doubt more work to be done, and readers may bring forth their own examples, helping to further cement our understanding of contemporary thought and theatre. Here I hope simply to have erected the scaffolding for future enquiry and, in doing so, to have underlined the significance of gesture to a historical moment in the grip of anxiety, yet on the cusp of reform.

Modernist reform, I should add. This couple of paragraphs makes for a neat conclusion, and one that may even endorse the general thrust of this book: what better way to promote the scholarly significance of dance than to proclaim the historical triumph of gesture over song, of ballet over opera? Yet I prefer to end with a few words on the specifically modernist implications of my historical thesis. 'Gesticulation', I think, may be understood as a theatrical phenomenon that ripples over into the broader contexts of modernist aesthetics.

The so-called language crisis provides one such context. As scholars have explained, the late nineteenth and early twentieth centuries witnessed a loss of confidence amongst artists and academic types in the expressive and epistemological authority of words. According to Harold B. Segel, suspicion of language and extreme aestheticism arose in the context of a widespread disillusion with the rational, cerebral bias of intellectual culture.[174] Segel describes modernism's fervour to 'revitalize' language, to variously manipulate syntax, word formations and even words themselves in order to expose 'strata of meaning previously enmeshed in coils of convention'.[175] But he also notes a concurrent enthusiasm, shared by artists and society at large, for specifically physical modes of expression. His book – titled *Body Ascendant* – explores the contemporary preoccupation with physicality, particularly on stage; chapters on pantomime and other forms of non-verbal theatre reveal the depreciation of verbal culture and the simultaneous appreciation and cultivation of gesture.

It seems more than likely, then, that the 'gesticulation' I have described owes something to this twofold contemporary condition. To put this another way, one might conceptualize the gestural phenomenon as an attempt to revitalize theatrical expression (a sign of Segel's 'body ascendant'), as well as a symptom of a newly non-rational philosophical outlook, one in which concrete, verbal exegesis gives way to intangible, physical expression.

Equally, the trend towards 'gesticulation' may have absorbed modernist suspicions of theatre itself. As is well known, from the perspective of modern artists and theorists, theatre posed a problem – namely, the actor on stage. His live presence, as well as his chief business of dramatic impersonation, was an obstacle to modernist methods: he frustrated attempts to block mimesis, to disembody theatrical signification and to develop a more abstract, non-representational theatre. Faced with this challenge, playwrights developed various dramaturgical and performance strategies in order to resist and undermine the actor's corporeal materiality: these included the use of puppets and masks, as well as a more general shift in emphasis from character, plot and point of view to the play between time and space, the patterning (or 'superposition') of dramatic and allegorical levels.[176] As a result, modernist theatre came to represent the non-representational: estrangement,

---

[174] Harold B. Segel, *Body Ascendant: Modernism and the Physical Imperative* (Baltimore, MD: The Johns Hopkins University Press, 1998).

[175] *Ibid.*, p. 2.

[176] Puchner provides a useful overview in the introduction to *Stage Fright*, pp. 1–28. Also see Jonas Barish, *The Antitheatrical Prejudice* (Berkeley and Los Angeles: University of California Press, 1981); William B. Worthen, *The Idea of the Actor: Drama and the Ethics of Performance* (Princeton University Press, 1984); and Joseph R. Roach, *The Player's Passion: Studies in the Science of Acting* (Ann Arbor: University of Michigan Press, 1993).

depersonalization, fragmentation, fracture, and the bypassing of realism, literalism and mimesis.

Examples from this chapter – such as Duncan's *Orphée* – come to mind. The dancer's embodiment of the Greek chorus (rather than any particular character); the abstract quality of her dancing (the detachment from pictorial meaning at the level of the sign); the allegorization of the Orpheus story: Duncan's danced version of Gluck's opera directed spectators' attention away from dramatic impersonation towards non-illustrative images, untrackable meanings and another, non-material plane of significance. Then there is *Le Coq d'or*. To repeat, the opera-ballet offered simultaneous yet disembodied singing and dancing, to say nothing of a plot that featured little in the way of psychological intrigue.[177] In other words, human identity was not only subordinated to action; it was fractured into earthly (gestural) and astral (sonorous) forms. Two levels of reality were held in ambiguous suspension: the multi-planar landscape became the new dramaturgical focus; the audience, abandoning the pursuit of character and plot, yet unable to absorb the entire *mise en scène* at once, scanned theatrical layers, trying to make sense of their superposition.

Both Duncan's *Orphée* and Diaghilev's *Coq d'or*, then, exemplify modernism's critique of the theatre – which is to say, of the conventional theatricality embodied in the onstage performer. Both also thematize what Elinor Fuchs has dubbed 'the death of character' – the loss of interest amongst turn-of-the-century theorists and playwrights in the principle of character as 'the motor or agency of dramatic structure' and the concomitant turn towards multi-planar forms.[178]

But readers will note the anomalous examples: the operas of Massenet, the performance styles of Calvé, Garden and their followers. These 'gesticulatory' phenomena, far from eclipsing character and dehumanizing the performer, tended to do the opposite: they proclaimed a triumphant theatricalism, going to great lengths to embody and individualize stage characters. Leaning on the scholarship of Martin Puchner, one might describe these examples as evidence of a second modernist tradition, one that Puchner calls 'pro-theatricalism'.[179] This tradition, indebted to Wagner, determined to promote the value of the theatre and of theatricality on stage. Character was exalted

---

[177] In *Padmâvatî*, too, characters are undeveloped in psychological terms: Richard Langham Smith describes 'cardboard puppets with minimal psychological development'; 'Padmâvatî', *New Grove Dictionary of Music and Musicians*, ed. Stanley Sadie and John Tyrell (London: Macmillan, 2001).

[178] Elinor Fuchs, *The Death of Character: Perspectives on Theatre after Modernism* (Bloomington: Indiana University Press, 1996), p. 22.

[179] Puchner, *Stage Fright*, p. 2.

rather than suppressed; performers celebrated the personal, the individual, the human and mimetic.

Puchner is keen to stress the slippage between the two traditions – that the boundary between modernist abstraction and pro-theatricalism was permeable, and related, ultimately, to the perceived agency of the theatre as a vehicle of social influence. I should like to stress a vehicle and an agency of a different kind: gesture, a means (on the one hand) of estranging, fragmenting and framing character, of ushering in a new symbolic order, and (on the other) of celebrating physicality, energy, spectacle and theatrical illusionism.[180] The malleability of gesture as a dramaturgical device: this is my point, and this, I wager, was gesture's trump card in the early twentieth century – particularly in face of a devolving operatic tradition. The 'gesticulation' of opera, then, may have reflected not only a contemporary disillusionment with singing, but a desire to offer something that singing alone could not – an engagement with modernist theatrical ideologies.[181] Gesture, put plainly, was opera's means of survival, its passport into the twentieth century. Without it, opera was without modern significance; with it, opera was ever more like ballet.

---

[180] To put this another way, one might describe gesture's 'absolute' and 'pictorial' (or 'programmatic') tendencies. I am grateful to Dean Sutcliffe for these terms.

[181] The well-known enthusiasm for gesture shared by Kurt Weill and Bertolt Brecht in the 1920s and 30s betrays the historical reach of this idea. For more on the pair and their theories of 'Gestus', see Albright, *Untwisting the Serpent: Modernism in Music, Literature and the Other Arts* (University of Chicago Press, 2000), pp. 110–22. Albright's volume also includes comments from Weill and others (Alban Berg, Ernst Krenek) on the developmental trends of opera during the period.

Select bibliography

Archives

Paris, Bibliothèque-musée de l'Opéra (F-Po)

Archives internationales de la danse

Dossiers d'artistes: Lucienne Bréval; Emma Calvé; Fyodor Chaliapin; Ivan Clustine; Jaques-Émile Dalcroze; Isadora Duncan; Loie Fuller; Mary Garden; Tamara Karsavina; Victor Maurel; Vaslav Nijinsky; Natalia Trouhanova; Jean d'Udine

Dossiers d'œuvres: *Esclarmonde* (1889); *Thaïs* (1894); *Salome* (1905); *Aphrodite* (1906); *Le Pavillon d'Armide* (1909); *Les Sylphides* (1909); *Schéhérazade* (1910); *Giselle* (1910); *La Fête chez Thérèse* (1910); *España* (1911); *La Roussalka* (1911); *Le Dieu bleu* (1912); *L'Après-midi d'un faune* (1912); *Les Bacchantes* (1912); *La Péri* (1912); *Le Sacre du printemps* (1913); *Suite de danses* (1913); *Le Coq d'or* (1914); *Philotis* (1914); *Hansli le bossu* (1914); *Les Noces* (1923); *Padmâvatî* (1923)

Fonds Bakst

Fonds Kochno

Fonds Rouché

Paris, Bibliothèque nationale de France (F-Pn, Département des Arts du spectacle)

Collection Auguste Rondel (Ro)

New York Public Library for the Performing Arts (US-NYpl)

Jerome Robbins Dance Division: Gabriel Astruc–Diaghilev Collection; Lincoln Kirstein Collection; Roger Pryor Dodge Collection

Robinson Locke Collection: Mary Garden Scrapbooks

Cambridge, MA, Houghton Library, Harvard University (US-CAh)

Theatre Collection: Howard D. Rothschild Collection on the Ballets Russes of Sergey Diaghilev; Marchioness of Ripon Scrapbooks; Michel Fokine Papers; S. L. Grigoriev Papers; Stravinsky–Diaghilev Foundation Collection

French newspapers and journals

L'Action française
Comœdia
Comœdia illustré
Le Correspondant
Le Courrier musical
La Critique indépendante
La Dépêche
L'Écho de Paris
L'Éclair
L'Excelsior
Le Feu
Le Figaro
Le Gaulois
Gazette des tribunaux
Gil Blas
La Grande Revue
Je sais tout
Le Journal
Journal des débats
La Liberté
Le Matin
Le Ménestrel
Le Mercure de France
Le Mercure musical
Le Miroir
Le Monde artiste
Le Monde musical
Montjoie!
Musica
La Nouvelle Revue française
L'Occident
La Parthénon
La Patrie
La Petite République
La Revue
La Revue blanche
La Revue de Paris
Revue des deux mondes
Revue française de musique

Revue générale
Revue musicale
Revue musicale S.I.M.
Le Temps
Le Théâtre
La Tribune musicale
Le Voltaire

Books, articles and unpublished theses

Abbate, Carolyn, *Unsung Voices: Opera and Musical Narrative in the Nineteenth Century*. Princeton University Press, 1991.

  In Search of Opera. Princeton University Press, 2001.

  'Music: Drastic or Gnostic?', *Critical Inquiry*, 30/3 (2004), pp. 505–36.

  'Cipher and Performance in Sternberg's *Dishonored*', in Karol Berger and Anthony Newcomb (eds.), *Music and the Aesthetics of Modernity*. Cambridge, MA: Harvard University Press, 2005, pp. 357–92.

Abel, Richard (ed.), *French Film Theory and Criticism, 1907–1939*. Princeton University Press, 1988.

Agathocleous, Tanya, *Urban Realism and the Cosmopolitan Imagination in the Nineteenth Century*. Cambridge University Press, 2010.

Albright, Ann Cooper, *Choreographing Difference: The Body and Identity in Contemporary Dance*. Middletown, CT: Wesleyan University Press, 1997.

  Traces of Light: Absence and Presence in the Work of Loïe Fuller. Middletown, CT: Wesleyan University Press, 2007.

Albright, Daniel, *Stravinsky: The Music Box and the Nightingale*. London: Gordon and Breach, 1989.

  Untwisting the Serpent: Modernism in Music, Literature, and the Other Arts. University of Chicago Press, 2000.

  'Golden Calves: The Role of Dance in Opera', *The Opera Quarterly*, 22/1 (2006), pp. 22–37.

Alda, Frances, *Men, Women and Tenors*. Boston, MA: Houghton Mifflin, 1937.

Allanbrook, Wye, *Rhythmic Gesture in Mozart: 'Le Nozze di Figaro' and 'Don Giovanni'*. University of Chicago Press, 1983.

Anthony, James R., 'The French *Opéra-Ballet* in the Early Eighteenth Century: Problems of Definition and Classification', *Journal of the American Musicological Society*, 18/2 (1965), pp. 197–20.

Antliff, Mark and Patricia Leighten, *Cubism and Culture*. London: Thames and Hudson, 2001.

Apollinaire, Guillaume, *Apollinaire on Art*, ed. LeRoy C. Breunig, trans. Susan Suleiman. New York: Viking Press, 1972.

Appia, Adolphe, *Œuvres complètes*, ed. Marie L. Bablet-Hahn, 4 vols. Lausanne: L'Âge d'Homme, 1988.

Armstrong, Isobel, *The Radical Aesthetic*. Oxford: Blackwell, 2000.

Armstrong, Tim, *Modernism, Technology and the Body: A Cultural Study*. Cambridge University Press, 1998.

Atlas, Allan W., 'Mimi's Death: Mourning in Puccini and Leoncavallo', *Journal of Musicology*, 14/1 (1996), pp. 52–79.

Audubert, Jules, *L'Art du chant, suivi d'un traité de maintien théâtral*. Paris: Brandus et Cie, 1876.

Austin, William W. (ed.), *Claude Debussy: Prelude to 'The Afternoon of a Faun', Norton Critical Score*. London: Norton, 1970.

d'Avenel, Georges, *Le Nivellement des jouissances*. Paris: Flammarion, 1913.

Baer, Nancy Van Norman (ed.), *The Art of Enchantment: Diaghilev's Ballets Russes*. San Francisco, CA: Universe Books, 1989.

Bailey, Peter, *Popular Culture and Performance in the Victorian City*. Cambridge University Press, 1998.

Barish, Jonas, *The Antitheatrical Prejudice*. Berkeley and Los Angeles: University of California Press, 1981.

Barnes, Clives, 'The Russians Have Come, the Russians Have Come', *Dance Magazine*, 72/2 (1998), p. 162.

Barrès, Maurice, *Contre les étrangers: étude pour la protection des ouvriers français*. Paris: Grande Imprimerie Parisienne, 1893.
   Scènes et doctrines du nationalisme. Paris: F. Juven, 1902.

Barthes, Roland, *Image-Music-Text*, trans. and ed. Stephen Heath. London: Fontana, 1977.

Batson, Charles, *Dance, Desire, and Anxiety in Early Twentieth-Century French Theater*. Aldershot: Ashgate, 2005.

Bazaillas, Albert, *Musique et inconscience: introduction à la psychologie de l'inconscient*. Paris: Félix Alcan, 1908.

Beacham, Richard C., *Adolphe Appia: Artist and Visionary of the Modern Theatre*. London: Routledge, 1994.

Benedetti, Jean, *Stanislavski: An Introduction*. London: Methuen, 1982.
   Stanislavski and the Actor. London: Methuen, 1998.

Benjamin, Roger, *Orientalist Aesthetics: Art, Colonialism and French North Africa, 1880–1930*. Berkeley and Los Angeles: University of California Press, 2003.

Benois, Alexandre, *Reminiscences of the Russian Ballet*, trans. Mary Britnieva. London: Putnam, 1941.

Berchtold, Alfred, 'Émile Jaques-Dalcroze et son temps', in Frank Martin (ed.), *Émile Jaques-Dalcroze: l'homme, le compositeur, le créateur de la rythmique*. Neuchâtel: Éditions de la Baconnière, 1965, pp. 27–158.

Berghaus, Günther, *Futurism and Politics: Between Anarchist Rebellion and Fascist Reaction, 1909–1944*. Oxford University Press, 1996.

   Italian Futurist Theatre, 1909–1944. Oxford University Press, 1998.

Berlanstein, Lenard R., *Daughters of Eve: A Cultural History of French Theater Women from the Old Regime to the Fin de Siècle*. Cambridge, MA: Harvard University Press, 2001.

   'Historicizing and Gendering Celebrity Culture: Famous Women in Nineteenth-Century France', *Journal of Women's History*, 16/4 (2004), pp. 65–91.

Berman, Jennifer Schiff, *Modernist Fiction, Cosmopolitanism, and the Politics of Community*. Cambridge University Press, 2001.

Berman, Marshall, *All That is Solid Melts into Air: The Experience of Modernity*. New York: Simon and Schuster, 1982.

Bhabha, Homi, *The Location of Culture*. 1994; repr. London: Routledge, 2005.

Bhogal, Gurminder Kaur, 'Debussy's Arabesque and Ravel's *Daphnis et Chloé* (1912)', *Twentieth-Century Music*, 3/2 (2006), pp. 171–99.

Bielecki, Emma, 'Faking It: Representations of Art Forgery from the Second Empire to the *Belle Époque*', in Louis Hardwick (ed.), *New Approaches to Crime in French Literature, Culture and Film*. New York: Peter Lang, 2009, pp. 35–50.

Blackmer, Corrine E. and Patricia Juliana Smith (eds.), *En Travesti: Women, Gender Subversion, Opera*. New York: Columbia University Press, 1995.

Bohn, Willard, *The Aesthetics of Visual Poetry, 1914–1928*. Cambridge University Press, 1986.

Bourneville, Désiré-Magloire and Paul Régnard, *Iconographie photographique de la Salpêtrière*, 3 vols. Paris: Progrès Médical/Delahaye et Lecrosnier, 1875–1880.

Bowlt, John E., 'Diaghilev and the Eighteenth Century', in Sjeng Scheijen (ed.), *Working for Diaghilev*. Groninger Museum, 2004, pp. 38–48.

Braun, Marta, *Picturing Time: The Work of Étienne-Jules Marey (1830–1904)*. University of Chicago Press, 1994.

Breckenridge, Carol A., Sheldon Pollock and Homi Bhabha (eds.), *Cosmopolitanism*. Durham, NC: Duke University Press, 2002.

Bretell, Richard R., *Modern Art, 1851–1929: Capitalism and Representation*. Oxford University Press, 1999.

Brillant, Maurice, *Problèmes de la danse*. 1953; repr. Paris: Librairie Théâtrale, 1979.

Bronfen, Elisabeth, *The Knotted Subject: Hysteria and its Discontents*. Princeton University Press, 1998.

Brown, Julia Prewitt, *Cosmopolitan Criticism: Oscar Wilde's Philosophy of Art*. Charlottesville: University of Virginia Press, 1997.

Bruneau, Alfred, *Musiques d'hier et de demain*. Paris: Bibliothèque Charpentier, 1900.

   Musiques de Russie et musiciens de France. Paris: Charpentier, 1903.

Buci-Glucksmann, Christine, 'Catastrophic Utopia: The Feminine as Allegory of the Modern', *Representations*, 14 (1986), pp. 220–9.

Buckle, Richard, *Nijinsky*. London: Weidenfeld and Nicolson, 1971.

   Diaghilev. London: Weidenfeld and Nicolson, 1979.

Bullard, Truman C., 'The First Performance of Igor Stravinsky's *Sacre du printemps*', PhD thesis, University of Rochester, 1971.

Caballero, Carlo, *Fauré and French Musical Aesthetics*. Cambridge University Press, 2001.

Cabanès, Jean-Louis, *Les Frères Goncourt: art et écriture*. Presses Universitaires de Bordeaux, 1997.

Calvé, Emma, *My Life*. London: Appleton, 1922.

Camard, Jean-Pierre, Paul Ricard and Lynne Thornton, *L'Art et la vie en France à la belle époque*. Paris: Paul Ricard, 1971.

Canudo, Ricciotto, *Le Livre de l'évolution de l'homme: psychologie musicale des civilisations*. Paris: E. Sansot et Cie, 1907.

Carter, Alexandra and Janet O'Shea (eds.), *The Routledge Dance Studies Reader*. 1998; rev. edn London: Routledge, 2010.

Chaliapin, Fyodor, *Man and Mask: Forty Years in the Life of a Singer*, trans. Phyllis Mégroz. London: Victor Gollancz, 1932.

Charbonnier, Georges, *Le Monologue du peintre*. Paris: Éditions Julliard, 1960.

Charcot, Jean Martin, *Œuvres complètes*, 9 vols. Paris: Progrès Médical/ Lecrosnier et Babé, 1886–9.

Charcot, Jean Martin and Paul Richer, 'Note on Certain Facts of Cerebral Automatism Observed in Hysteria during the Cataleptic Period of Hypnotism', *Journal of Nervous and Mental Disease*, 10 (1883), pp. 1–13.

Charle, Christophe, *Paris fin de siècle: culture et politique*. Paris: Éditions du Seuil, 1998.

Chu, Petra ten-Doesschate and Gabriel P. Weisberg (eds.), *The Popularization of Images: Visual Culture under the July Monarchy*. Princeton University Press, 1994.

Clark, Maribeth, 'Understanding French Grand Opéra through Dance', PhD thesis, University of Pennsylvania, 1998.

   'The Quadrille as Embodied Musical Experience in 19th-Century Paris', *Journal of Musicology*, 19/3 (2002), pp. 503–26.

   'The Body and the Voice in *La Muette de Portici*', *19th-Century Music*, 27/ 2 (2003), pp. 116–31.

'The Role of *Gustave, ou le bal masqué* in Restraining the Bourgeois Body of the July Monarchy', *Musical Quarterly*, 88/2 (2005), pp. 204–31.

Clark, T. J. *The Painting of Modern Life: Paris in the Art of Manet and his Followers*. New York: Knopf, 1984.

Farewell to an Idea: Episodes from a History of Modernism. New Haven, CT, and London: Yale University Press, 1999.

Code, David J., 'Hearing Debussy Reading Mallarmé: Music *après Wagner* in the *Prélude à l'après-midi d'un faune*', *Journal of the American Musicological Society*, 54/3 (2001), pp. 493–554.

Copeland, Roger and Marshall Cohen (eds.), *What is Dance? Readings in Theory and Criticism*. Oxford University Press, 1983.

Cottington, David, *Cubism and its Histories*. Manchester University Press, 2004.

Counsell, Colin, *Signs of Performance*. London: Routledge, 1996.

Crary, Jonathan, *Techniques of the Observer: On Vision and Modernity in the Nineteenth Century*. Cambridge, MA: The MIT Press, 1992.

Suspensions of Perception: Attention, Spectacle and Modern Culture. Cambridge, MA: The MIT Press, 1999.

Cui, César, *La Musique en Russie*. Paris: Fischbacher, 1880.

Current, Richard Nelson and Marcia Ewing Current, *Loie Fuller: Goddess of Light*. Boston, MA: Northeastern University Press, 1997.

Curtis, Michael, *Three Against the Third Republic: Sorel, Barrès and Maurras*. Princeton University Press, 1959.

Dagognet, François, *Étienne-Jules Marey: A Passion for the Trace*, trans. Robert Galeta. Cambridge, MA: The MIT Press, 1992.

Daly, Ann, *Done into Dance: Isadora Duncan in America*. Bloomington: Indiana University Press, 1995.

'The Natural Body', in Ann Dils and Ann Cooper Albright (eds.), *Moving History/Dancing Cultures*. Middletown, CT: Wesleyan University Press, 2001, pp. 288–99.

Daudet, Léon, *Hors du joug allemand*. Paris: Nouvelle Librairie Nationale, 1915.

L'Entre-deux-guerres. Paris: Nouvelle Librairie Nationale, 1915.

Davies, James Q., 'Dancing the Symphonic: Beethoven-Bochsa's *Symphonie Pastorale*, 1829', *19th-Century Music*, 27/1 (2003), pp. 25–47.

Davis, Mary E., *Classic Chic: Music, Fashion, and Modernism*. Berkeley and Los Angeles: University of California Press, 2006.

Erik Satie. London: Reaktion Books, 2007.

Ballets Russes Style: Diaghilev's Dancers and Paris Fashion. London: Reaktion Books, 2010.

Deak, Frantisek, *Symbolist Theatre: The Formation of an Avant-Garde*. Baltimore, MD, and London: The Johns Hopkins University Press, 1993.

Deane, Basil, *Albert Roussel*. London: Barrie and Rockliff, 1961.

Debon, Claude, *'Calligrammes' de Guillaume Apollinaire*. Paris: Gallimard, 2004.

Denby, Edwin, *Dance Writings*. New York: Knopf, 1986.

Denis, Maurice, *Journal*, 3 vols. Paris: Éditions du Vieux Colombier, 1957.

Desmond, Jane C. (ed.), *Meaning in Motion: New Cultural Studies of Dance*. Durham, NC: Duke University Press, 1997.

Doane, Mary Ann, 'The Voice in the Cinema: The Articulation of Body and Space', *Yale French Studies*, 60/1 (1980), pp. 33–50.

Dobie, Madeleine, *Foreign Bodies: Gender, Language and Culture in French Orientalism*. Stanford University Press, 2001.

Drain, Richard (ed.), *Twentieth-Century Theatre: A Sourcebook*. London: Routledge, 1995.

Driault, Édouard, *Plus rien d'allemand*. Paris: Tenin, 1918.

Duchamp, Marcel, *The Writings of Marcel Duchamp*, ed. Michel Sanouillet and Elmer Peterson. Oxford University Press, 1973.

Duncan, Isadora, *Écrits sur la danse*. Paris: Éditions du Grenier, 1927.
  My Life. 1928; repr. London: Gollancz, 1996.

Eksteins, Modris, *Rites of Spring: The Great War and the Birth of the Modern Age*. Boston, MA: Houghton Mifflin, 1989.

Ellis, Katharine, *Interpreting the Musical Past: Early Music in Nineteenth-Century France*. Oxford University Press, 2005.

Esslin, Martin, *Theatre of the Absurd*. Garden City, NY: Doubleday, 1961.

Evans, David and Kate Griffiths (eds.), *Pleasure and Pain in Nineteenth-Century French Literature and Culture*. New York: Rodopi, 2008.

Fauser, Annegret, 'Visual Pleasures–Musical Signs: Dance at the Paris Opéra', *South Atlantic Quarterly*, 104/1 (2005), pp. 99–121.
  (ed.), *Dossier de presse parisienne: Jules Massenet, 'Esclarmonde' (1889)*. Heilbronn: Édition Lucie Galland, 2001.

Fauser, Annegret and Mark Everist (eds.), *Music, Theatre, and Cultural Transfer: Paris, 1830–1914*. University of Chicago Press, 2009.

Fédorovski, Vladimir, *L'Histoire secrète des Ballets Russes*. Paris: Éditions du Rocher, 2002.

Féré, Charles, *Sensation et mouvement*. Paris: Félix Alcan, 1887.

Ferguson, Priscilla Parkhurst, *Paris as Revolution: Writing the 19th-Century City*. Berkeley and Los Angeles: University of California Press, 1994.

Fine, Robert, *Cosmopolitanism*. London: Routledge, 2007.

Flam, Jack, *Matisse: The Dance*. Washington, DC: National Gallery of Art, 1993.
  (ed.), *Matisse on Art*. 1978; rev. edn Berkeley and Los Angeles: University of California Press, 1995.

Fleischer, Mary, *Embodied Texts: Symbolist Playwright-Dancer Collaborations*. New York: Rodopi, 2007.

Fokine, Michel, *Memoirs of a Ballet Master*, ed. Anatole Chujoy, trans. Vitale Fokine. London: Constable, 1961.

Foster, Hal, 'The "Primitive" Unconscious of Modern Art', *October*, 34 (1985), pp. 45–70.

Foster, Susan Leigh (ed.), *Choreographing History*. Bloomington: Indiana University Press, 1995.

Francastel, Pierre, *La Création du musée historique de Versailles et la transformation du palais, 1832–1848*. Paris: Les Presses Modernes, 1930.

Franko, Mark, *Dancing Modernism/Performing Politics*. Bloomington: Indiana University Press, 1995.

Frolova-Walker, Marina, 'Russian Opera: Between Modernism and Romanticism', in Mervyn Cooke (ed.), *The Cambridge Companion to Twentieth-Century Opera*. Cambridge University Press, 2005, pp. 181–96.

Fuchs, Elinor, *The Death of Character: Perspectives on Theatre after Modernism*. Bloomington: Indiana University Press, 1996.

Fulcher, Jane, *French Cultural Politics and Music: From the Dreyfus Affair to the First World War*. Oxford University Press, 1999.

The Composer as Intellectual: Music and Ideology in France. Oxford University Press, 2005.

Fuller, Loie, *Fifteen Years of a Dancer's Life*. 1913; repr. New York: Dance Horizons, 1977.

Garafola, Lynn, *Diaghilev's Ballets Russes*. 1989; repr. New York: Da Capo, 1998.

Legacies of Twentieth-Century Dance. Middletown, CT: Wesleyan University Press, 2005.

(ed.), *Rethinking the Sylph: New Perspectives on the Romantic Ballet*. Hanover, NH: University Press of New England, 1997.

Garden, Mary and Louis Biancolli, *Mary Garden's Story*. London: Michael Joseph, 1952.

Garelick, Rhonda, *Electric Salome: Loie Fuller's Performance of Modernism*. Princeton University Press, 2007.

Geminiani, Francesco, *Treatise of Good Taste in the Art of Music*. London: n.p., 1749; facsimile Wyton: King's Music, 1988.

Genrich, Tom, *Authentic Fictions: Cosmopolitan Writing of the Troisième République, 1908–1940*. New York: Peter Lang, 2004.

Gillis, Patrick, '*Thaïs* dans tous ses états: genèse et remaniements', *L'Avant-scène opéra: 'Thaïs'*, 109 (1988), pp. 66–74.

'*Thaïs* à l'Opéra: du roman à la comédie lyrique, pertes et profits', in Marie-Claire Bancquart and Jean Dérens (eds.), *Anatole France:*

humanisme et actualité. Paris: Bibliothèque Historique de la Ville de Paris, 1994, pp. 107–34.

Goehr, Lydia, *The Imaginary Museum of Musical Works: An Essay in the Philosophy of Music*. 1992; rev. edn Oxford University Press, 2007.

Goetz, Christopher G., *Charcot the Clinician: The Tuesday Lessons*. New York: Raven Press, 1987.

Goetz, Christopher G., Michel Bonduelle and Toby Gelfand, *Charcot: Constructing Neurology*. Oxford University Press, 1995.

Goncourt, Edmond de and Jules de Goncourt, *Journal: mémoires de la vie littéraire*, 9 vols. Paris: Charpentier, 1887–96.

Gorce, Jérôme de la, 'De l'opéra-ballet aux fragments', *XVIIe siècle*, 198 (1998), pp. 37–50.

Gosling, Nigel, *Paris, 1900–1914: The Miraculous Years*. London: Weidenfeld and Nicolson, 1978.

Gradmann, Christoph, 'Invisible Enemies: Bacteriology and the Language of Politics in Imperial Germany', *Science in Context*, 13 (2000), pp. 9–30.

Greskovic, Robert, *Ballet 101: A Complete Guide to Learning and Loving the Ballet*. 1998; rev. edn Milwaukee, WI: Limelight Editions, 2005.

Grey, Thomas S. (ed.), *Richard Wagner and his World*. Princeton University Press, 2009.

Gritten, Anthony and Elaine King (eds.), *Music and Gesture*. Aldershot: Ashgate, 2006.

  New Perspectives on Music and Gesture. Aldershot: Ashgate, 2010.

Groberg, Kristi A., 'The Shade of Lucifer's Dark Wing: Satanism in Silver Age Russia', in Bernice Glatzer Rosenthal (ed.), *The Occult in Russian and Soviet Culture*. Ithaca, NY: Cornell University Press, 1997, pp. 99–133.

Groos, Arthur and Roger Parker (eds.), *Giacomo Puccini, 'La bohème'*. Cambridge University Press, 1986.

Guest, Anne Hutchinson and Claudia Jeschke, *Nijinsky's 'Faune' Restored*. Philadelphia, PA: Gordon and Breach, 1991.

Guest, Igor, *Le Ballet de l'Opéra de Paris: trois siècles d'histoire et de tradition*. 1976; repr. Paris: Flammarion, 2001.

Guichard, Léon, *La Musique et les lettres en France au temps du wagnérisme*. Paris: Presses Universitaires de France, 1963.

Guillain, Georges, *J.-M. Charcot (1825–1893): sa vie, son œuvre*. Paris: Masson, 1955.

Gumbrecht, Hans Ulrich, *The Production of Presence: What Meaning Cannot Convey*. Stanford University Press, 2004.

  'Production of Presence, Interspersed with Absence: A Modernist View on Music, Libretti, and Staging', trans. Matthew Tiews, in Karol Berger and

Anthony Newcomb (eds.), *Music and the Aesthetics of Modernity.* Cambridge, MA: Harvard University Press, 2005, pp. 343–55.

In Praise of Athletic Beauty. Cambridge, MA: Harvard University Press, 2006.

Hahn, Reynaldo, *Du Chant* (1920), in *On Singers and Singing*, trans. Leopold Simoneau. London: Christopher Helm, 1990.

Haldey, Olga, *Mamontov's Private Opera: The Search for Modernism in Russian Theater.* Bloomington: Indiana University Press, 2010.

Hamon, Philippe and Alexandrine Viboud, *Dictionnaire thématique du roman de mœurs, 1850–1914.* Paris: Presses de la Sorbonne Nouvelle, 2003.

Harris, Jonathan P., *Writing Back to Modern Art.* London: Routledge, 2005.

Hart, Brian, '"Le Cas Debussy": Reviews and Polemics about the Composer's "New Manner"', in Jane F. Fulcher (ed.), *Debussy and His World.* Princeton University Press, 2001, pp. 363–82.

Harvey, David, *Paris: Capital of Modernity.* London: Routledge, 2003.

Heisler, Wayne, *The Ballet Collaborations of Richard Strauss.* University of Rochester Press, 2009.

Hemmings, F. J., *The Russian Novel in France, 1884–1914.* Oxford University Press, 1950.

Henson, Karen, 'In the House of Disillusion: Augusta Holmès and *La Montagne noire*', *Cambridge Opera Journal*, 9/3 (1997), pp. 233–62.

'Verdi, Victor Maurel and *Fin-de-Siècle* Operatic Performance', *Cambridge Opera Journal*, 19/1 (2007), pp. 59–84.

Hepokoski, James, *Giuseppe Verdi: 'Otello'.* Cambridge University Press, 1987.

Herbert, Robert L. (ed.), *Modern Artists on Art.* 1964; rev. edn Mineola, NY: Dover, 2000.

Hibberd, Sarah (ed.), *Melodramatic Voices: Understanding Music Drama.* Aldershot: Ashgate, 2011.

Higgonet, Patrice, *Paris, Capital of the World.* Cambridge, MA: Harvard University Press, 2002.

Hindson, Catherine, *Female Performance Practice on the Fin-de-Siècle Popular Stages of London and Paris.* Manchester University Press, 2007.

Hodson, Millicent, *Nijinsky's Crime Against Grace: Reconstruction of the Original Choreography for 'Le Sacre du printemps'.* Hillsdale, NY: Pendragon, 1995.

Holford-Strevens, Leofranc, 'Sirens in Antiquity and the Middle Ages', in Lynda Phyllis Austern and Inna Naroditskaya (eds.), *Music of the Sirens.* Bloomington: Indiana University Press, 2006, pp. 16–51.

Honigwachs, L., 'The Edwardian Discovery of Russia, 1900–1917', PhD thesis, Columbia University, 1977.

Hoobler, Dorothy and Thomas Hoobler, *The Crimes of Paris: A True Story of Murder, Theft, and Detection*. Boston, MA: Little, Brown and Company, 2009.

Horne, Alistair, *Seven Ages of Paris: Portrait of a City*. London: Macmillan, 2002.

Howard, Kathleen, *Confessions of an Opera Singer*. London: Kegan Paul, 1920.

Huebner, Steven, *French Opera at the Fin de Siècle: Wagnerism, Nationalism, and Style*. Oxford University Press, 1999.

Hutcheon, Linda and Michael Hutcheon, *Bodily Charm, Living Opera*. Lincoln: University of Nebraska Press, 2000.

Huyssen, Andreas, *After the Great Divide: Modernism, Mass Culture, Postmodernism*. Bloomington: Indiana University Press, 1986.

Järvinen, Hanna, 'Dancing without Space: On Nijinsky's *L'Après-midi d'un faune* (1912)', *Dance Research*, 27/1 (2009), pp. 28–64.

   'Failed Impressions: Diaghilev's Ballets Russes in America, 1916', *Dance Research Journal*, 42/2 (2010), pp. 76–108.

Jones, Colin, *Paris: Biography of a City*. London: Allen Lane, 2004.

Jordan, Stephanie, 'Debussy, the Dance, and the Faune', in James Briscoe (ed.), *Debussy in Performance*. New Haven, CT, and London: Yale University Press, 1999, pp. 119–34.

   Stravinsky Dances: Re-Visions Across a Century. London: Dance Books, 2007.

Joseph, Charles, *Stravinsky and Balanchine: A Journey of Invention*. New Haven, CT, and London: Yale University Press, 2002.

Jowitt, Deborah, 'The Ballets Russes Revolution', *Dance Magazine*, 83/2 (2009), pp. 26–9.

Kahane, Martine and Nicole Wild (eds.), *Wagner et la France*. Paris: Bibliothèque Nationale de France, 1983.

Kelkel, Manfred (ed.), *Albert Roussel: musique et esthétique*. Paris: Vrin, 1989.

Kendall, Elizabeth, '1900, A Doorway to Revolution', *Dance Magazine*, 73/1 (1999), pp. 80–3.

Kennan, George F., *The Decline of Bismarck's European Order: Franco-Russian Relations 1875–1890*. Princeton University Press, 1979.

   The Fateful Alliance: France, Russia, and the Coming of the First World War. New York: Pantheon, 1984.

Kern, Stephen, *The Culture of Time and Space: 1880–1918*. Cambridge, MA: Harvard University Press, 1983.

Kirby, Michael, *Futurist Performance*. New York: E. P. Dutton, 1971.

Knapp, Bettina L., *The Reign of the Theatrical Director: French Theatre, 1887–1924*. New York: Whitston, 1988.

Kochno, Boris, *Diaghilev and the Ballets Russes*, trans. Adrienne Foulke. London: The Penguin Press, 1971.

Kopelson, Kevin, *The Queer Afterlife of Vaslav Nijinsky*. Stanford University Press, 1997.

Kregor, Jonathan, *Liszt as Transcriber*. Cambridge University Press, 2010.

Kreuzer, Gundula, *Verdi and the Germans: From Unification to Third Reich*. Cambridge University Press, 2010.

Kurth, Peter, *Isadora: A Sensational Life*. Boston, MA: Little, Brown and Company, 2001.

Landels, John G., *Music in Ancient Greece and Rome*. London: Routledge, 1999.

Launay, Elisabeth, *Les Frères Goncourt, collectionneurs de dessins*. Paris: Arthena, 1991.

Leader, Darian, *Stealing the Mona Lisa: What Art Stops Us From Seeing*. New York: Counterpoint, 2002.

Lecoq, Jacques, *Le Théâtre du geste* (1987), in *Theatre of Movement and Gesture*, trans. David Bradby. London: Routledge, 2006.

Le Guin, Elizabeth, *Boccherini's Body: An Essay in Carnal Musicology*. Berkeley and Los Angeles: University of California Press, 2005.

Leopold, Silke (ed.), *Musikalische Metamorphosen: Formen und Geschichte der Bearbeitung*. Kassel: Bärenreiter, 1992.

Lepecki, André, *Exhausting Dance: Performance and the Politics of Movement*. London: Routledge, 2006.

  (ed.), *Of the Presence of the Body: Essays on Dance and Performance Theory*. Middletown, CT: Wesleyan University Press, 2004.

Levitz, Tamara, 'In the Footsteps of Eurydice: Gluck's *Orpheus und Eurydice* in Hellerau, 1913', *Echo*, 3/2 (2001), no page numbers.

  'Syvilla Fort's Africanist Modernism and John Cage's Gestic Music: The Story of *Bacchanale*', *The South Atlantic Quarterly*, 104/1 (2005), pp. 123–49.

Lista, Giovanni, *Loïe Fuller: danseuse de la belle époque*. Paris: Somogy, 1995.

Lowenthal, Lillian, *The Search for Isadora: The Legend and Legacy of Isadora Duncan*. Pennington, NJ: Dance Horizons, 1993.

MacMillan, James F., *Twentieth-Century France: Politics and Society*. New York and London: Edward Arnold, 1992.

Maehder, Jürgen, 'Paris-Bilder: Zur Transformation von Henry Murgers Roman in den Bohème-Opern Puccinis und Leoncavallos', *Jahrbuch für Opernforschung*, 2 (1986), pp. 109–76.

Mallarmé, Stéphane, *Œuvres complètes*, ed. G. Jean-Aubry and Henri Mondor. Paris: Gallimard, 1945.

Marchesi, Mathilde, *Marchesi and Music: Passages from the Life of a Famous Singing Teacher*. New York: Harper, 1897.

Marks, Steven G., *How Russia Shaped the Modern World: From Art to Anti-Semitism, Ballet to Bolshevism*. Princeton University Press, 2003.

Marrinan, Michael, *Painting Politics for Louis-Philippe: Art and Ideology in Orleanist France*. New Haven, CT, and London: Yale University Press, 1988.

Massenet, Jules, *Mes souvenirs*. Paris: Lafitte, 1912.

Mauclair, Camille, *Trois crises de l'art actuel*. Paris: Fasquelle, 1906.
    Histoire de la musique européenne, 1850–1914. Paris: Fischbacher, 1914.

Maurras, Charles, *Kiel et Tanger*. Paris: Nouvelle Librairie Nationale, 1910.
    Mes Idées politiques. Paris: Fayard, 1937.

Mawer, Deborah, *The Ballets of Maurice Ravel: Creation and Interpretation*. Aldershot: Ashgate, 2006.

McCarren, Felicia, *Dance Pathologies: Performance, Poetics, Medicine*. Stanford University Press, 1998.
    Dancing Machines: Choreographies of the Age of Mechanical Reproduction. Stanford University Press, 2003.

Merlin, Bella, *Konstantin Stanislavski*. London: Routledge, 2003.

Merlin, Olivier, *L'Opéra de Paris*. Fribourg: Hatier, 1975.

Meyerheim, Jane, *L'Art du chant technique*. Paris: Costallat, 1905.

Meyerhold, Vsevolod, *Meyerhold on Theatre*, ed. Edward Braun. New York: Hill and Wang, 1969.

Micale, Mark (ed.), *The Mind of Modernism: Medicine, Psychology, and the Cultural Arts in Europe and America, 1880–1940*. Stanford University Press, 2004.

Michelis, Marco de, 'Modernity and Reform: Heinrich Tessenow and the Institute Dalcroze at Hellerau', *Perspecta*, 26 (1990), pp. 143–70.

Migot, Georges, *Essais pour une esthétique générale*. Paris: Eugène Figuière et Cie, 1920.
    Appogiatures résolues et non résolues. Paris: Éditions de la Douce France, 1922.

Morrison, Simon, 'The Origins of *Daphnis et Chloé* (1912)', *19th-Century Music*, 28/1 (2004), pp. 50–76.

Moseley, Roger, 'Work or Play? Brahms's Performance of His Own Music', in Kevin C. Karnes and Walter Frisch (eds.), *Johannes Brahms and His World*. Princeton University Press, 2009, pp. 137–65.

Munthe, Axel, *The Story of San Michele*. London: John Murray, 1930.

Murphy, Kerry, 'Melba's Paris Debut: Another White Voice?', *Musicology Australia*, 33/1 (2011), pp. 1–11.

Musset, Alfred de, *Poésies nouvelles*. 1851; repr. Paris: Gilbert, 1962.

Nava, Mica, *Visceral Cosmopolitanism: Gender, Culture and the Normalization of Difference*. New York: Berg, 2007.

Navarette, Susan J., *The Shape of Fear: Horror and the Fin de Siècle*. Lexington: University Press of Kentucky, 1998.

Nead, Lynda, *Victorian Babylon: People, Streets and Images in Nineteenth-Century London*. New Haven, CT, and London: Yale University Press, 2000.

   The Haunted Gallery: Painting, Photography and Film c.1900. New Haven, CT, and London: Yale University Press, 2007.

Nectoux, Jean-Michel (ed.), *Nijinsky: 'Prélude à l'après-midi d'un faune'*. London: Thames and Hudson, 1990.

Ngal, Sianne, *Ugly Feelings*. Cambridge, MA: Harvard University Press, 2004.

Nijinsky, Romola, *Nijinsky*. London: Victor Gollancz, 1933.

Offen, Karen, 'Depopulation, Nationalism, and Feminism in *Fin-de-Siècle* France', *American Historical Review*, 89/3 (1984), pp. 648–76.

Opstad, Gillian, *Debussy's Mélisande: The Lives of Georgette Leblanc, Mary Garden and Maggie Tayte*. Woodbridge: The Boydell Press, 2009.

Orenstein, Arbie (ed.), *A Ravel Reader: Correspondence, Articles, Interviews*. New York: Dover, 2003.

Orledge, Robert, *Debussy and the Theatre*. Cambridge University Press, 1982.

Ory, Pascal, *Les Expositions universelles de Paris*. Paris: Ramsay, 1982.

   (ed.), *Nouvelle histoire des idées politiques*. Paris: Hachette, 1987.

Otis, Laura, *Membranes: Metaphors of Invasion in Nineteenth-Century Literature, Science and Politics*. Baltimore, MD: The Johns Hopkins University Press, 1999.

Parker, Roger, *Remaking the Song: Operatic Visions and Revisions from Handel to Berio*. Berkeley and Los Angeles: University of California Press, 2006.

Pasler, Jann, *Composing the Citizen: Music as Public Utility in Third Republic France*. Berkeley and Los Angeles: University of California Press, 2009.

Péladan, Joséphin, *La Guerre des idées*. Paris: Flammarion, 1916.

Perloff, Marjorie, *The Futurist Moment: Avant-Garde, Avant-Guerre, and the Language of Rupture*. 1985; rev. edn University of Chicago Press, 2003.

Peter, René, *Le Théâtre et la vie sous la Troisième République*, 2 vols. Paris: Marchot, 1947.

Pistone, Danièle, 'Wagner à Paris (1839–1900)', *Revue internationale de musique française*, 1 (1980), pp. 7–84.

Poesio, Giannandrea, 'Perpetuating the Myth: Sergey Diaghilev and the Ballets Russes', *Modernism/Modernity*, 18/1 (2011), pp. 161–73.

Poole, Mary Ellen, 'Gustave Charpentier and the Conservatoire Populaire de Mimi Pinson', *19th-Century Music*, 20/3 (1997), pp. 231–52.

Preston, Carrie J., 'The Motor in the Soul: Isadora Duncan and Modernist Performance', *Modernism/Modernity*, 12/2 (2005), pp. 273–89.

Pritchard, Jane (ed.), *Diaghilev and the Golden Age of the Ballets Russes, 1909–1929*. London: Victoria and Albert Museum, 2010.

Prochasson, Christophe, *Paris 1900: essai d'histoire culturelle*. Paris: Calmann-Lévy, 1999.

Proust, Marcel, *À la recherche du temps perdu*. 1913–27; repr. Paris: Gallimard, 1954.

Puchner, Martin, *Stage Fright: Modernism, Anti-Theatricality and Drama*. Baltimore, MD, and London: The Johns Hopkins University Press, 2002.

Rainey, Lawrence, 'Taking Dictation: Collage Poetics, Pathology and Politics', *Modernism/Modernity*, 5/2 (1998), pp. 123–53.

Rambert, Marie, *Quicksilver*. London: Macmillan, 1972.

Rasponi, Lanfranco, *The Last Prima Donnas*. London: Gollancz, 1984.

Rearick, Charles, *Pleasures of the Belle Époque: Entertainment and Festivity in Turn-of-the-Century France*. New Haven, CT, and London: Yale University Press, 1985.

Reed, Susan A., *Dance and the Nation: Performance, Ritual and Politics in Sri Lanka*. Madison: University of Wisconsin Press, 2009.

Rimsky-Korsakov, Nikolay, *My Musical Life*, trans. Judah A. Joffe. 1923; repr. London: Faber and Faber, 1989.

Rioux, Jean-Pierre, *Chronique d'une fin de siècle: France, 1889–1900*. Paris: Seuil, 1991.

Ripa, Yannick, *Women and Madness: The Incarceration of Women in Nineteenth-Century France*, trans. Catherine du Pelous Menagé. Minneapolis: University of Minnesota Press, 1990.

Roach, Joseph R., *The Player's Passion: Studies in the Science of Acting*. Ann Arbor: University of Michigan Press, 1993.

Robinson, Harlow, 'The Case of Three Russians: Stravinsky, Prokofiev, and Shostakovich', *Opera Quarterly*, 6/3 (1989), pp. 59–75.

Rochas, Albert de, *Les Sentiments, la musique et le geste*. Grenoble: H. Falque and F. Perrin, 1900.

Rolland, Romain, *La Vie de Léon Tolstoï*. Paris: Hachette, 1911.

Ross, Dorothy (ed.), *Modernist Impulses in the Human Sciences, 1870–1930*. Baltimore, MD: The Johns Hopkins University Press, 1994.

Rouché, Jacques, *L'Art théâtral moderne*. 1910; rev. edn Paris: Bloud et Gay, 1924.

Rudorff, Raymond, *The Belle Époque: Paris in the Nineties*. London: Hamish Hamilton, 1972.

Rutherford, Susan, 'Wilhelmine Schröder-Devrient: Wagner's Theatrical Muse', in Maggie B. Gale and Viv Gardner (eds.), *Women, Theatre and Performance: New Histories, New Historiographies*. Manchester University Press, 2000, pp. 60–80.

The Prima Donna and Opera, 1815–1930. Cambridge University Press, 2006.

Ryan, Judith, *The Vanishing Subject: Early Psychology and Literary Modernism.* University of Chicago Press, 1991.

Sabatier, Pierre, *L'Esthétique des Goncourts.* Geneva: Slatkine, 1970.

Sadoff, Diane F., *Sciences of the Flesh: Representing Body and Subject in Psychoanalysis.* Stanford University Press, 1998.

Said, Edward, *Orientalism.* New York: Pantheon, 1978.

Saint-Saëns, Camille, *Portraits et souvenirs.* Paris: Société d'Édition Artistique, 1900.

Samson, Jim (ed.), *The Cambridge History of Nineteenth-Century Music.* Cambridge University Press, 2002.

Scheijen, Sjeng, *Diaghilev: A Life.* Oxford University Press, 2010.

Schmid, Marion, 'À bas Wagner! The French Press Campaign against Wagner during World War I', in Barbara L. Kelly (ed.), *French Music, Culture, and National Identity, 1870–1939.* University of Rochester Press, 2008, pp. 77–91.

Schneider, William H., *An Empire for the Masses: The French Popular Image of Africa.* Westport, CT: Greenwood, 1982.

Schouvalov, Alexander (ed.), *The Art of Ballets Russes.* New Haven, CT, and London: Yale University Press, 1997.

Schumacher, Claude (ed.), *Naturalism and Symbolism in European Theatre, 1850–1918.* Cambridge University Press, 1996.

Schwartz, Vanessa R., *Spectacular Realities: Early Mass Culture in Fin-de-Siècle Paris.* Berkeley and Los Angeles: University of California Press, 1998.

Segel, Harold B., *Body Ascendant: Modernism and the Physical Imperative.* Baltimore, MD: The Johns Hopkins University Press, 1998.

Seigel, Jerrold, *Bohemian Paris: Culture, Politics, and the Boundaries of Bourgeois Life, 1830–1930.* New York: Viking, 1986.

Shattuck, Roger, *The Banquet Years: The Origins of the Avant-Garde in France, 1885 to World War I.* 1958; rev. edn London: Vintage, 1968.

Shead, Richard, *Ballets Russes.* London: The Apple Press, 1989.

Silver, Kenneth E., *Esprit de Corps: The Art of the Parisian Avant-Garde and the First World War, 1914–1925.* London: Thames and Hudson, 1989.

Silverman, Debora L., *Art Nouveau in Fin-de-Siècle France: Politics, Psychology and Style.* Berkeley and Los Angeles: University of California Press, 1989.

Singer, Barnett, *Modern France: Mind, Politics, Society.* Seattle: University of Washington Press, 1980.

Smart, Mary Ann, *Mimomania: Music and Gesture in Nineteenth-Century Opera.* Berkeley and Los Angeles: University of California Press, 2004.

(ed.), *Siren Songs: Representations of Gender and Sexuality in Opera*. Princeton University Press, 2000.

Smith, Marian, *Ballet and Opera in the Age of 'Giselle'*. Princeton University Press, 2000.

Sokolova, Lydia, *Dancing for Diaghilev: The Memoirs of Lydia Sokolova*, ed. Richard Buckle. London: John Murray, 1960.

Solenière, Eugène de, *Massenet: étude critique et documentaire*. Paris: Bibliothèque d'Art de la Critique, 1897.

Sommer, Sally, 'Loie Fuller', *Drama Review*, 19/1 (1975), pp. 53–67.

Sonn, Richard, *Anarchism and Cultural Politics in Fin-de-Siècle France*. Lincoln: University of Nebraska Press, 1989.

Sontag, Susan, *Against Interpretation and Other Essays*. New York: Farrar, Straus and Giroux, 1966.

Spencer, Charles, *Léon Bakst and the Ballets Russes*. 1973; rev. edn London: Academy Editions, 1995.

Stanislawski, Michael, *Zionism and the Fin de Siècle: Cosmopolitanism and Nationalism from Nordau to Jabotinsky*. Berkeley and Los Angeles: University of California Press, 2001.

Sternhell, Zeev, *Maurice Barrès et le nationalisme français*. Paris: A. Colin, 1972.

'National Socialism and Anti-Semitism: The Case of Maurice Barrès', *Journal of Contemporary History*, 8/4 (1973), pp. 47–66.

Stokes, Sewell, *Isadora Duncan: An Intimate Portrait*. London: Brentano, 1928.

Stravinsky, Igor and Robert Craft, *Expositions and Developments*. 1959; repr. London: Faber and Faber, 1962.

Sutton, Michael, *Nationalism, Positivism, Catholicism: The Politics of Charles Maurras and French Catholics, 1890–1914*. Cambridge University Press, 2002.

Svétlov, Valérien, *Le Ballet contemporain*, trans. Michel Dimitri Calvocoressi. Paris: Brunhoff, 1912.

Symons, Arthur, *Studies in Seven Arts*. London: Constable, 1906.

Taruskin, Richard, *Stravinsky and the Russian Traditions: A Biography of the Works through 'Mavra'*, 2 vols. Berkeley and Los Angeles: University of California Press, 1996.

Defining Russia Musically: Historical and Hermeneutical Essays. Princeton University Press, 1997.

On Russian Music. Berkeley and Los Angeles: University of California Press, 2009.

The Danger of Music and Other Anti-Utopian Essays. Berkeley and Los Angeles: University of California Press, 2009.

Taylor, Christiana J., *Futurism: Politics, Painting and Performance*. Ann Arbor, MI: UMI Research Press, 1974.

Téry, Gustave, *Les Allemands chez nous*. Paris: L'Œuvre, 1918.

Thomas, Helen, *The Body, Dance and Cultural Theory*. New York: Palgrave Macmillan, 2003.

Thomas, Valérie and Jérôme Perrin (eds.), *Loïe Fuller, danseuse de l'art nouveau*. Paris: Éditions de la Réunion des Musées Nationaux, 2002.

Timms, Edward and David Kelley (eds.), *Unreal City: Urban Experience in Modern European Literature and Art*. Manchester University Press, 1988.

Tombs, Robert (ed.), *Nationhood and Nationalism in France: From Boulangism to the Great War, 1889–1918*. London: Harper Collins, 1991.

Tomlinson, Gary, *Metaphysical Song: An Essay on Opera*. Princeton University Press, 1999.

Townsend, Julie, 'Alchemic Visions and Technological Advances: Sexual Morphology in Loie Fuller's Dance', in Jane C. Desmond (ed.), *Dancing Desires: Choreographing Sexualities on and off the Stage*. Madison: University of Wisconsin Press, 2001, pp. 73–96.

Turbow, Gerald D., 'Art and Politics: Wagnerism in France', in David C. Large and William Weber (eds.), *Wagnerism in European Culture and Politics*. Ithaca, NY: Cornell University Press, 1984, pp. 134–66.

Turnbull, Michael, *Mary Garden*. Aldershot: Scolar Press, 1997.

Udine, Jean d', *L'Orchestration des couleurs, analyse, classification et synthèse mathématiques des sensations colorées*. Paris: A. Joanin, 1903.
L'Art et le geste. Paris: Félix Alcan, 1910.
Traité complet de géométrie rythmique. Paris: Heugel, 1926.

Vaillat, Léandre, *Ballets de l'Opéra de Paris*. Paris: Compagnie Française des Arts Graphiques, 1943.

Van der Linden, Albert, 'Albert Roussel et Octave Maus', *Revue belge de musicologie*, 4/4 (1950), pp. 198–206.

Van Vechten, Carl, *Music after the Great War*. New York: Schirmer, 1915.
Interpreters and Interpretations. New York: Knopf, 1927.

Vertovec, Steven and Robin Cohen (eds.), *Conceiving Cosmopolitanism*. Oxford University Press, 2003.

Vuillermoz, Émile, *L'Art cinématographique*. Paris: Félix Alcan, 1927.

Wachtel, Andrew (ed.), *'Petrushka': Sources and Contexts*. Evanston, IL: Northwestern University Press, 1998.

Wagner, Richard, *Richard Wagner's Prose Works*, trans. William Ashton Ellis, 8 vols. London: Kegan Paul, 1896.

Waters, Lindsay, 'Literary Aesthetics: The Very Idea', *The Chronicle of Higher Education*, 16 December 2005, page numbers unknown.

Watkins, Glenn, *Pyramids at the Louvre: Music, Culture, and Collage from Stravinsky to the Postmodernists*. Cambridge, MA: The Belknap Press, 1994.

Waxman, Samuel, *Antoine and the Théâtre Libre*. Cambridge, MA: Harvard University Press, 1926.

Weber, Adna Ferrin, *The Growth of Cities in the Nineteenth Century: A Study in Cities*. Ithaca, NY: Cornell University Press, 1968.

Weber, Eugen, *The Nationalist Revival in France, 1905–1914*. Berkeley and Los Angeles: University of California Press, 1959.

'Gymnastics and Sports in *Fin-de-Siècle* France: Opium of the Classes?', *American Historical Review*, 76 (1971), pp. 70–98.

France: Fin de Siècle. Cambridge, MA: Harvard University Press, 1986.

My France: Politics, Culture, Myth. Cambridge, MA: The Belknap Press, 1991.

Weitsman, Patricia, *Dangerous Alliances: Proponents of Peace, Weapons of War*. Stanford University Press, 2004.

Wesseling, H. L., 'Pierre de Coubertin: Sport and Ideology in the Third Republic, 1870–1914', *European Review*, 8/2 (2000), pp. 167–71.

West, T. G. (ed.), *Symbolism: An Anthology*. London: Methuen, 1980.

Wiley, Roland John, 'Alexandre Benois' Commentaries on the First *Saisons Russes*', *The Dancing Times*, 71/841 (1980), pp. 28–30.

Tchaikovsky's Ballets. Oxford University Press, 1985.

Williams, Robert C., *Russia Imagined: Art, Culture and National Identity, 1840–1995*. New York: Peter Lang, 1997.

Willms, Johannes, *Paris, Capital of Europe: From the Revolution to the Belle Époque*, trans. Eveline L. Kanes. New York: Holmes and Meier, 1997.

Winestein, Anna, 'Still Dancing: Photographs and Postcards of the Ballets Russes', in Alston Purvis, Peter Rand and Anna Winestein (eds.), *The Ballets Russes and the Art of Design*. New York: Random House, 2009, pp. 95–124.

Wood, Jane, *Passion and Pathology in Victorian Fiction*. Oxford University Press, 2001.

Worthen, William B., *The Idea of the Actor: Drama and the Ethics of Performance*. Princeton University Press, 1984.

Wright, Alastair, *Matisse and the Subject of Modernism*. Princeton University Press, 2004.

Yaraman, Sevin, *Revolving Embrace: The Waltz as Sex, Steps and Sound*. Hillsdale, NY: Pendragon, 2002.

Zbikowski, Lawrence, 'Dance Topoi, Sonic Analogues and Musical Grammar: Communicating with Music in the Eighteenth Century', in Danuta Mirka and Kofi Agawu (eds.), *Communication in Eighteenth-Century Music*. Cambridge University Press, 2008, pp. 283–309.

Index